# Google Chromebook SENIORS GUIDE

The Most User-Friendly Seniors and Beginners Guide to Learn Chromebook's Essential Features

- Install Chromebook
- Setting Up Your Security
- Set up Email
- Find Lost Files
- Use Social Media
- Have News Delivered to Your Desktop
- Add Shortcuts to Your Favorite Apps

Master Your New Chromebook with Pictures, Simple Explanations and the Best Tips and Tricks!

STEVE WHITE

# © COPYRIGHT 2023 - ALL RIGHTS RESERVED.

The content contained within this book may not be reproduced, duplicated or transmitted without direct written permission from the author or the publisher. Under no circumstances will any blame or legal responsibility be held against the publisher, or author, for any damages, reparation, or monetary loss due to the information contained within this book. Either directly or indirectly.

## LEGAL NOTICE:

This book is copyright protected. This book is only for personal use. You cannot amend, distribute, sell, use, quote or paraphrase any part, or the content within this book, without the consent of the author or publisher.

## DISCLAIMER NOTICE:

Please note the information contained within this document is for educational and entertainment purposes only. All effort has been executed to present accurate, up to date, and reliable, complete information. No warranties of any kind are declared or implied. Readers acknowledge that the author is not engaging in the rendering of legal, financial, medical or professional advice. The content within this book has been derived from various sources. Please consult a licensed professional before attempting any techniques outlined in this book. By reading this document, the reader agrees that under no circumstances is the author responsible for any losses, direct or indirect, which are incurred as a result of the use of information contained within this document, including, but not limited to, errors, omissions, or inaccuracies.

## TRADEMARK:

Chromebook Seniors Guide" is an independent publication and has not been authorized, sponsored, or otherwise approved by Microsoft Windows.

All trademarks and brands within this book are for clarifying purposes only and are owned by the owners themselves, not affiliated with this document

# TABLE OF CONTENTS

GLOSSARY .............................. 8

INTRODUCTION ................... 9

**CHAPTER 1: SETTING UP YOUR CHROMEBOOK ....... 11**

Initial Setup ........................................ 11
Creating a Google Account ....... 12
Personalize Your Chromebook .. 12

    Desktop Wallpaper ...................... 12
    Using Your Own Photos ............ 13
    Account Images .......................... 14
    Sync and Google Services ....... 15

Transferring Your File to a Chromebook ................................. 16

    Using Google Drive ..................... 16
    Using External Drive .................. 17

Setting up Printers ....................... 17

    Cloud-Enabled Wireless Printers ........................................... 17
    Traditional Printers ..................... 18

Adding Bluetooth Devices ......... 19
Connect Your Phone to Chromebook ................................... 19
Connect to Wi-Fi .......................... 20
Managing Users ............................ 22

    Adding Users ............................... 22
    Deleting Users ............................. 23

Parental Controls ......................... 23

    Add Child Accounts .................... 23
    Set up Parental Controls ......... 24
    Monitoring Child Accounts with Family Links ........................ 24
    Allow or Blocks Apps ................. 24
    Manage Web Browsing ............. 24

Configuring Other Settings ...... 25

    Mouse and Touchpad ............... 25
    Internal Display Settings .......... 26
    External Display Settings ........ 27
    Time Zone ..................................... 27
    Change Language ..................... 28
    Keyboard Layout ....................... 29
    Keyboard Settings ..................... 29
    Network Settings ....................... 30
    Power Options ............................ 30

Integrate Dropbox ....................... 30
Integrate One-Drive .................... 31
Remote Desktop ........................... 32

    Setup .............................................. 32
    Connecting .................................. 32

## CHAPTER 2: GETTING AROUND CHROMEBOOK. 34

- Power Up and Power Down ....... 34
- The Login Screen .......................... 34
- The TouchPad .............................. 35
- The Keyboard ............................... 36
  - Onscreen Keyboard Help ......... 36
- Chromebook Task Manager ...... 37
- Desktop and the App Shelf ....... 38
- System Tray ................................. 39
- Notifications ................................ 40
- Pinned Files and Holding Space 41
- App Launcher .............................. 42
  - Opening .................................... 42
  - App Types ................................. 42
  - Create App Folders .................. 43
  - Pin apps to Your app Shelf ...... 43

## CHAPTER 3: MANAGEMENT FILES IN CHROMEBOOK .. 44

- Creating Folders .......................... 44
- Moving Files ................................. 46
- Copying Files ............................... 47
  - Copying Using a Mouse or Touchpad .................................. 48
  - Copying Using Touchscreen ... 49
- Renaming Files ............................ 49
  - Renaming Through Right Clicking ................................... 49
  - Renaming Using Keys ............... 50
- Sorting Files ................................. 51
- Searching Files ............................ 51
- External Drivers .......................... 52
  - Formatting External Drives ..... 53
- Nearby Share ............................... 53
  - Sharing Content With Other Devices ..................................... 54
  - Receiving Content From Someone ................................... 55
  - Nearby Share Using Android ..................................... 55
- Screen Capture ............................ 55
  - Chromebook Screenshots ...... 56
  - Record the Screen ................... 57
- Talk to Your Chromebook .......... 57

## CHAPTER 4: USING CHROME APPS ...... 59

- Browsing Chrome App Store .... 59
- Searching the Store ................... 60
- Removing Chrome Extensions .................................. 60
- Useful Online Apps for Your Chromebook ................................. 62
- Android Apps on Chromebooks ............................... 62
- Enable Google Play Store .......... 63
- Searching, Browsing, and Downloading Apps ....................... 63
- Managing Apps ........................... 65
- Removing Apps ........................... 65
- Using Linux Apps ........................ 66
  - How to Turn on Linux? ............. 67

# TABLE OF CONTENTS

    Turning Linux off ........................... 67
    Installing Linux Apps ................. 68

How to Install FileZilla FTP? ....... 69

How to Install Audacity on Chromebook? ..................................... 71

Install Gimp Image Editor ......... 72

Install LibreOffice on Chromebook ..................................... 73

Install Python on Your Chromebook ..................................... 75

Removing Linux Apps ................. 77

## CHAPTER 5: WEB, EMAIL, AND COMMUNICATION ... 79

**Google Chrome** ............................. 79
    Browser Tabs ................................ 80
    Browse Incognito ......................... 80
    Browsing History ........................ 81
    Bookmaking a Site ..................... 82
    Bookmark Folders ...................... 82
    Site Shortcuts .............................. 82
    Downloads .................................... 83
    Printing a Webpage ................... 84
    Saving Passwords ....................... 84
    Managing Passwords ................ 85
    Chrome Security ......................... 85

**Gmail App** ...................................... 86
    Reading Email ............................. 86
    Reply an email ............................ 86
    Writing a New Message ........... 87
    Adding Attachments ................. 88
    Recover Deleted Messages .... 88

    Search messagges ..................... 89
    Adding Other Email Accounts  90

**Calendar App** ................................ 90
    Adding Events ............................. 91
    Adding Reminders ..................... 91
    Adding Tasks ............................... 92
    Add a Goal .................................... 92

**Gmail on the Web** ....................... 92
    Inserting Images ........................ 92

**Contacts Web App** ...................... 93
    View Contact Details ................ 93
    Add New Contacts ..................... 93
    Add a Contact From Message ....................................... 94

**Google Meet** ................................. 94
    Starting a Google Meet ........... 94
    Creating a Meeting for Later.  95
    Start Instant Meeting .............. 96
    Schedule Meeting in the Calendar ................................ 97
    Joining a Meeting ..................... 97
    In-Call Options ........................... 97
    Present and Share Desktops ..................................... 98
    Whiteboard ................................. 99
    Change Background ............... 100
    Captions ..................................... 100

**Google Chat** ................................ 101
    Starting Google Chat ............. 101
    Group Conversation ............... 101

| | |
|---|---|
| Chat Rooms | 103 |
| Creating a Room and Chatting | 103 |
| Share Files on google chat | 103 |
| Assign a Task | 103 |

**Google Duo** .................................. 103

| | |
|---|---|
| Starting Google Duo | 104 |
| Setup | 104 |
| Start a Conversation on google duo | 104 |
| Group Conversation on google duo | 104 |
| Invite a Friend on google duo | 105 |

## CHAPTER 6: ENTERTAINMENT ............ 106

**Google Photos** ............................. 106

| | |
|---|---|
| Photos in Chrome OS: Viewing and Editing | 107 |
| View Local Photos | 107 |
| Rotate a Photograph | 108 |
| Zoom | 110 |
| Use the Auto-Correct Feature. | 110 |
| Make Adjustments to the Exposure | 110 |
| Color Saturation can be Adjusted | 111 |
| Apply Advanced Modifications | 112 |
| Cropping and Rotation | 112 |

**Music Enjoyment** ....................... 113

| | |
|---|---|
| Listening to Music | 113 |
| Playing a Song From a Playlist | 113 |
| Listening to Music Streaming Services | 114 |
| Using Spotify to Listen to Music | 115 |

**Video Streaming** ......................... 116

| | |
|---|---|
| WebM | 116 |
| Using Online Video Streaming Services | 117 |

**Google Play Books** ..................... 119
**Library** ........................................... 120
**Sharing Files** ................................ 121

## CHAPTER 7: PRODUCTIVITY WITH GOOGLE SUITE .... 122

**Getting Around Google Docs** .. 122

| | |
|---|---|
| Using Paragraph Styles | 122 |
| Justify Text | 124 |
| Bullet Lists | 124 |
| Numbered Lists | 125 |
| Cut, Copy, and Paste | 126 |
| Adding Images | 126 |
| Adding Tables | 127 |
| Saving Documents | 128 |
| Printing Documents | 129 |
| Sharing Documents | 130 |

**Google Sheets** ............................ 131

| | |
|---|---|
| Spreadsheets | 131 |
| Getting Around Google Sheets | 132 |
| Using Functions | 134 |

# TABLE OF CONTENTS

    Insert Table ............................... 135

**Google Slides** ................................. 136

    Designing a Slide ..................... 136

    Printing Presentations ........... 140

    Giving Your Presentation ...... 141

**Present With Chromecast** ...... 141

## CHAPTER 8: MAINTENANCE ............... 142

**Battery Care for Chromebooks** ............................. 142

**Diagnostics** ................................. 143

    Opening the Diagnostics App ....................... 144

    Utilizing the Diagnostics App ....................... 145

**Updating Chrome OS** ................ 145

    Access Settings ........................ 146

    Check for New Information . 146

**Powerwash** .................................. 147

**Recovery** ...................................... 148

    The Recovery Process ............ 148

    Traditional Recovery .............. 148

**VPNs** .............................................. 149

    How Do VPNs Work? ............... 149

    Is a VPN Required for Your Chromebook? ........................... 149

    Installing a VPN on a Chromebook .......................... 150

## CHAPTER 9: TIPS AND TRICKS FOR CHROMEBOOK ............... 151

Run Windows Applications on Chrome OS ............................ 151

Use an Android Phone to Unlock Chromebook ................. 151

Access the Overview Mode .... 152

Use Chromebook Extras .......... 153

Security When Sharing Your Chromebook ................................ 153

Opening Apps Using Keys ........ 154

Add Restart Button on Chromebook ................................ 154

Chromebook Shortcuts ............ 155

Enable the Offline mode for Google Docs ........................ 156

Reset Your Chromebook .......... 157

**CONCLUSION** .................. 158

**REFERENCES** ................... 165

**Free Bonus Page 158**

# Glossary

**Bluetooth:** This is a short-range wireless internet connection that allows you to share information between various devices.

**Bookmarking a site:** The act of adding a certain design to a page so that it becomes easier to find it when you want to use it.

**Browsing Incognito:** The ability to surf the internet in private.

**Chat Room:** This refers to a space that is created with the purpose of having certain conversations.

**Chrome OS:** This is a Google-owned operating system that is Linux-based.

**Family Link app:** This describes an application that gives parents control over how their children use the computer.

**Google Meet:** It's a business-related video conferencing tool that has been developed by Google.

**Holding space:** This is a storage place that accommodates the most current screenshots and downloads.

**Powerwash:** It's an option that you find on your Chromebook that allows you to clear all user information and reset the settings.

**Spotify:** This is a service that allows you to get access to music and various forms of content from creators, the world over.

**Spreadsheet:** It's an electronic document that contains rows and columns with labels and figures that you can use in calculations.

**Whiteboard:** This is a tool that permits you to demonstrate certain concepts to the audience during a video meeting.

# Introduction

There are several similarities between a Chromebook and a laptop. What you need to do on a laptop, you can simply do it on a Chromebook. The Chromebook has the advantage that it comes at a much cheaper price. You can get some of the models for less than $300. If you want to purchase a Chromebook, check with major retailers such as Best Buy and Target. In case you want to buy online, it is advisable to purchase from Amazon or NewEgg (gcfglobal, 2021).

**Chromebooks do not run on Windows, as most computers do. They have their own Chrome Operating System (Chrome OS)**, which is the equivalent of the Google Chrome web browser. With the Chrome OS, you are able to use your Chromebook to do different tasks online. For instance, you can check your email, watch videos online, and read websites.

You may be used to working with Windows software such as Adobe Photoshop and Microsoft Office but these are not compatible with the Chromebook. Bear in mind that you can use alternatives that are compatible with your Chromebook such as Pixlr, Google Docs, and Office Online. Actually, there are many software alternatives that you can utilize when using the Chromebook. We will look at these as we proceed with the book.

In comparison with the normal laptop, the **Chromebook is cloud-based**. This means that you can run most of its applications from the cloud, contrary to other laptops which store their programs on an internal hard drive. Being a cloud-based gadget, the Chromebook tends to be extremely lightweight because it does not require as much memory and processing power as the normal laptop. Please note that your internet connection has to be reliable if you desire to use a Chromebook. It is possible to use some of the apps while offline but keep in mind that you will have to be connected to the internet in order to get the maximum use of your Chromebook.

**Due to the fact that Chromebooks are mostly cloud-based, they usually possess smaller built-in storage. Depending on the Chromebook you can afford, built-in storage will range from 16GB to 256GB..** Instead of the common desktop on most laptops, a Chromebook has a shelf or launcher that you can access your apps from. If you want to play music on your Chromebook, you can play it from saved files or a USB drive. You cannot play your DVDs or CDs from here because they do not have built-in DVD or CD drives.

# INTRODUCTION

Although using a Chromebook may seem to be difficult, **this book will help you to use your gadget with ease**. We will look at how to set up your Chromebook and the general navigation process. In addition to that, we will discuss the ways in which you could manage your files by creating, naming, and sharing them with others. The Chromebook has applications with which it is compatible. This book will provide you with the know-how to use Chrome apps as well as others that are compatible with the Chromebook.

In these times, people commonly communicate using email and the Web. Tips will be provided that will help you to communicate with ease when it comes to online communication using the Chromebook. We will also discuss entertainment in relation to the Chromebook. Under entertainment, we will look at Google photos, Spotify, YouTube Music, Netflix, and more. As we proceed, we will also explain how you can be productive using the Google suite. This will include changing the color, style and size of fonts, adding tables and images to documents as well as sharing them, if need be.

If you have to give presentations at some point in time, then this book can walk you through doing that. Also, provided in this book are maintenance tips such as diagnostics and Chrome OS update information. We will also provide tips and tricks that you can utilize in order to maximize your use of the Chromebook.

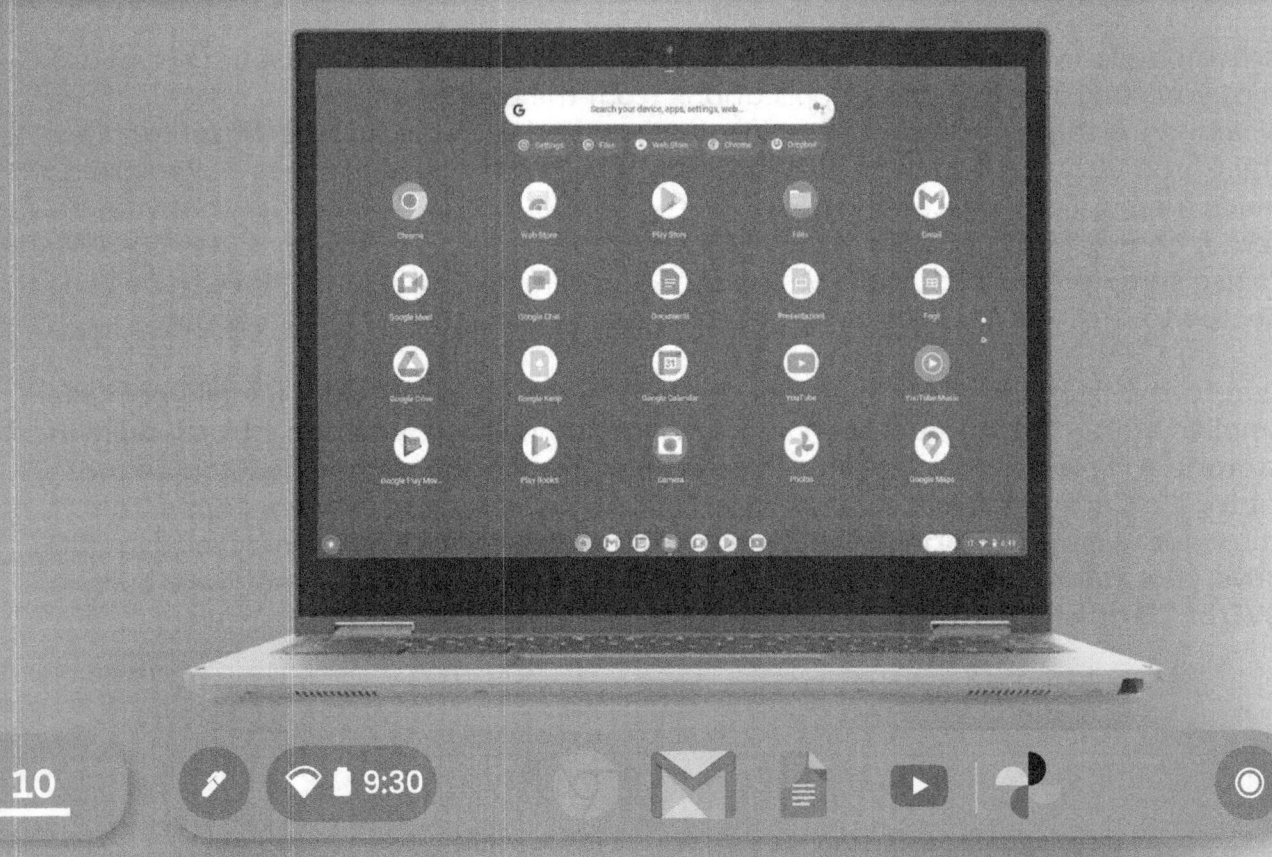

# Chapter 1: Setting Up Your Chromebook

After reading this chapter, you will have in-depth knowledge about the basics of how to use your Chromebook. Information will be provided that will help you with setting up your Chromebook, creating accounts, and doing file transfers, among other tasks. In addition to that, you will also get information on how to set up parental controls. Let's begin with the initial setup.

## INITIAL SETUP

**When setting up your Chromebook, you will need your Google Account username, password, and access to the internet.**

The **FIRST STEP** is to turn on your Chromebook. Make sure the power cord is plugged in, then switch your Chromebook on by pressing the power button for a few seconds. The next step is to select the language that you prefer to use, as well as the keyboard settings. If you want, you can turn on your accessibility features by selecting **Accessibility**. Afterward, select your network and agree to the terms of service.

Power Button

**CHAPTER 1**

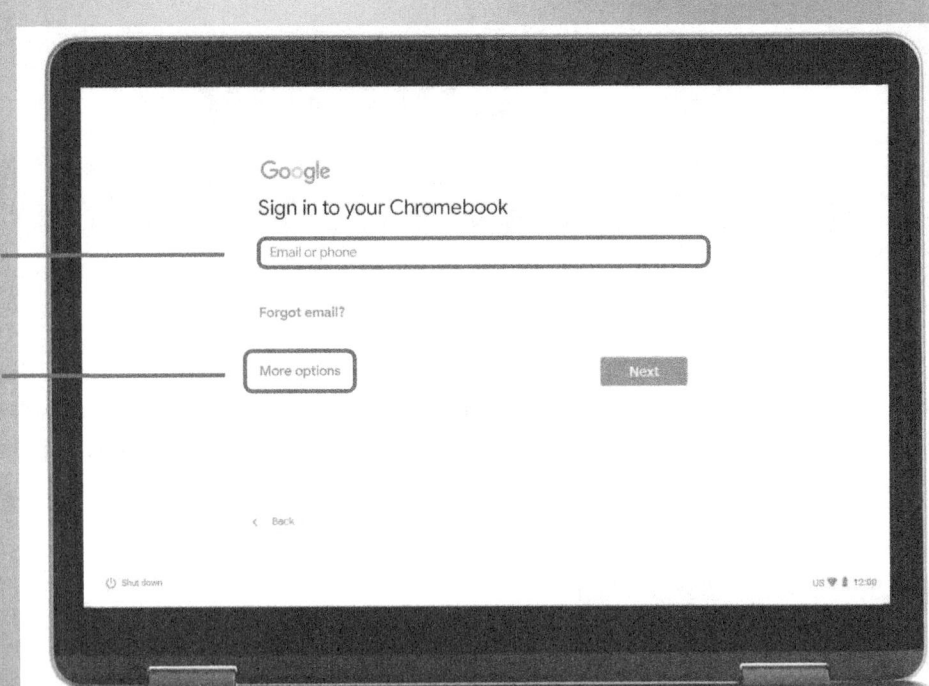

*If you already have a Google Account enter your email*

*To create a Google Account, choose More options*

## CREATING A GOOGLE ACCOUNT

To create a Google Account, choose **More options**, then click on **Create new account**. Enter your name and password. Verify your password by re-entering it in the designated field. Please note that if you prefer to use your Chromebook without an account, you can choose the option which says, **"Browse as guest."** However, in case you are facing challenges in signing in using your Google Account, you can choose the **Sign-in troubleshooter** option. Once you are successfully signed in, you will automatically see your extensions, apps, and bookmarks.

## PERSONALIZE YOUR CHROMEBOOK

Although to a limited extent, it is possible to customize your Chromebook. The operating system of Chrome is quite simple and it has been the same for quite some time. Because of its [Y1] simplicity, anyone can easily start using a Chromebook.

### DESKTOP WALLPAPER

If you like, you can change the wallpaper on your Chromebook. Chrome's OS has one of the best default wallpaper pickers. The wallpaper picker is straightforward, simple, and has the advantage that it provides you with more choices. Chrome's built-in

## SETTING UP YOUR CHROMEBOOK

wallpaper picker has numerous wallpapers. In addition to that, there is also an option to choose from a particular category that allows you to have a different wallpaper each day. The categories on offer include compositions, patterns, original designs, cityscape, and landscape shots.

- To alter your wallpaper, go to your desktop and right-click on it, then choose **Set wallpaper**.

- A left column will appear, from which you have to choose the category of your choice.

- Select any wallpaper that you prefer on the right, and it will be automatically applied.

*Press the right button anywhere on the Desktop then choose "Set wallpaper"*

### USING YOUR OWN PHOTOS

You may desire to use your own photos as your Chromebook's wallpaper. The process is slightly different when compared to using the default images. Proceed as follows:

1. Go to your Chrome desktop and **right-click**. Select **Set wallpaper** from the options that appear on-screen.

2. To choose an image from your own photos, choose the **My Images** option that appears at the bottom of the list.

**CHAPTER 1**

## ACCOUNT IMAGES

Due to the fact that it is a requirement of the Chrome OS for you to provide a Google account in order to sign in, your profile picture is automatically used as your account image. In addition to setting up static images, you are also able to set animated ones as your account image. However, it is noteworthy that the choice of animations is a bit limited because you cannot utilize your own (Ankur, 2021).

1. To customize your account images, click on the **Settings** app.

2. Afterward, select **Personalization** on the column to your left, or simply scroll downwards until you see the Personalization option.

3. Next, select **Change device account image** under the Personalization option.

4. Last, choose an animated account picture from the available options.

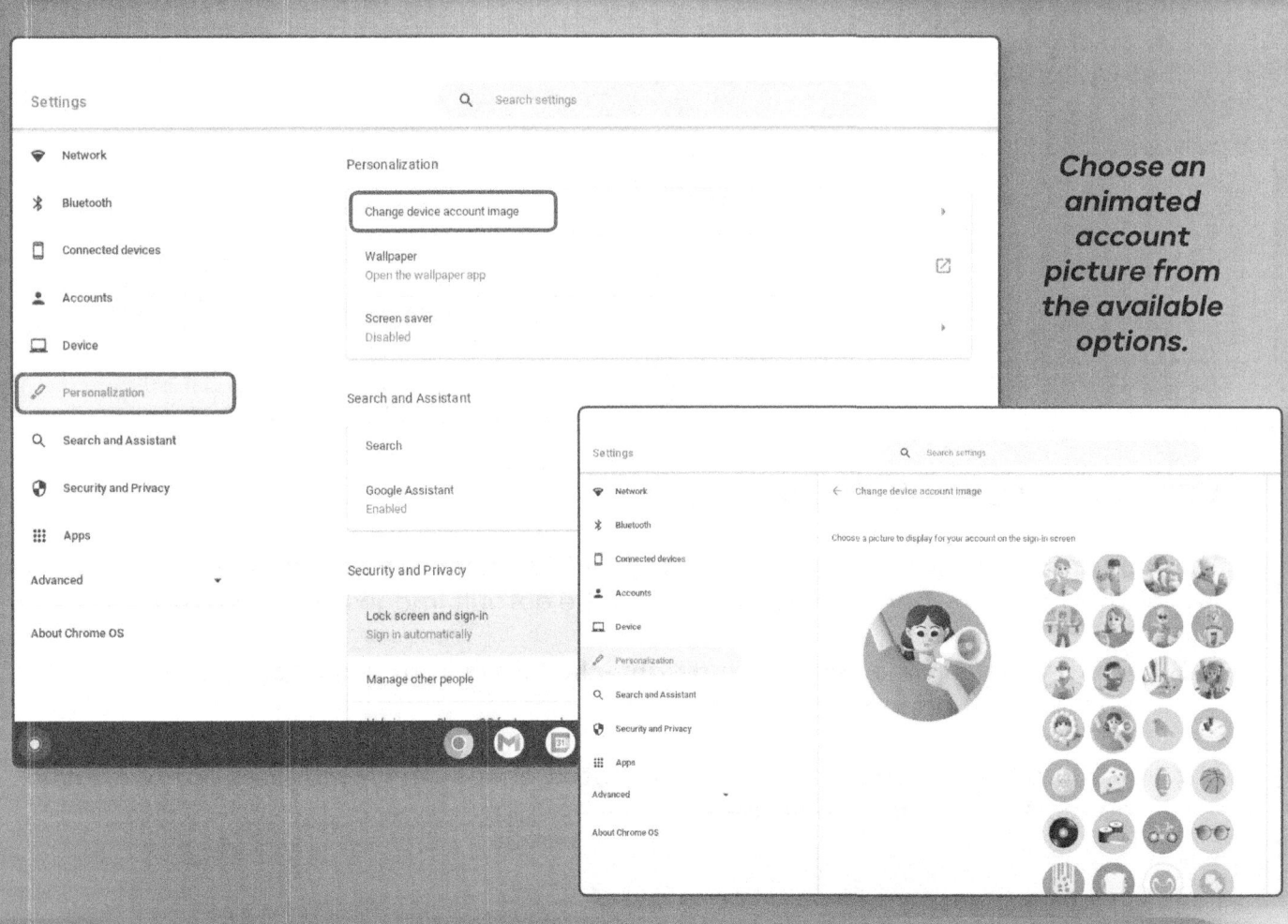

*Choose an animated account picture from the available options.*

# SETTING UP YOUR CHROMEBOOK

## SYNC AND GOOGLE SERVICES

It is possible to save and sync your bookmarks, passwords, Wi-Fi networks and history to your Google account. When you do that, you will always have access to these on any Chromebook that you use. You can also access your information on Google Chrome from any other device if you have synced your account settings. Bear in mind that you can only sync your data if you are using the Chrome OS version 18 or later versions.

1. Choose the time, at the bottom right, then click on **Settings**.

2. Click on **Sync and Google services** under the **Accounts option**.

3. Afterward, select **Manage what you sync**

4. You should then select what you prefer to sync.

In case you want to use similar settings on every Chromebook that you use, you should choose the option that says, **"Sync everything."** It is advisable to turn this setting on for any device that you want to sync. Sometimes you may want to sync various settings in each Chromebook that you sign in. If so, click on the **Customize sync** option. Afterward, go to Sync data, then turn on the settings that you would like to sync.

Please note that if you are using your Chromebook at school or at work, your administrator may turn off sync. If this is the case, it will not be possible for you to sync your information.  - *See the images in the next page -*

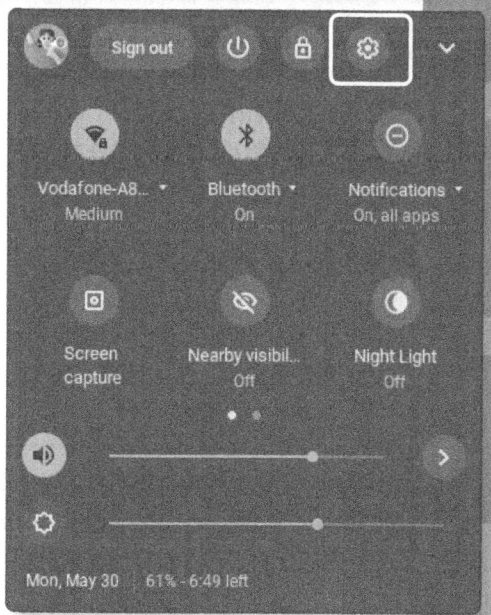

# CHAPTER 1

## TRANSFERRING YOUR FILE TO A CHROMEBOOK

There are times when you have to transfer files to and from your Chromebook. You can either transfer the files using Google Drive or an external drive. Let's explore more information on how to do this.

### USING GOOGLE DRIVE

Due to the fact that Chromebooks are cloud-based, you can easily download files from Google Drive to your Chromebook. However, when you want to transfer huge files, this method of transfer will need excessive time and data. Using Google Drive to transfer files is advantageous because you can do it without having a second device close by and it is possible to use it on any operating system. On the other hand, Google Drive will require you to have an Internet connection in order to send files. When it comes to transferring huge files, it requires a lot of data.

# SETTING UP YOUR CHROMEBOOK

## USING EXTERNAL DRIVE

To transfer files using an external drive,

1. Click the **Files app** on your Chromebook.

2. Connect your external drive so that it appears in the left navigation panel, as a folder in the **Files app**.

3. Next, mark the files and folders that you want to copy by placing checkmarks on them.

4. Afterward, copy the files by dragging and dropping them on your Chromebook.

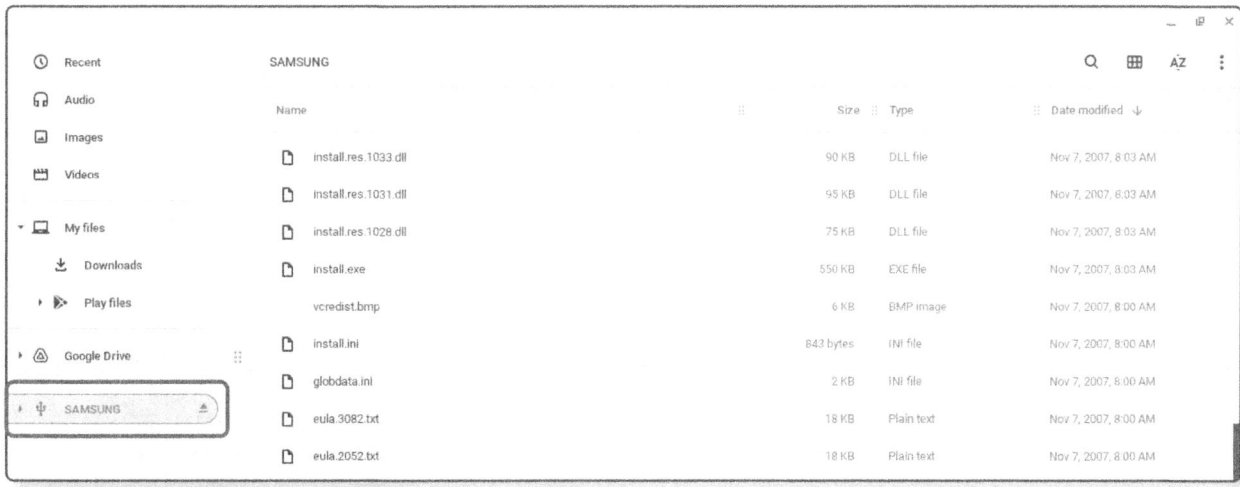

## SETTING UP PRINTERS

As a Chromebook user, you may need to use a printer so that you print your documents or other files. This section will provide more information on how you can set up both traditional and cloud-enabled wireless printers. Here are the details.

### CLOUD-ENABLED WIRELESS PRINTERS

To begin with, make sure that your printer and Chromebook are connected to the same Wi-Fi network.

# CHAPTER 1

1. First, go to the bottom right of your Chromebook screen and **select the Time.**

2. Click on **Advanced**, then choose **Printing**. Afterward, select **Printers.**

3. The next step is to choose the option which says, **Available printer to save**. Next, click on **Save** when you see the name of your printer.

4. Afterward, you should be able to see the name of your wireless printer at the top part of the screen and under **Saved printers** as well.

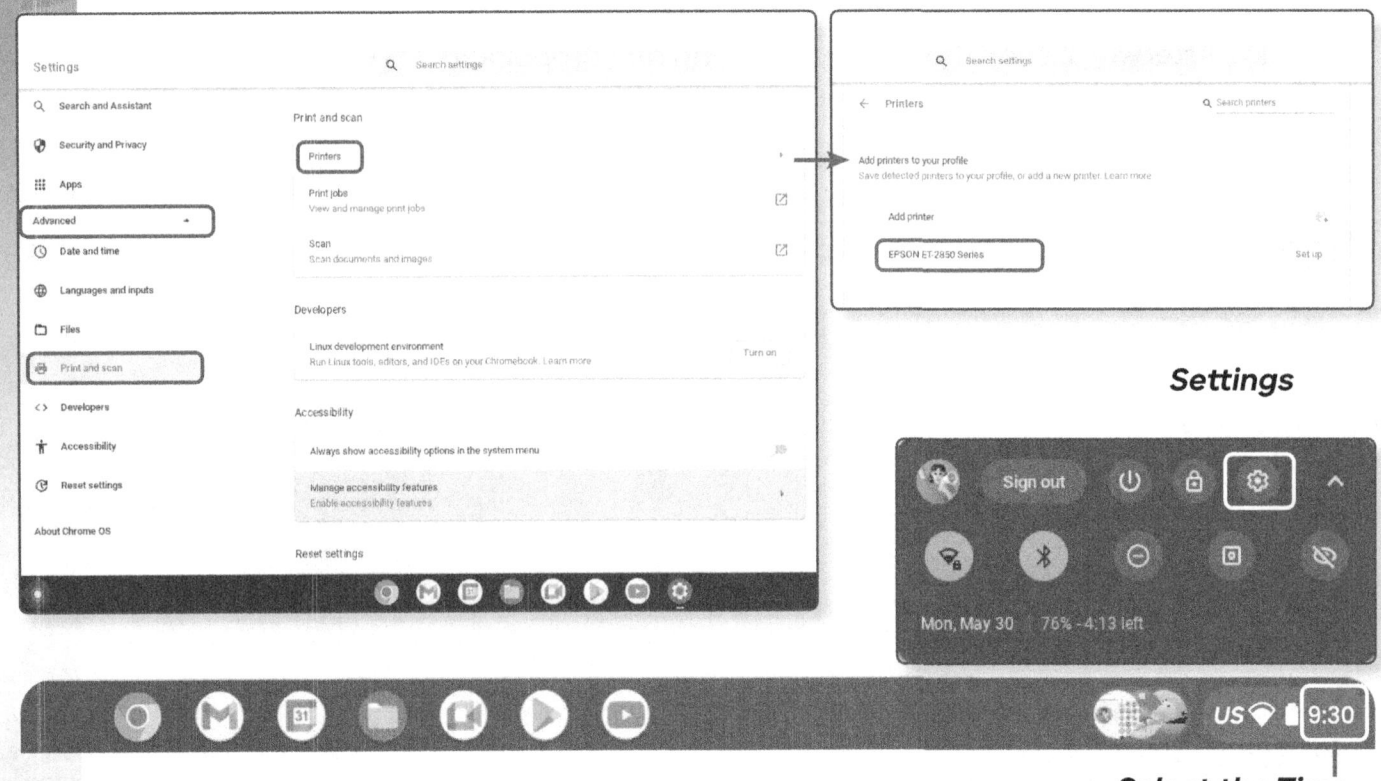

*Settings*

*Select the Time*

## TRADITIONAL PRINTERS

In case you cannot connect your printer to the wireless route, you can always do it using a USB cable. The process is more or less the same as you do when connecting wirelessly (Stanton, 2021). However, when going the traditional way, you will need to connect the printer by use of a USB cable. Your laptop will recognize the printer, then you can go ahead and add it.

## SETTING UP YOUR CHROMEBOOK

## ADDING BLUETOOTH DEVICES

You can connect your Chromebook to Bluetooth devices such as headphones, keyboards, printers, and mice. To know if there has been a successful Bluetooth connection, check in the Bluetooth status notification area. Let's discuss how to add Bluetooth devices to your Chromebook in this section.

1. Ensure that the Bluetooth device that you want to add is ready to pair. It should also be within close range.

2. At the bottom right of your screen, select the **Quick Settings Panel** option, then choose **Bluetooth**.

3. Afterward, you should then choose your **Bluetooth accessory**.

4. Last, confirm the **passkey** and click on **Accept**.

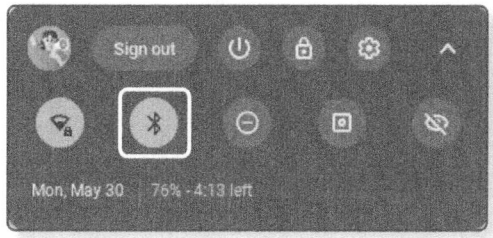
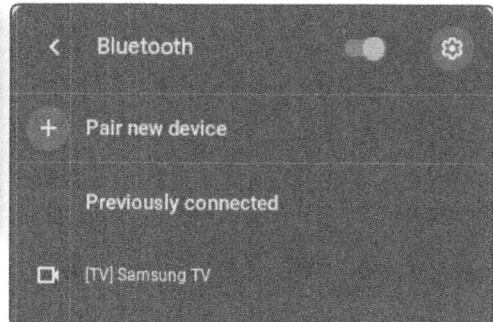

## CONNECT YOUR PHONE TO CHROMEBOOK

If you want to connect your phone to your Chromebook, you can make use of Phone Hub. This will allow you to have instant access to both your devices. By using Phone Hub, you can check your phone's battery life, view the recent browser history of your phone, respond to your text messages, as well as do other phone-related tasks from your Chromebook. When you want to use Phone Hub, ensure that your Chromebook is updated to the recent version. To connect your Android phone to a Chromebook:

1. Select the **Settings** option and choose **Connected Devices**.

2. To see whether or not your phone is connected, click on **Connected Devices**, at the top. In case your phone is already connected, go to Setting up the

# CHAPTER 1

connected phone.

3. If it is not connected, choose **Set-up**.

4. If your devices are using the same Wi-Fi network, you should be able to see your phone appearing under **Detected**.

5. Afterward, choose **Accept and Continue**.

6. The on-screen instructions will require you to enter your password. Once you have done that, you should then press **Done**.

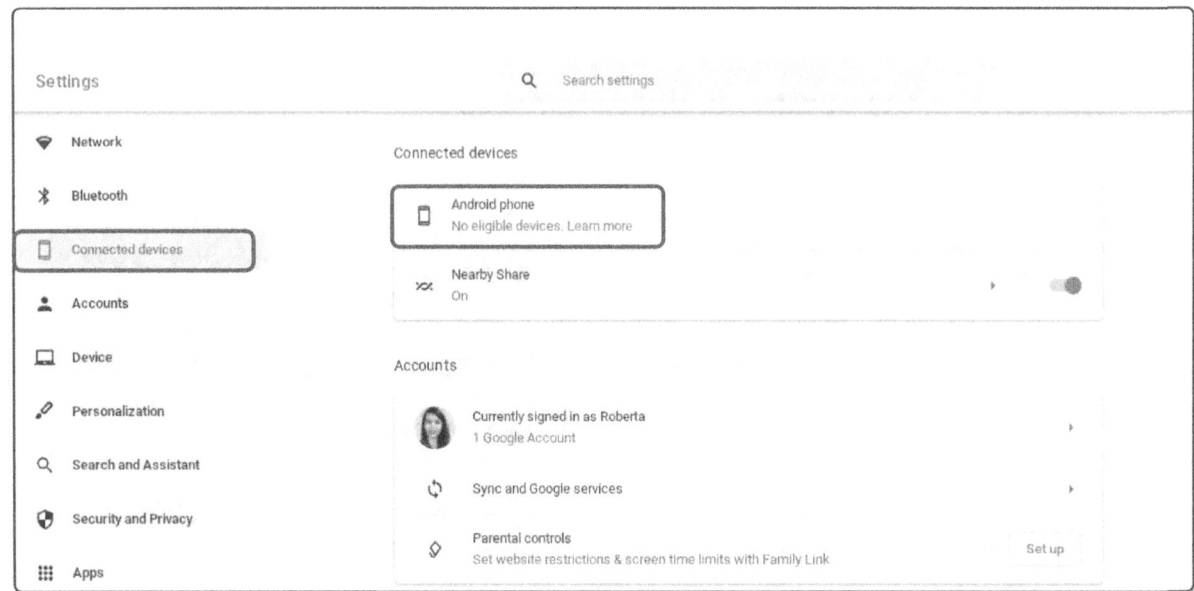

## CONNECT TO WI-FI

Chromebooks commonly use Wi-Fi networks that are usually found in public places such as cafés and libraries. Generally, they have built-in network cards. In addition to that, the Chrome OS is created in such a way that it is easy to view and connect to Wi-Fi networks that are near you. It is, therefore, important to know how to easily connect to Wi-Fi, using your Chromebook. The first step in connecting to a Wi-Fi network is to view the available nearby networks, be it open or password-protected ones.

1. To see the available networks, go to the lower right of your screen and click on

## SETTING UP YOUR CHROMEBOOK

**Wi-Fi** network. Afterward, click on the **Wi-Fi icon** that pops up on your screen. Please note that if your Chromebook is already configured to connect to a network, the status of your connectivity will appear as **Connected**. If not configured, it will read **Not connected**.

2. After clicking on **Wi-Fi network**, a Network window will be opened, and this will show you the list of all the available networks.

3. Select the network that you want to connect to. In case the network that you have just selected is an open one, simply click on **Connect**. You will then see your status update appearing as **Connected**.

4. In the event that the network that you have chosen is a secure one, go ahead and choose Configure so that a configuration window is opened. This window will present you with the name of the network, security type, and a field where you should input the password of the network.

5. In cases where you are connecting to your home Wi-Fi network, or any other that you frequently connect to, ensure that you enable the options which are labeled **Prefer this network** and **Automatically connect to this network**. Once you activate these options, your Chromebook will automatically connect to the network each time you are close.

6. When you finish entering your password and activating the automatic options, click on **Connect**. The Wi-Fi network status will then change to **Connected**. When you see that notification, you will successfully be connected to the Wi-Fi network.

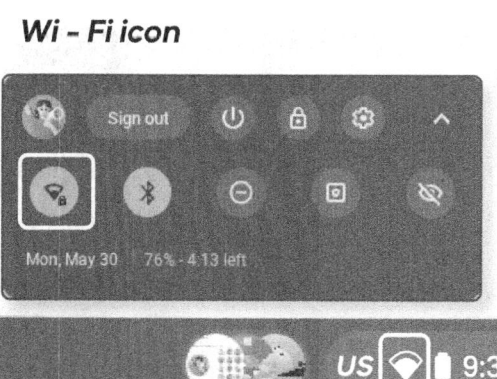

*Wi - Fi icon*

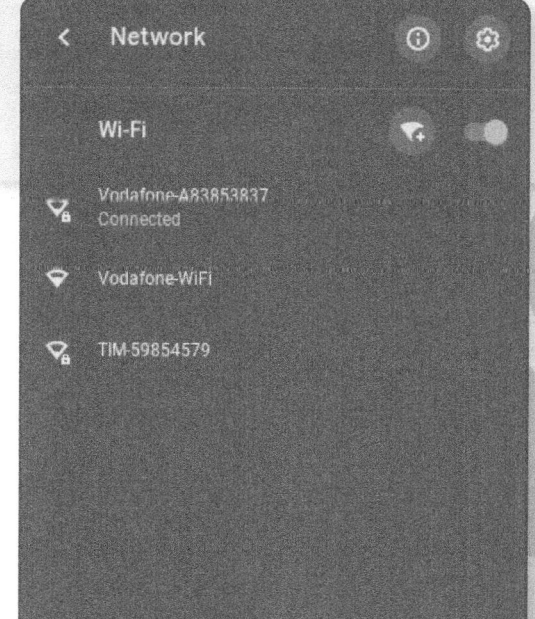

*List of all available networks*

# CHAPTER 1

## MANAGING USERS

It is possible for many users to use a single Chromebook to log in to their accounts. This allows each of the users to use the Chromebook without interfering with others' work. Let's get more information on how to manage users in this section.

### ADDING USERS

You can let other people sign in to your Chromebook using their Google Accounts. At the bottom right, **select the time.**

Select **Sign Out**, then select **Add person**.

Enter the **Google Account email address** and select **Next**.

Once added, the user will have their individual account with which they can log into your Chromebook.

*Sign out*

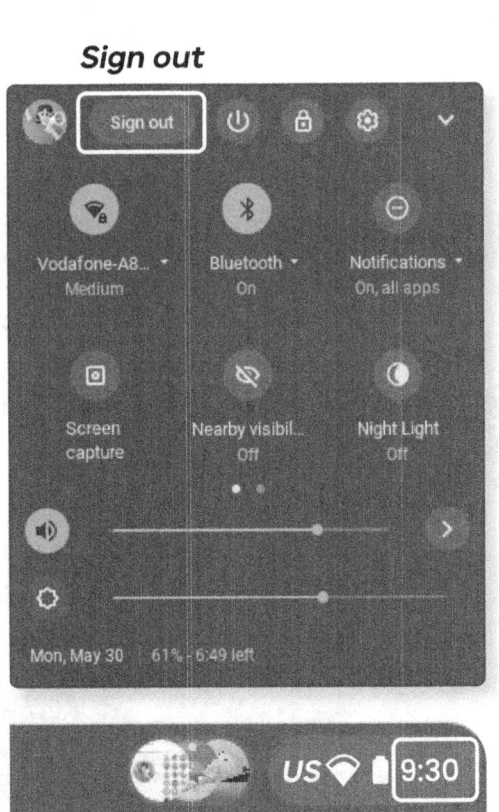

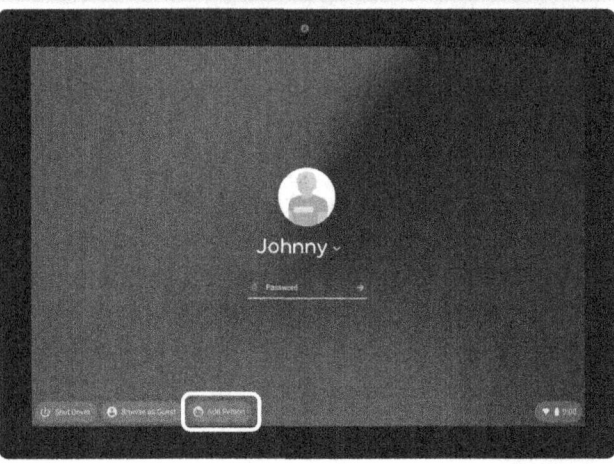

*Add Person*

## SETTING UP YOUR CHROMEBOOK

### DELETING USERS

To delete a user, you should begin by signing in as the administrator. Afterward, open the **Users section** and click on the user that you wish to remove. Select the **Remove option**, prior to confirming your choice. Once there is confirmation, the user will automatically be deleted from the Chromebook.

## PARENTAL CONTROLS

To set up parental controls for a child's Chromebook, you will have to use the Google Family Link. In order to utilize Chromebook parental controls with Google Family Link, you will require android devices that run Android 5.0 Lollipop or a later version. If you are an Apple user, your device has to be compatible with iOS 11 or above. Your Chromebook will have to be running Chrome OS 71 or better. Android devices that are compatible with Android 7.0 Nougat or the newer version allow you to install the Google Family Link. In case your Chromebook is not updated, ensure to do so.

### ADD CHILD ACCOUNTS

To add a child's account, it is important to initially download and start using the Google Family Link app on your phone.

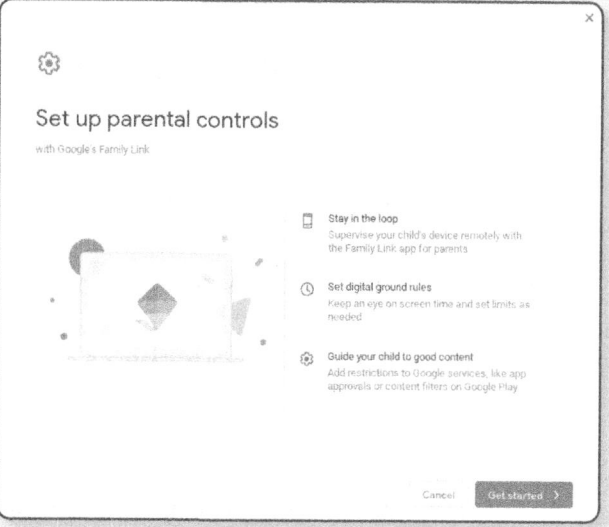

1. In case you are using a new Chromebook, you will need to do the setup process, then sign in with your parental account. This is crucial because the first account that signs in automatically becomes the owner account, thereby giving you special privileges.

2. Afterward, you can add the account of your child to the Chromebook. Simply click on the **Notification** area, then **Settings**. Afterward, click on the **People** option prior to clicking your account. Choose **Add account**. You will be required to have their Google account, email, and password.

3. Please note that it is advisable to disable the guest mode so that you are able to control who gets to sign in to your child's Chromebook. Without doing so, your child might bypass parental controls.

# CHAPTER 1

## SET UP PARENTAL CONTROLS

To set up parental controls, sign in to your child's account and go to the **Notification** area. Choose the **Settings** option, then select **People**. Afterward, choose **Parental controls** setup, then click on the **child's account** that you wish to activate the parental controls for. After that, you can now list the devices that you prefer to be protected. Once you finish with the list, make the confirmation that the parent account will do the supervision. When you complete the confirmation, input the email, password, and any necessary authentication. The system will then take you through what it can and cannot do. Afterward, your child has to enter their password in order to confirm the supervision.

## MONITORING CHILD ACCOUNTS WITH FAMILY LINKS

1. Monitoring child accounts using family links requires that you first open the **family link app**, then select your child.

2. Next, click **Manage settings** and select your desired family setting.

3. Afterward, select **Manage sites** so that you can manually block or allow particular sites.

## ALLOW OR BLOCKS APPS

1. If you want to allow or block apps, go ahead and open the **Family Link app**.

2. Afterward, select your **child's account**, then click on Apps installed.

3. After that, select **More** and click the **app name** that you wish to block or allow.

4. You should then go to the **Allow app** option and switch it on or off.

## MANAGE WEB BROWSING

1. To manage web browsing, go to the **Family Link app** and open it.

2. Click on your **child's account** and select **Settings**.

3. Afterward, choose **Manage settings**, then click on **Filters,** on Google Chrome.

# SETTING UP YOUR CHROMEBOOK

4. Select the right setting for your family from **Allow all sites, Only allow certain sites**, or **Try to block mature sites**.

5. Click on **Manage sites** so that you can block or allow certain sites.

## CONFIGURING OTHER SETTINGS

In addition to the above-mentioned settings, there are also other settings that you will find on your Chromebook. Some of the settings include internal, and external display settings, time zone, and keyboard settings. Let's discuss these and more in this section.

### MOUSE AND TOUCHPAD

With the Chromebook touchpad, you can execute many tasks such as switching between tabs, right-clicking, and scrolling vertically or horizontally. If you are interested in changing how your touchpad works, you may as well change the settings.

1. Go to the bottom right of your screen and select the time.

2. Choose **Settings**, then go to the **Device** option. After that, choose **Touchpad and mouse**.

3. From here, there are several available options from which you can choose your desired settings. For example, you can switch on tap dragging or pick the type of scrolling that you prefer.

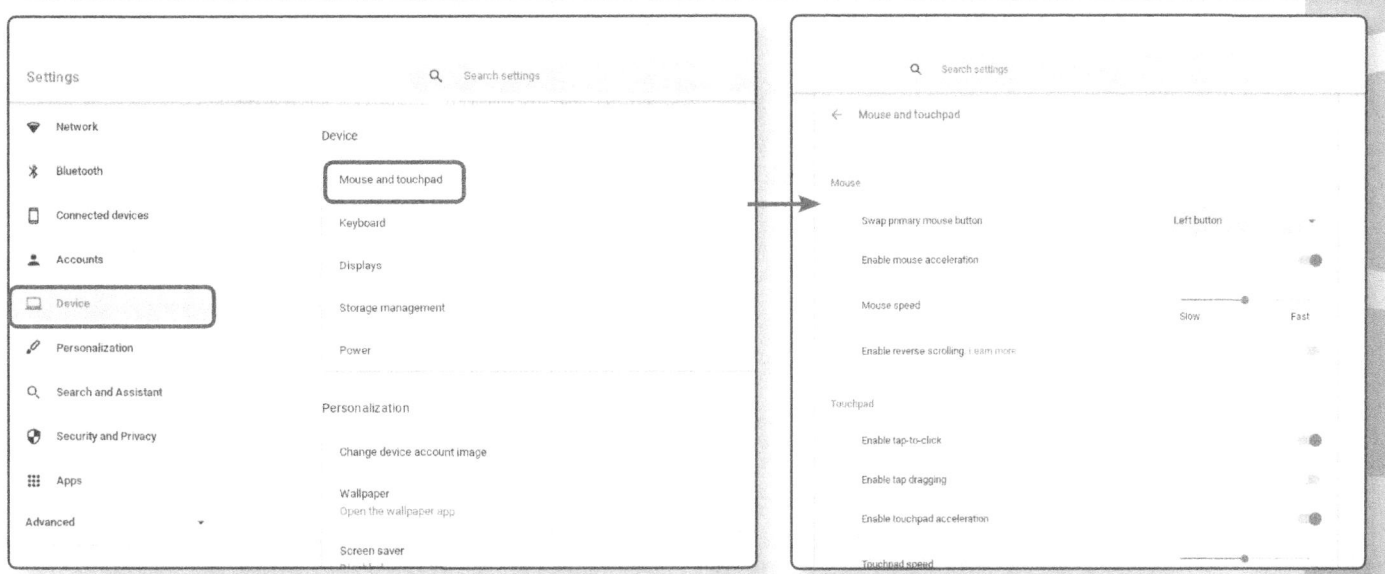

# CHAPTER 1

## INTERNAL DISPLAY SETTINGS

In case you are interested in changing your Chromebook's settings,

1. Open your **Chrome browser** and click on the **three vertical dots** that are located in the upper-right corner of your screen.

2. From the drop-down menu, choose **Settings**.

3. After that, go to the **Device section** and tap on **Displays**. This is where you choose your desired display options such as orientation and display size.

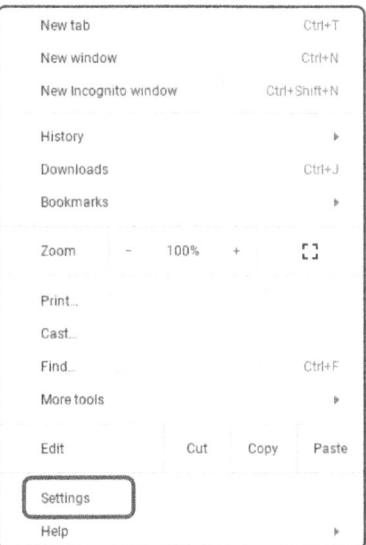

*Settings > Device > Displays*

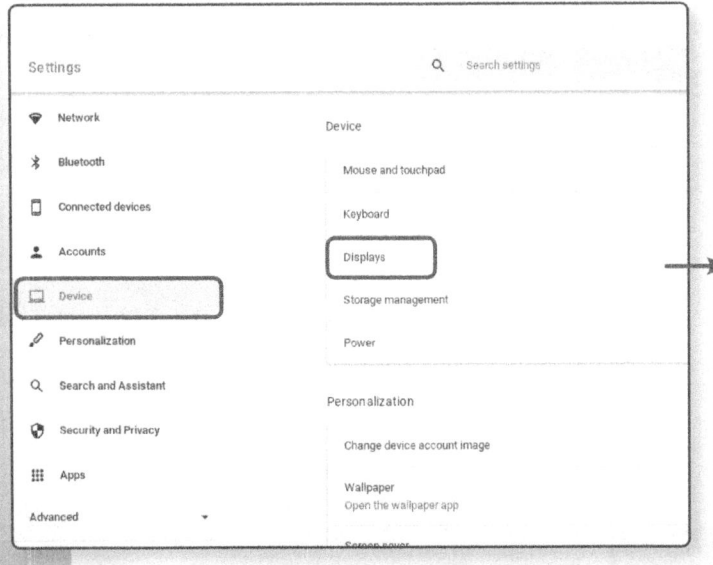
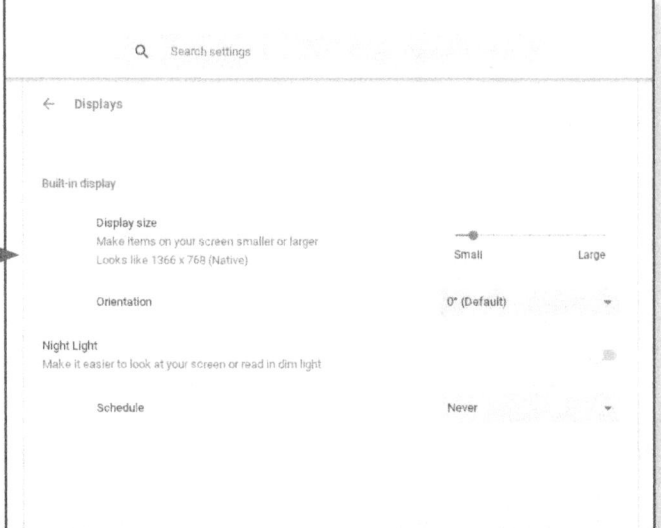

# SETTING UP YOUR CHROMEBOOK

## EXTERNAL DISPLAY SETTINGS

You can use a cable to externally display things on your Chromebook to another monitor or TV screen. Simply connect the cable from the Chromebook to the external display. Afterward, go to **Settings**, then **Device**, and finally click on **Displays**.

You could also do an external display through Chromecast on a wireless connection. To proceed, you can tap **Options**, then **Cast**. This is possible if you have a modern Chromebook.

## TIME ZONE

It is possible for your Chromebook to detect the location and then change the time accordingly. For this to occur, you have to be connected to the internet. However, you can also manually change the date and time, if you wish. To manually change the date and time on your Chromebook,

1. Click on the **Settings** app, to open it.
2. Next, click on **Advanced**, then go to the **Date and time** option.
3. Tap the **Time zone** option.
4. After that, click on **Choose from list**, then tap on the new time zone.

*Settings > Advanced > Date and time*

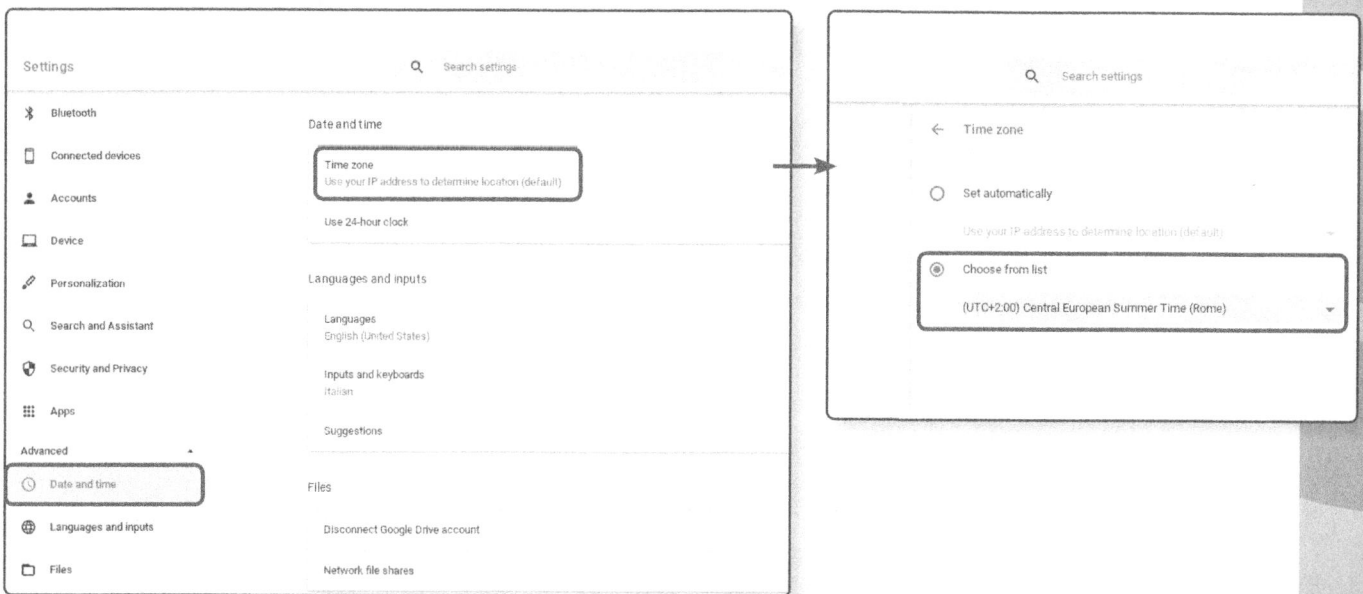

# CHAPTER 1

## CHANGE LANGUAGE

To change the language on your Chromebook:

1. Go to the **bottom right corner** of your screen and tap the **time icon**.

2. To access your **Settings menu**, click on the **gear icon**.

3. Next, click **Advanced**, which you will find at the bottom of the page.

4. You will then see an option that says **Languages and input**, from here, choose **Language** from the drop-down list.

5. If you do not find your desired language, tap **Add language**, then enter the language of choice.

6. After that, tap on the **three dots** next to the language you prefer to use.

*Settings > Advanced > Languages and inputs*

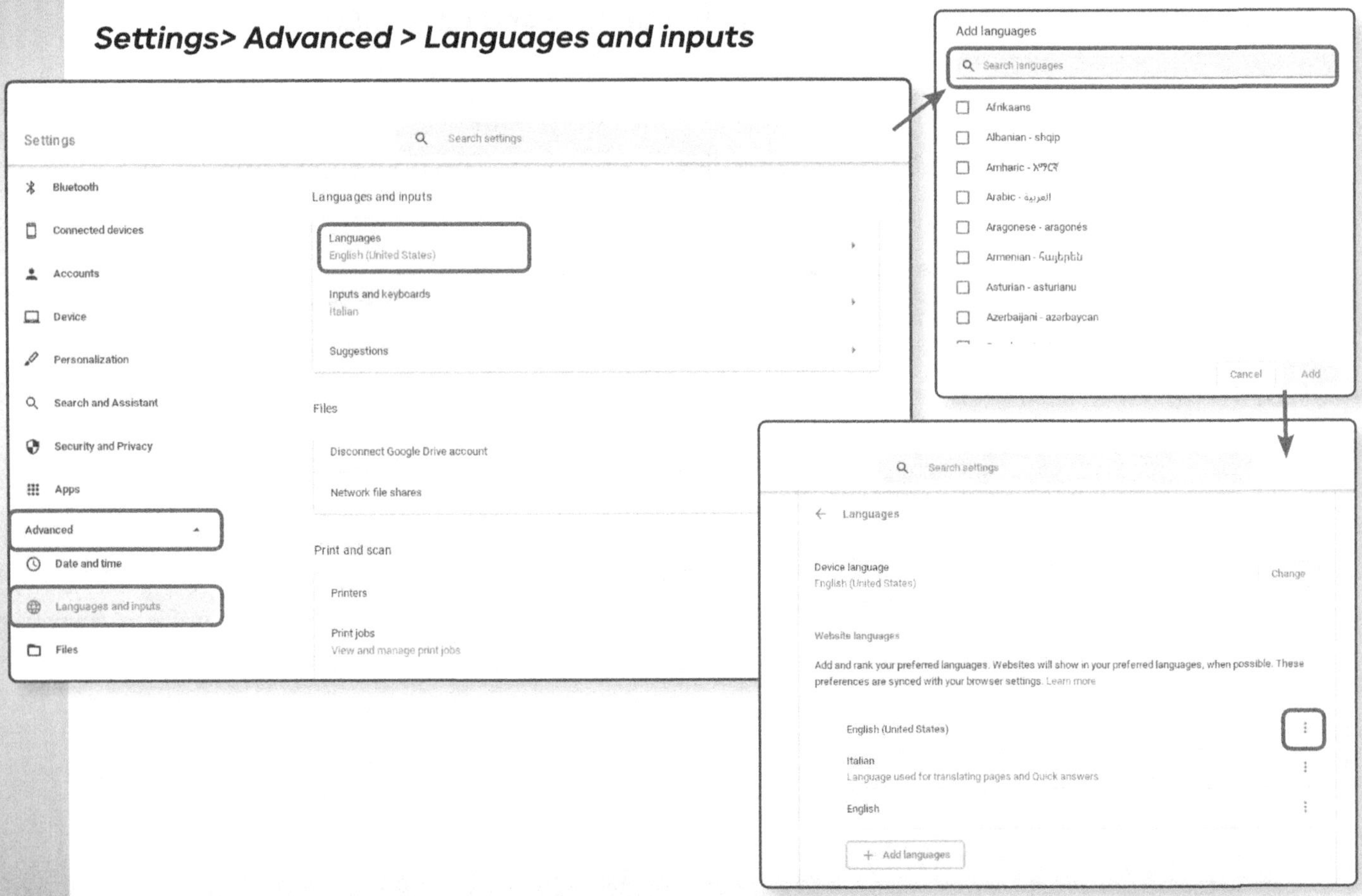

# SETTING UP YOUR CHROMEBOOK

## KEYBOARD LAYOUT

When it comes to the layout of a Chromebook's keyboard, there are a few differences from that of a Windows laptop. A search key is present on a Chromebook's keyboard, whereas there is normally a Caps Lock on a Windows PC. Instead of the function keys on the top rows of most computers, the Chromebook has shortcut keys for refreshing the web page and controlling the volume. In case you prefer a traditional layout, you can customize your Chromebook's keyboard so that it appears similar to what you are used to.

## KEYBOARD SETTINGS

To change your Chromebook's keyboard settings:

1. Go to the lower right corner of your screen and select the **Settings gear** in your Chrome browser.

2. On the left menu pane, select **Device** then **Keyboard.**

3. From this point, it is possible to change the function of certain keys by selecting options from the Ctrl drop-down menu. For example, to enable function keys, you can choose **Treat top-row keys as function keys**.

*Settings > Device > Keyboard*

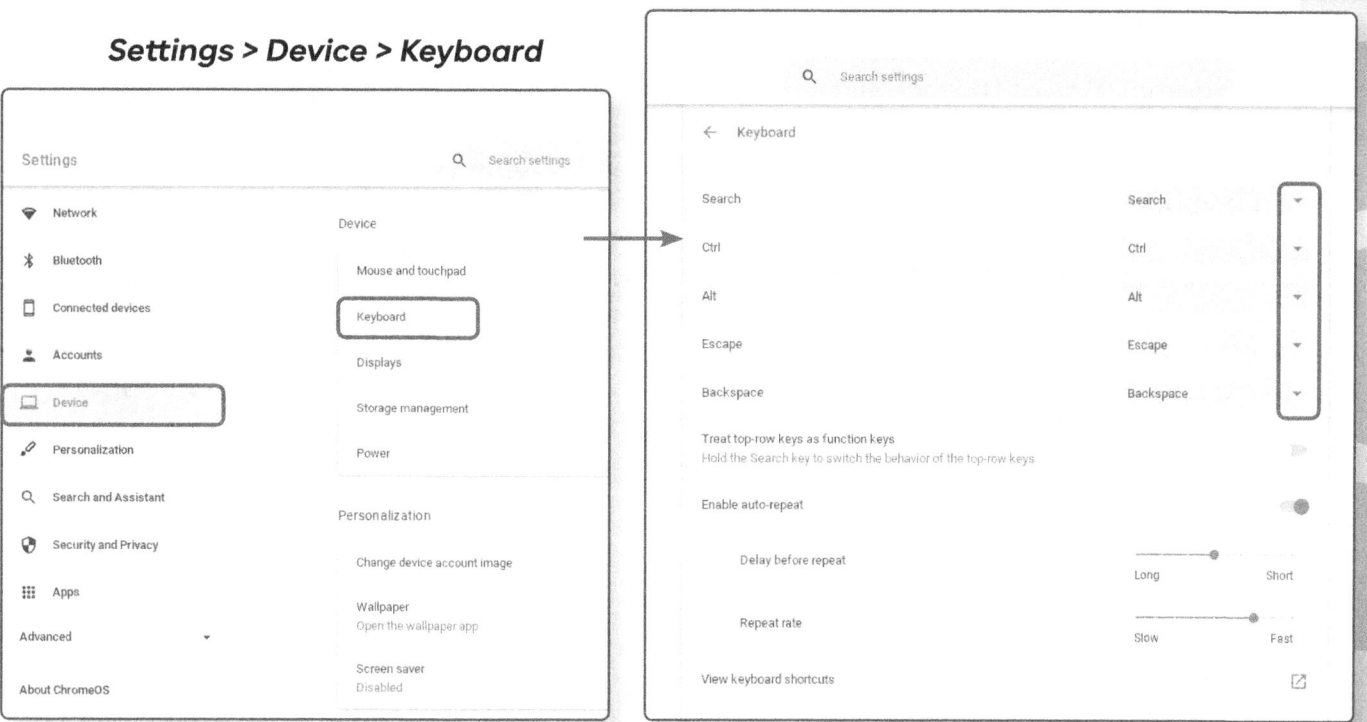

# CHAPTER 1

## NETWORK SETTINGS

If your Chromebook has multiple networks saved on it, it is possible for you to choose which type of network your device should automatically connect to. The default order of preference for which your Chromebook tries to connect is a wired local area network, secure wireless network, unsecured wireless network, and the mobile data network. However, the mobile data network can only be used if your Chromebook possesses a data plan.

## POWER OPTIONS

Keeping your Chromebook awake even when the lid is not open is feasible. The device can be controlled in such a manner that it can go to 'sleep' or "stay awake" when the lid is closed. Even when idle, you can choose to turn off the display or keep it on.

## INTEGRATE DROPBOX

If you want to easily access your Dropbox files, you have to integrate your Dropbox into your Chromebook. You can do this by installing the File System for the Dropbox extension from Chrome's Web Store.

Go to website: *chrome.google.com/webstore/category/extensions* and search for **'FILE SYSTEM FOR DROPBOX'**.

Upon completion of the installation process, you have to grant it access to your Dropbox account so that your Dropbox folder will be positioned on the left panel of your Chromebook's file manager. Once you do this, it becomes easier for you to drag and drop your Google Drive folders and download files to your Dropbox.

You can easily transfer files from your Dropbox to your Google Drive and download them as well. Please note that although the integration process will have been successful, the file system for the Dropbox extension does not provide you with offline access to your files that are on Dropbox. To have access to your Dropbox account in your Chromebook's Files app:

1. Click on the **Files app**, to open it.

2. Afterward, tap the **Menu icon**, then click on your **Dropbox** folder.

If your personal and work Dropbox accounts are connected to your Chromebook, you will be able to see both folders.

## SETTING UP YOUR CHROMEBOOK

*Go to website > chrome.google.com/webstore/category/extensions*

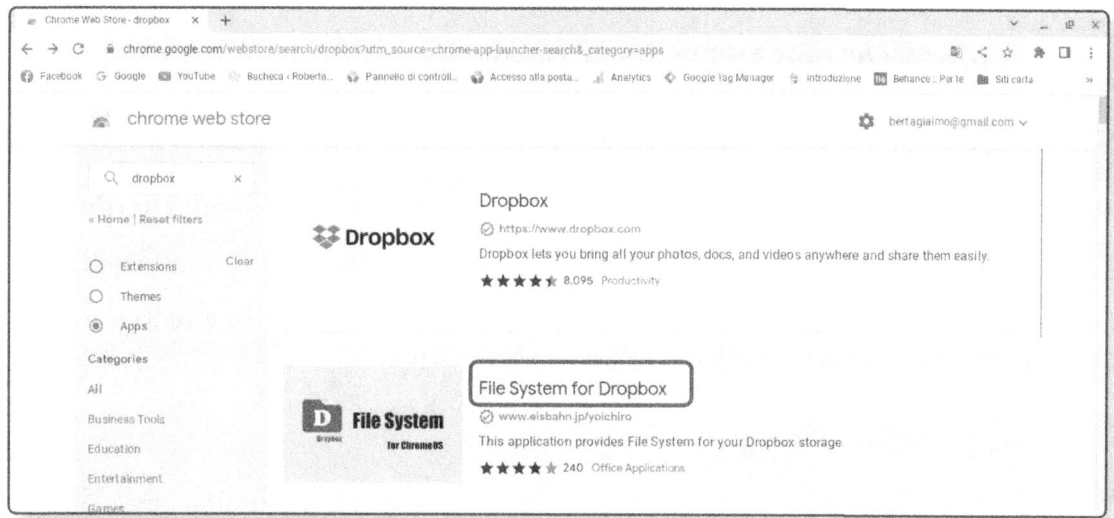

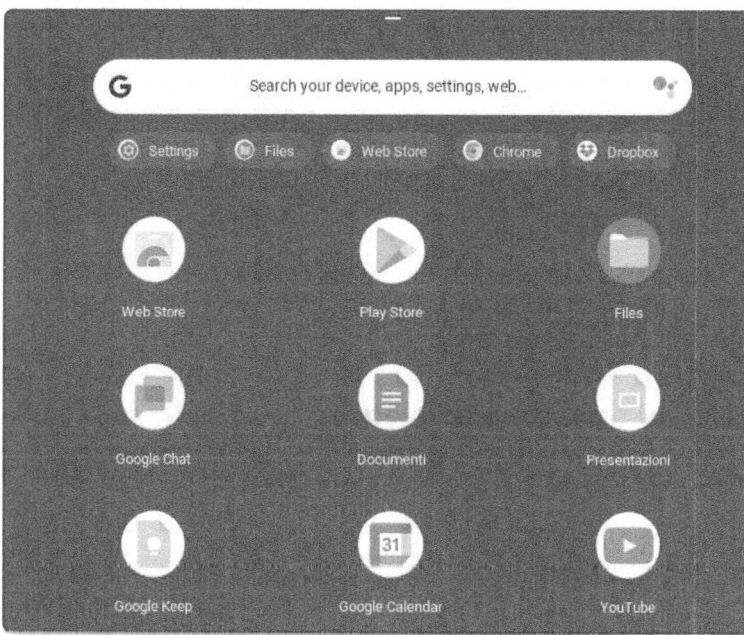

*Files App > Dropbox*

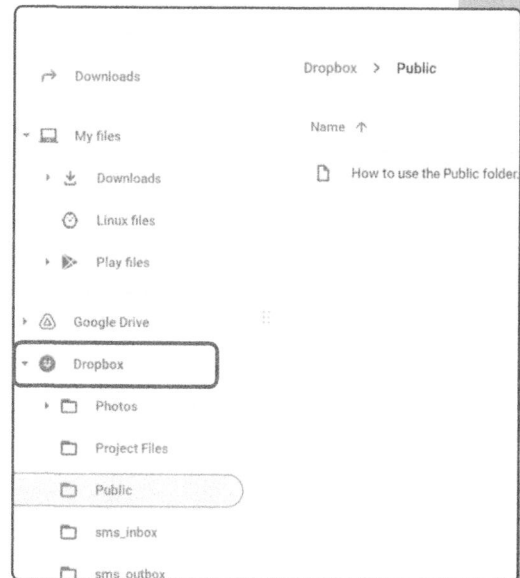

## INTEGRATE ONE-DRIVE

You can also integrate your One-Drive into your Chrome's OS in order to easily access them on the cloud. To do this, you need to:

1. Go to your Chromebook and open the **Files app**.

# CHAPTER 1

2. Choose the **Add** new services option that you will find on the sidebar.

3. After that, tap **Install and Add** the One-Drive app.

4. Upon seeing a pop-up window, go ahead and select **Mount**.

5. You have to then sign in with your One-Drive details when the login screen pops up.

6. After logging in, you will see a new folder in your file menu from which you can click to see your saved folders and files in One-Drive.

## REMOTE DESKTOP

In recent times, it has now become possible to utilize a mobile device or computer to access applications and files on another computer through the use of the Chrome Remote Desktop. This is feasible if you have internet connectivity. For remote access, you will require to download the Chrome Remote Desktop app. Let's get more details in this section.

### SETUP

1. To set up the remote desktop, open **Chrome** web browser and enter *"remotedesktop.google.com/access"* in the address bar.

2. Choose **Set up remote access** and then tap **Download**.

3. After that, follow the instructions that will pop up on-screen.

### CONNECTING

Upon finishing the setup process, you can now access your host computer from another computer or device.

1. Simply go to your Chrome browser and enter *"remotedesktop.google.com/access"* It is important that you sign in to Chrome with the same Google account that you used on the host computer.

2. You will then see your computer's name. By clicking on it, you will be prompted to **enter your pin**.

## SETTING UP YOUR CHROMEBOOK

**3.** Once you enter your pin, you will now have full access to your computer, much like you are sitting in front of it.

*Go to website > remotedesktop.google.com/access*

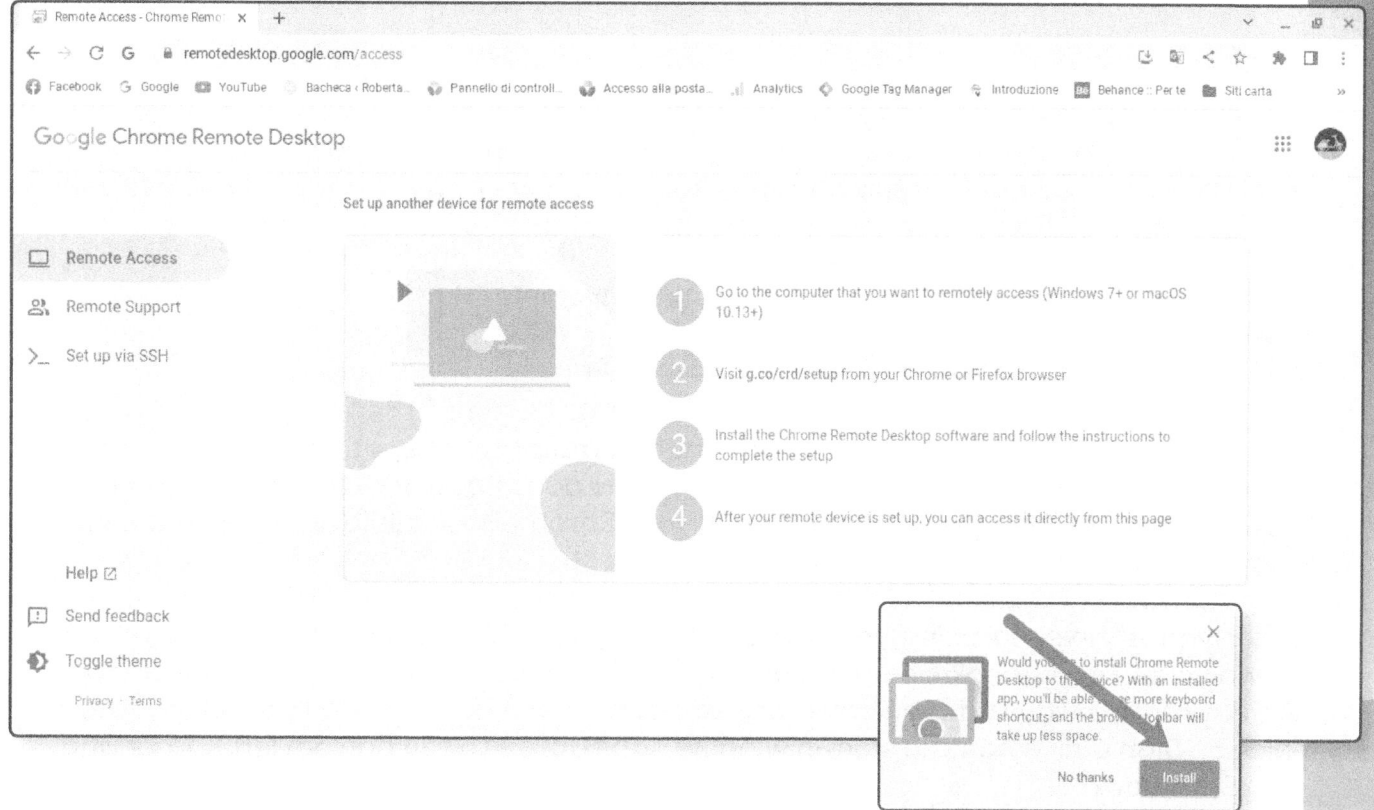

# Chapter 2: Getting Around Chromebook

You can find out some tips that will make it easier for you to use your Chromebook in this chapter. Some of them include the different gestures that you can do using your touchpad. Also, included in this chapter are discussions about the Task Manager and the System tray. Read on to understand these features and more.

## POWER UP AND POWER DOWN

To power up your Chromebook, go to the top-right area of the keyboard and press the **Power button**. If the power button is not located at this spot, search for it in the lower and top corners of your device. In case this does not work, close the device and connect it to the charger. After that, open your Chromebook's lid. Some Chromebooks may be powered up by simply opening their lids.

After you've finished using your Chromebook, you should power it down. To power down your Chromebook, go ahead and tap on the **System tray**, then the **Power icon**. An alternative way that you could use to power down is to go to **System tray**, then click on **Sign out**. When the sign-in window pops up, go to the bottom left corner and tap Shut down.

An additional way that you could use to power down your Chromebook is to go to the **Lock key** and press it for about three seconds. Afterward, tap the **Shutdown** option that you will see at the bottom left corner.

## THE LOGIN SCREEN

There have been advances in technology in most aspects of life. Even more so for the Chromebook's login screen. Upon entering passwords, they are not aligned in the center of the login page anymore. In the new update, the field has also become remarkably smaller (Duke, 2021).

## GETTING AROUND CHROMEBOOK

## THE TOUCHPAD

The Chromebook touchpad allows you to do movements and points to things on your screen. Some of the movements include scrolling, clicking, and dragging. Let's discuss these movements and several others that the touchpad supports.

- **One finger tap:** This gesture is used when you want to click on an item or on your screen. You can do this by pressing down the touchpad's bottom half until you hear a clicking sound.

- **Two-finger tap:** The two-finger tap is used when you want to right-click. Simply, use two fingers to click on the touchpad.

- **One-finger click and drag:** In order to drag and drop an item, use one finger to click on it. Using another finger, move the item. To drop the item to its new location, you should then release both fingers.

- **Two-finger scroll:** To do a two-finger scroll, go ahead and put two fingers on your touchpad. If you prefer to do vertical movements, move them up and down. If you want to do a horizontal movement, scroll from left to right.

- **Two-finger swipe:** The two-finger swipe allows you to place two fingers on the touchpad, then quickly move them to the left or the right. This is mostly used when you want to go in a forward or backward motion on web pages. You can also do this motion if you desire to move between apps.

- **Three-finger swipe:** In case you would like to see all of your open windows, you can do the swiping up motion using three fingers. Sometimes, you may have multiple browsers open. You can move between tabs by swiping left and right with three fingers.

# CHAPTER 2

## THE KEYBOARD

Apart from the normal keyboard, it is also possible to use an onscreen one (AbilityNet, 2021). If you want to add images to emails, files, and documents or handwrite text, you can utilize your Chromebook's on-screen keyboard. We will discuss how to use your on-screen keyboard in this section.

### ONSCREEN KEYBOARD HELP

1. To use your onscreen keyboard, go to the lower right corner of your screen and tap the **Time** widget. Afterward, select **Settings**.

2. After selecting **Settings**, a window will appear on which you have to click **Accessibility**, on the left-hand column. In case you do not see Accessibility, tap on **Advanced** so that you can see more menu items.

3. On your right-hand panel, select **Manage Accessibility Features**.

4. You will then see the **Accessibility settings** option and have to scroll down to the section which says **Keyboard and text input**. Click on **Enable** on-screen keyboard to activate the switch to **On**.

5. Now you can go to the **Status bar** so that you are able to activate the on-screen keyboard by tapping on the icon that is located on the lower right-hand corner of the screen.

*Settings> Advanced>Accessibility > Manage accessibility features*

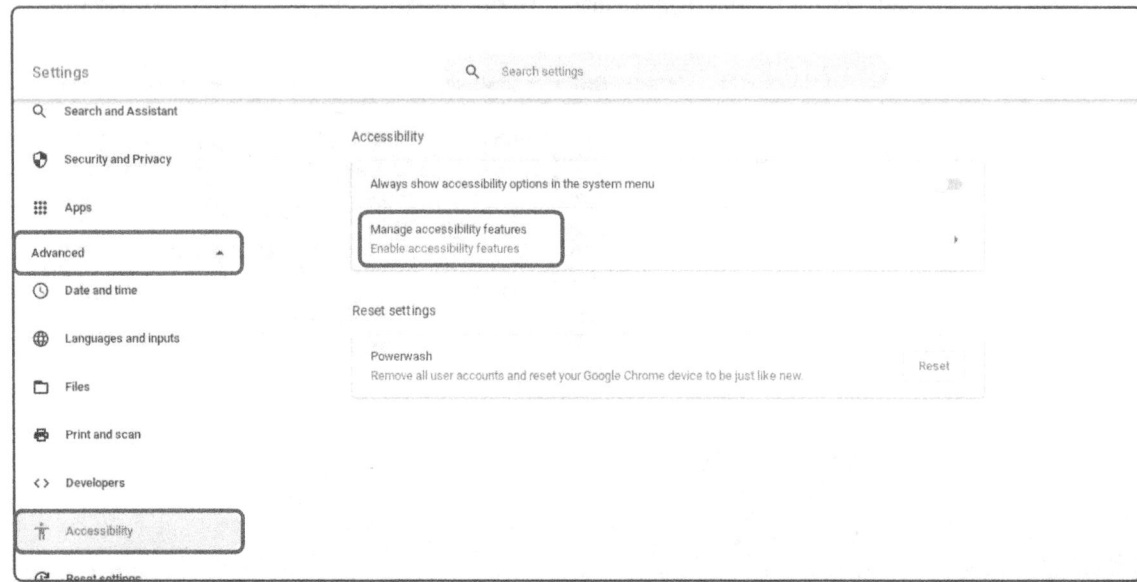

# GETTING AROUND CHROMEBOOK

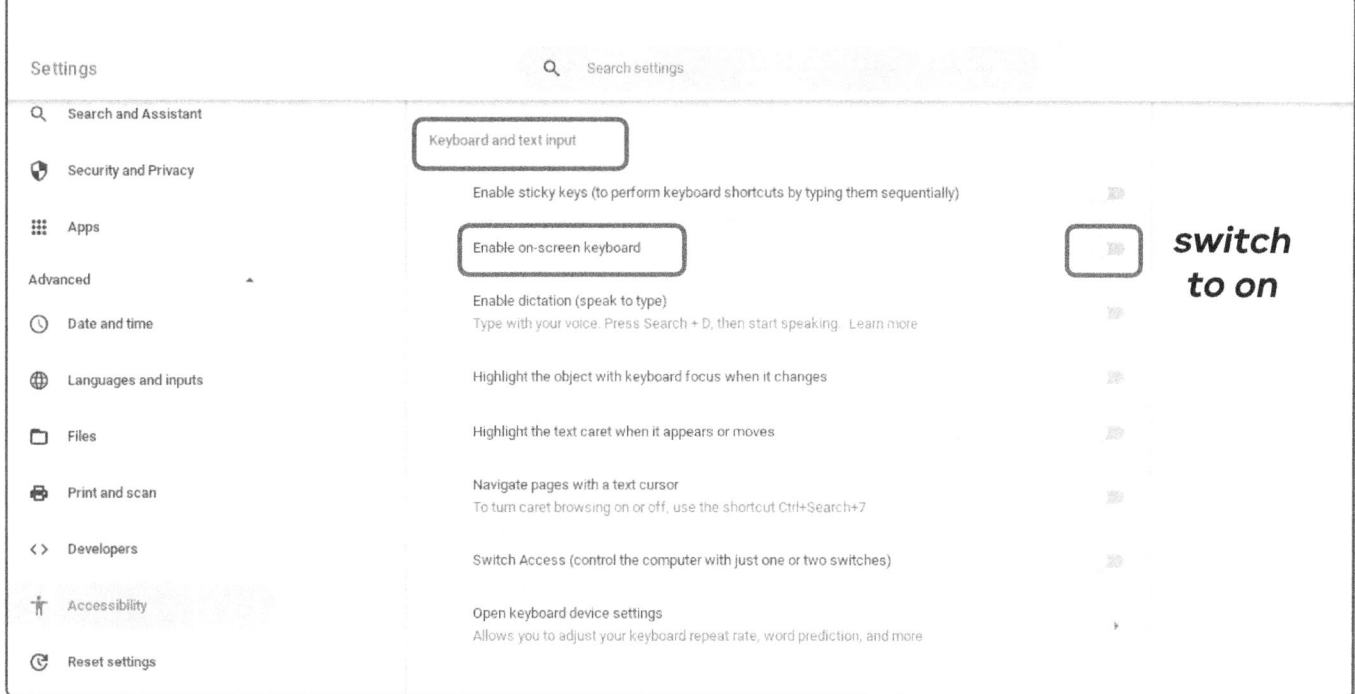

## CHROMEBOOK TASK MANAGER

Your Chromebook possesses a built-in task manager. This task manager is responsible for letting you see active processes and programs that are running on your computer. **The Chrome web browser also possesses a task manager that helps you to deal with troublesome tabs and extensions.**

To open your Task Manager, tap on the **Three dots** that are located at the top right corner of your screen. Afterward, click on **More tools**, then **Task manager**. An alternative way to open the Task manager on your Chromebook is to press **Search and Escape**, on your keyboard. Upon opening the Task Manager, you can see the activity currently running in the browser, list of tabs, and extensions.

In case a certain extension or tab has stopped responding, and you want to end it, you can easily do it on the **Task manager**. Simply, tap **on the process**, then click on **End process**. If you are interested in simultaneously ending multiple processes, just highlight the processes from the list by pressing the **Control or Shift** key, then click on **End process**.

# CHAPTER 2

**Chrome Web Browser**

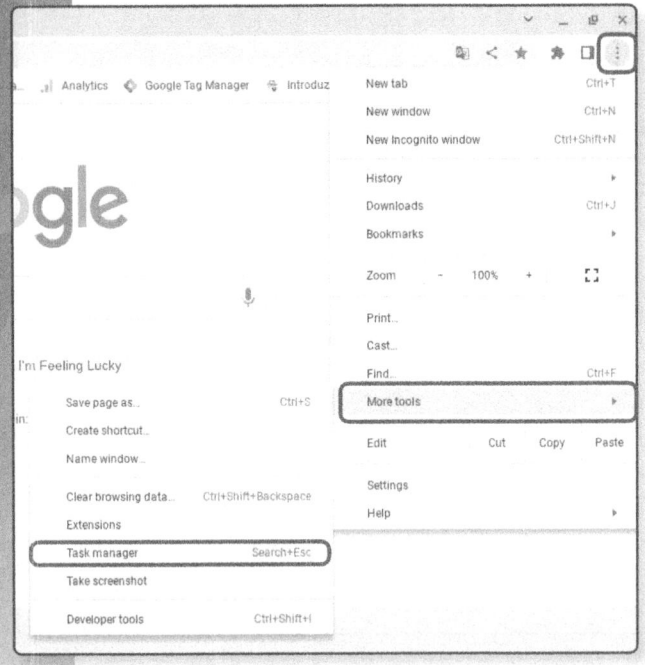

**Task Manager**

## DESKTOP AND THE APP SHELF

Although you can't put icons or apps on your Chromebook's desktop, it is possible to pin them to your App shelf so that you can quickly access them. Being an equivalent of the Windows taskbar, the Shelf is a row of apps that are located at the screen's bottom. The following steps will help you to pin apps to your App Shelf.

1. Tap on the **Launcher** and click on the **Up arrow**.

2. Afterward, find the app that you wish to add to your **Shelf**.

3. **Right-click** on the icon of the desired app prior to selecting **Pin to shelf**.

4. When you look at the bottom of your screen you will now see your newly pinned app on the Shelf.

Please note that you can arrange the apps in your desired order. Simply highlight, hold an app, and drag it to the desired position. Afterward, drop the app to its new position. If for some reason you decide to remove an app from the Shelf, right-click on it and click **Unpin**. Upon finishing this action, the app will immediately be removed from your Chromebook's shelf.

## GETTING AROUND CHROMEBOOK

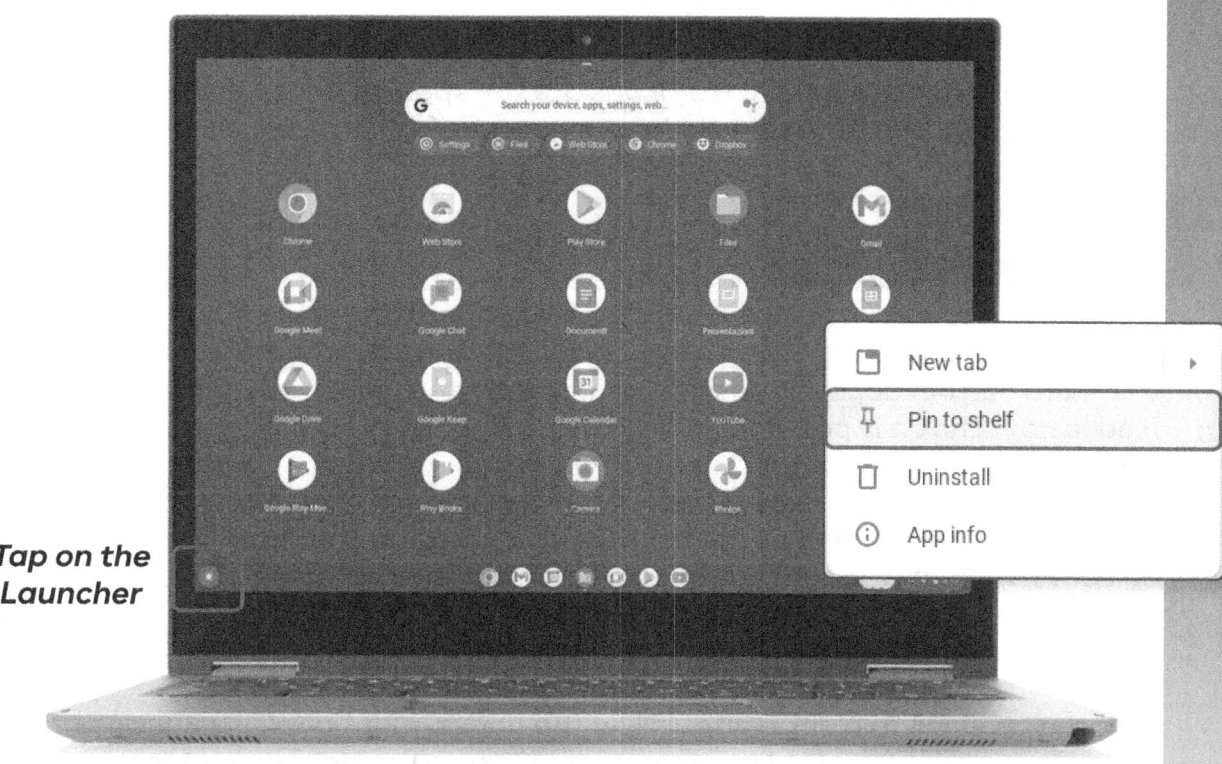

*Tap on the Launcher*

## SYSTEM TRAY

You can find the System tray on the lower-right corner of your Chromebook's screen. The system tray functions to display the battery power of your Chromebook, Wi-Fi strength, and time. This means that, by taking a peek at your System tray, you can quickly tell what time it is, how you are doing on battery power and the strength of your Wi-Fi connection. In the event that your Chromebook is charging, a lightning bolt icon will appear in the battery.

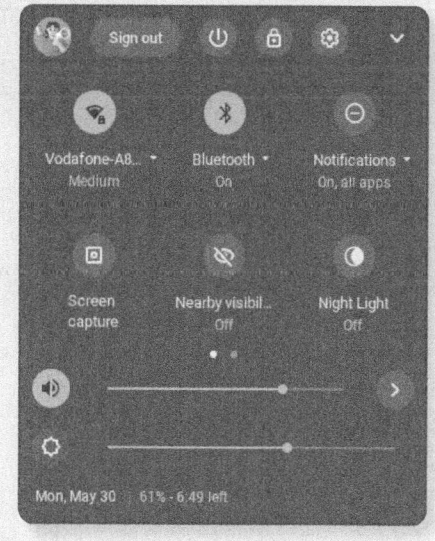

Apart from displaying the battery, Wi-Fi strength, and time, it is important to note that when you click on the System tray icon, you are able to see several other options. For example, the Sign out button will appear, which you can tap to sign out of your Chromebook.

You will also see the power icon, for shutting down your device. The Settings icon helps to access the settings page so that it becomes possible for you to customize or update your account.

# CHAPTER 2

Also, available on the System tray icons are the speaker and sun icons which assist in adjusting your volume as well as the brightness of the screen, respectively.

## NOTIFICATIONS

It is possible to get notifications such as reminders and meetings from apps, extensions, and websites on your Chromebook. By default, Chrome can alert you when there are certain apps, extensions, or websites that want to send you notifications. Please note that it is possible for you to change this setting if you wish.

To change the default settings on your computer, go ahead and open your Chrome browser. Go to the top right of your screen and tap on the **three dots**, then **Settings**. Select **Privacy and security**, click on **Site settings**, then on **Notifications**. After that, choose the option that you wish to be your default setting. These can be **Block a site**, **Allow a site**, or **Allow quieter notification prompts**.

In case you want to block a site, follow the above-mentioned instructions then click on **Block a site**. You will then see an option that says, **Not allowed to send notifications**. Next to this option, you should tap on **Add**, then enter the address of the website. Last, select **Add**.

To allow a site, click on the **Add** option, that appears next to **Allowed to send notifications**. Next, enter the address of the website, then click **Add**.

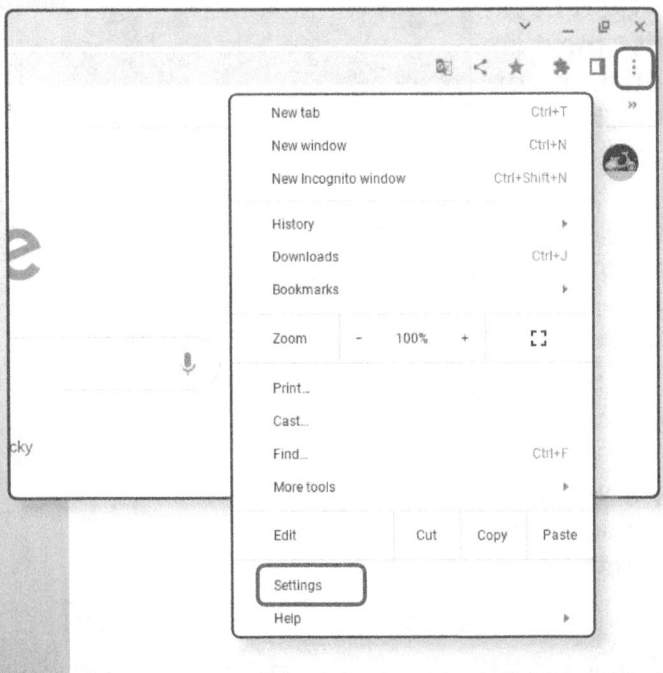
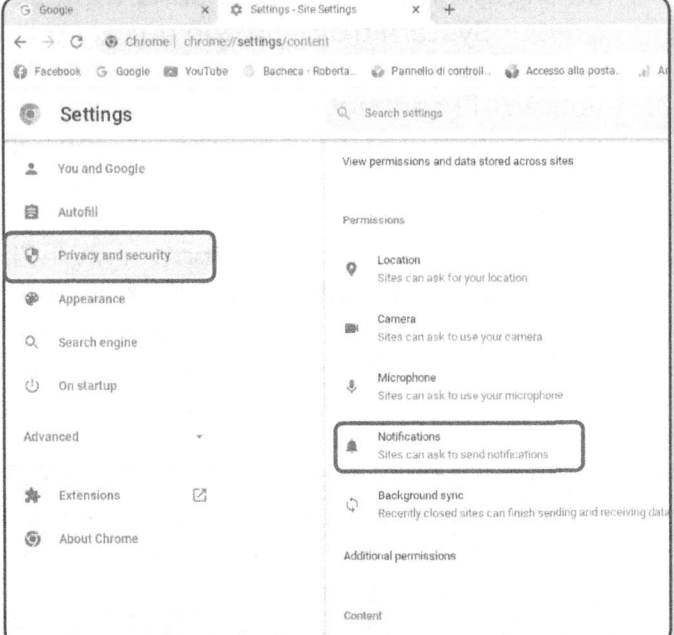

# GETTING AROUND CHROMEBOOK

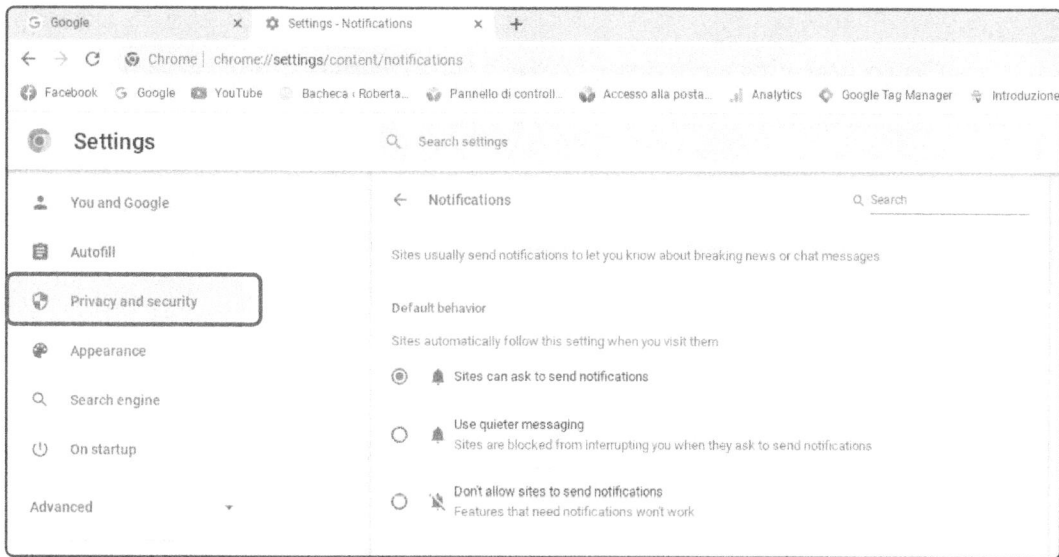

## PINNED FILES AND HOLDING SPACE

Most of the work that you do on your Chromebook is done online. However, you may want to quickly access a local file or folder offline. The best way to quickly access it is by pinning it to your Chromebook's Shelf or taskbar.

To pin an item on your taskbar, you have to first enable a flag (Burgess, 2021). **When you want to enable a flag, open your Chrome browser and enter the address *"chrome://flags/#enable-holding-space"*, then press Enter.**

This will bring you to the option which says **Quick access to screenshots, downloads, and files**. Select the **dropdown menu** and activate **Enabled**. For the flag to be activated, you will have to restart your Chromebook.

Upon restarting your computer, a **Holding space** icon will appear at the lower right corner of the taskbar that is next to the clock. When you tap on the Holding space icon, you will quickly access your most current downloads and screenshots.

Once you finish creating a holding space, you will now be able to pin your desired folders or files to the taskbar. To pin your desired folder or file, click on the **Files app**, then tap the item you wish to pin. Bear in mind that this also works for the Linux and Play Store partitions that are on your Chromebook.

After tapping the item, right-click on it. From the menu, select **Pin to shelf**. Once the pinning process is complete, your folder or file will be available in the Holding space.

# CHAPTER 2

*Go to website> chrome://flags/#enable-holding-space*

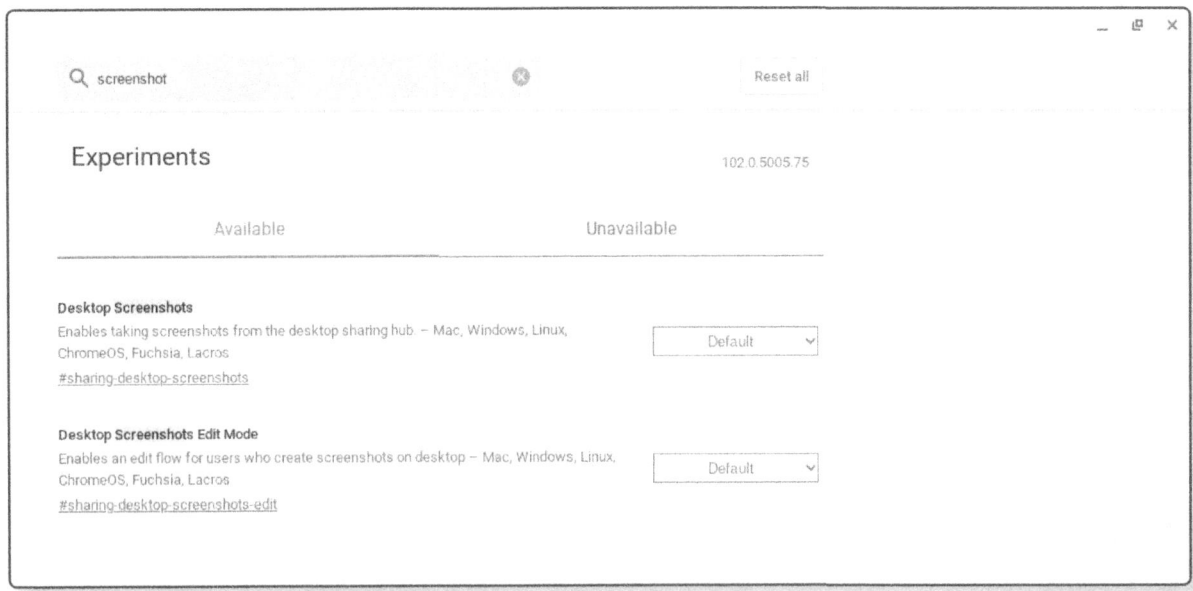

## APP LAUNCHER

**On your Chromebook's shelf, at the lower-left corner, you will see a circle icon, which is the Launcher icon.** This icon is responsible for bringing up the search field so that you are able to open websites, search for apps, and search Google. Just underneath the search field, your recently used apps will be visible. Upon clicking the arrow on top of the search field, you will get to see all of your apps.

### OPENING

To open apps on your keyboard, you can use a keyboard shortcut. For example, if you want to open Google Play, and it is the sixth app on your shelf, go ahead and press Alt and the number of the app, which is six. Simply put, if you want to access Google Play, press **Alt and 6**.

### APP TYPES

The types of apps that are present in the App launcher are the default ones and others that are linked to your Google Account. A total of up to 16 apps can be held in the App launcher. However, as you continue to install additional apps, the Chrome OS will add more windows to accommodate your new applications. In the event that you have more than 16 apps, you will see horizontal-shaped buttons at the bottom part

## GETTING AROUND CHROMEBOOK

of your screen. These buttons are a sign of extra windows that contain applications. To navigate between windows, you can just click these buttons.

### CREATE APP FOLDERS

To create app folders, it is advisable to click and drag **Google Apps launchers** into an individual folder. This will help by creating space in that App menu. On completion of adding the launchers to a folder, you can then open the folder by clicking on it and assigning a name to it.

### PIN APPS TO YOUR APP SHELF

For you to quickly access your favorite apps, it is possible to pin them to the Shelf. To pin one of your favorite apps to the shelf, **right-click** any clear part of your desktop. Once you do that, a screen will pop up, which has several options including one which says **Pin to shelf**. Afterward, select the app that you wish to pin. - See also pag. 41 -

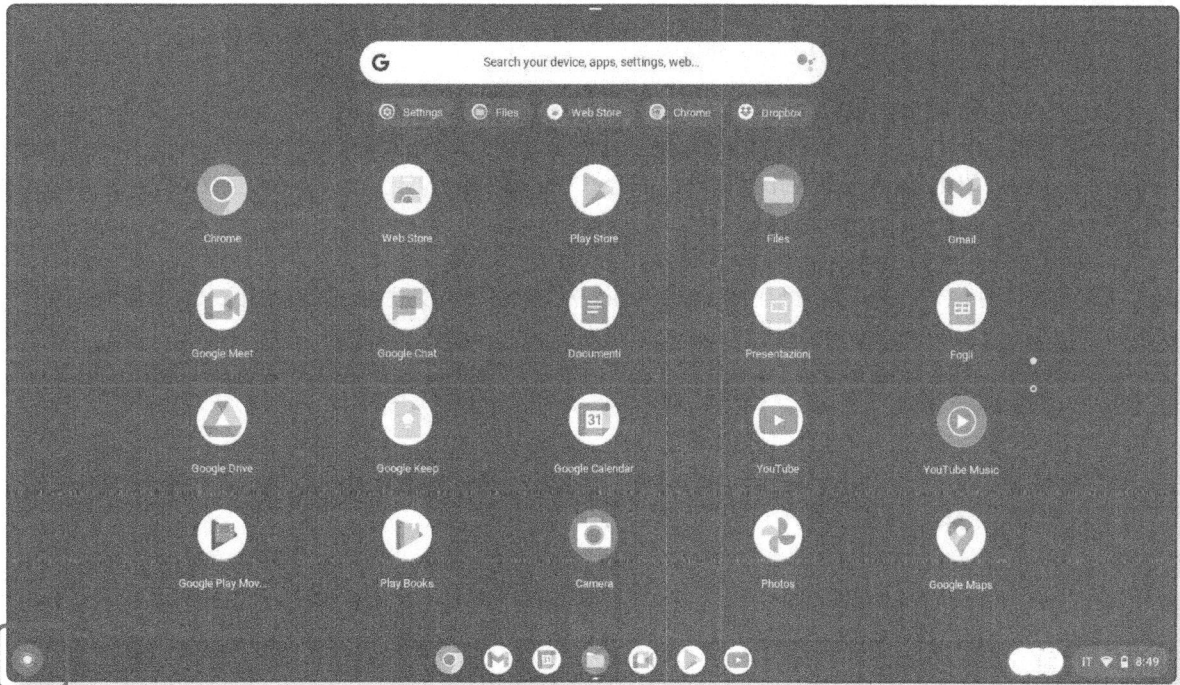

*Launcher icon*

# Chapter 3: Management Files in Chromebook

The chrome OS's file manager is known as 'files.' In this chapter, we will take a closer look at some of the important functions with regard to management files. We will also explore how you can access them with ease on your Chromebook.

## CREATING FOLDERS

The Chromebook **Files App** gives you an option to create, save, and store your documents or files on the cloud. Folders are created to organize and sort your files so that you can access them easily when you need them. Now, follow these steps to create a new folder on your Chromebook.

1. Go to the left side of the files window and select the **Downloads folder**.

2. If you look at the window's top right corner, you will see the **settings widget** and click on it.

3. After clicking on the settings widget, the **File Setting** menu will appear and then click **New folder**.

4. A new folder will appear and its name will be highlighted to show that it can be changed if necessary.

5. Type in your preferred name for the new folder and press **Enter** and the name will be saved.

To cross-check if your created folder has been saved, you can try opening it by double-clicking or double-tapping the created folder's icon. A window for this folder will be opened and it will be empty since nothing will have been added to it yet.

# MANAGEMENT FILES IN CHROMEBOOK

Bear in mind that **there are two types of folders**, which are **parent and child folders. A folder that contains another one or more folders defines the parent folder. The folder that you find inside another is the child folder.** In the path, you will find the parent folder appearing to the left of a child folder. In case you want to return to the parent folder, you have to click the folder's name in the path.

*Files app > Downloads*

*Settings widget*

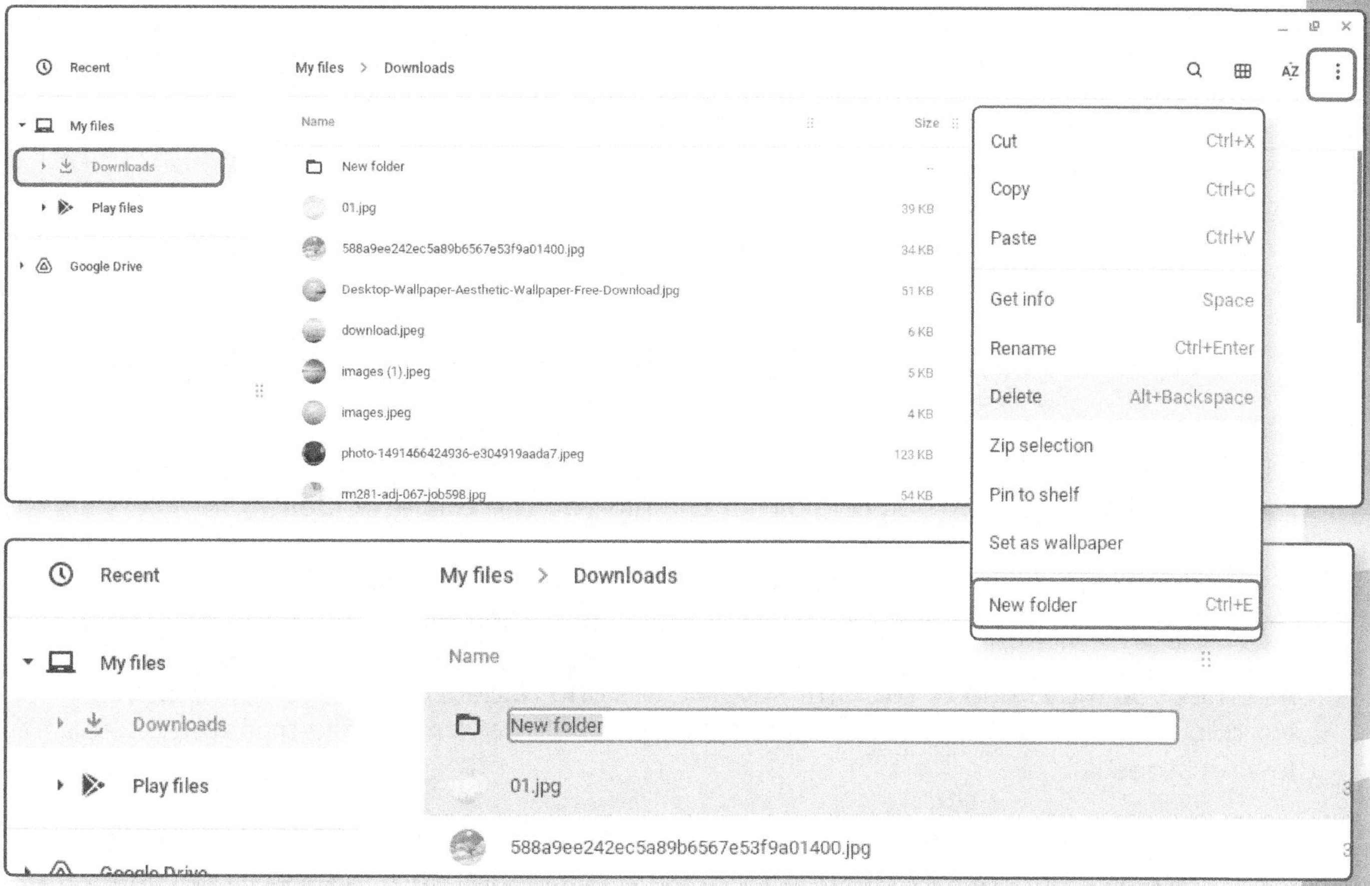

Considering that you may be using the Chromebook consistently, you may need to create several folders and continuously clicking the **Settings widget** can become monotonous. A folder can be created faster and easily by pressing **Ctrl + E**. Follow these steps to rename the folder for your convenience.

1. First click the desired folder icon.

## CHAPTER 3

2. Press **Ctrl + Enter** and the name of the folder will be highlighted and will be editable.

3. Type in the desired folder name and press **Enter** to save.

## MOVING FILES

You can use Files to organize or move your files on your Chromebook. Creating several folders allows you to group your files accordingly. For example, you may not want to mix pictures, documents, music, and videos in the same folder. For convenience and easy access to your files, you need to group these files into separate folders.

Follow these steps to move your files and folders.

1. Locate and click the **App Launcher** icon which you will find at the bottom left corner of the screen.

2. Go on and click on the **Files** icon. Files will open in a window separate from a Chrome browser.

3. If you are using the touchpad, click and hold the file you need to move. Use another finger to drag and direct the file into the target folder.

4. Hanging the file over the folder highlights the underneath folder and if it is the right target. Release to drop your file into the folder.

At times you may need to transfer several files and folders at once rather than picking and moving a single item each time. You can carry out multi-file transfers by following steps

1. Click the **Files application** and open a window. Now, press and hold the **Ctrl key** and click the desired files or folders. These files and folders will become highlighted.

2. Click on any part of the highlight, hold, and then drag the selection to the target location.

3. When you hover the selection over a folder, it will be highlighted. Now you can drop the files into the selected location by releasing.

There are times when you need to select the entire file collection for moving. In that

# MANAGEMENT FILES IN CHROMEBOOK

case, take the following steps.

1. Press the **Shift key**, click with a single finger, and move the pointer with another finger so that you highlight several successive or consecutive files at once.

2. Now, click and hold any part of the highlighted selection and drag it to your desired selection

3. Hold the files over the desired location and the destination folder will be highlighted to indicate that you can now drop the files.

4. Release your finger from the touchpad and drop the files into the desired folder.

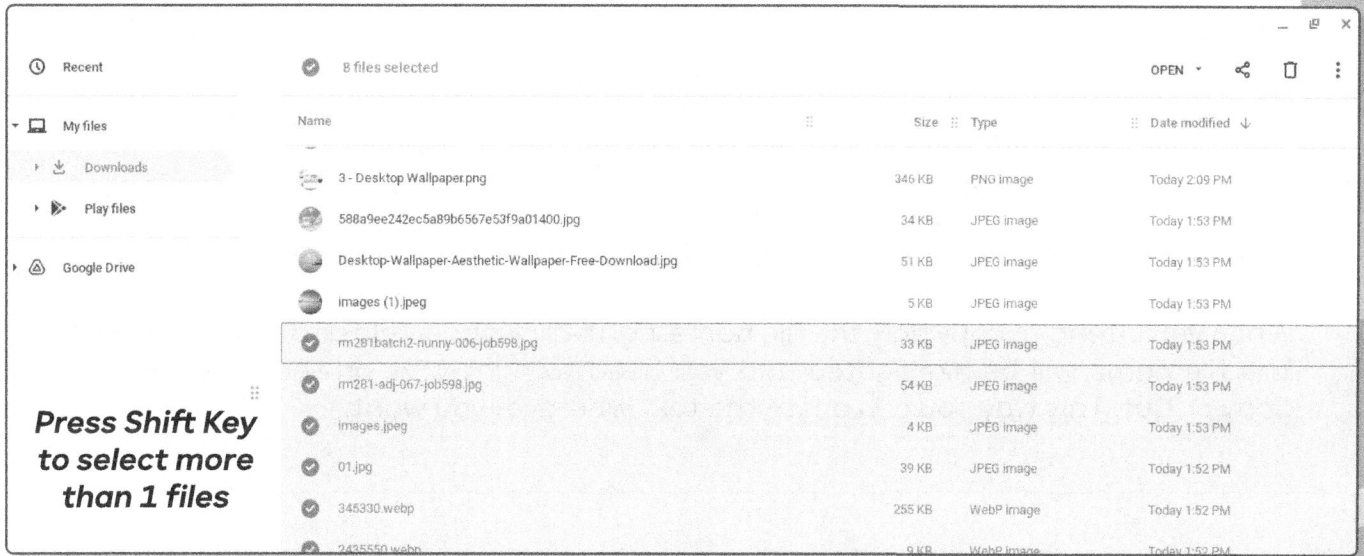

*Press Shift Key to select more than 1 files*

## COPYING FILES

Google has done its best to make sure that Chromebooks are as user-friendly as possible. Copying and pasting files is something you may need to do regularly. Follow these steps to learn how to copy and paste files on your Chromebook using the keyboard.

1. If you want to copy specific files and folders, press **Ctrl** and click on the files or folders you need to copy. Also, you can select multiple files by pressing

# CHAPTER 3

**Shift** and clicking on the first and last files. To copy a single file, click on the file or folder you need to copy. In the event that you want to copy all the files press **Ctrl + A**.

2. Now that you have chosen the files you need to copy, press **Ctrl + C** for copying or **Ctrl + X** to move.

3. Drag the files or folders to the desired location you need to paste them.

4. Press **Ctrl + V** to paste.

It is possible to copy a file name without the file extension. Click on the file and press **Ctrl + Enter**. This way you only copy the file name, not the entire file and its contents.

## COPYING USING A MOUSE OR TOUCHPAD

1. First, **right-click** on the file or folder you need to copy

2. Now, select **Cut** to move the entire file or **Copy** to make a copy of the file.

3. Move to the desired location and click on the free space.

4. Finally, click **Paste** to copy or move the files to the new location.

When you intend to copy only the file name, right-click on the file and select **Rename**. The file name will be highlighted and you need to right-click on the text and click **Copy** or **Cut**. This way you can paste the text wherever you want.

## MANAGEMENT FILES IN CHROMEBOOK

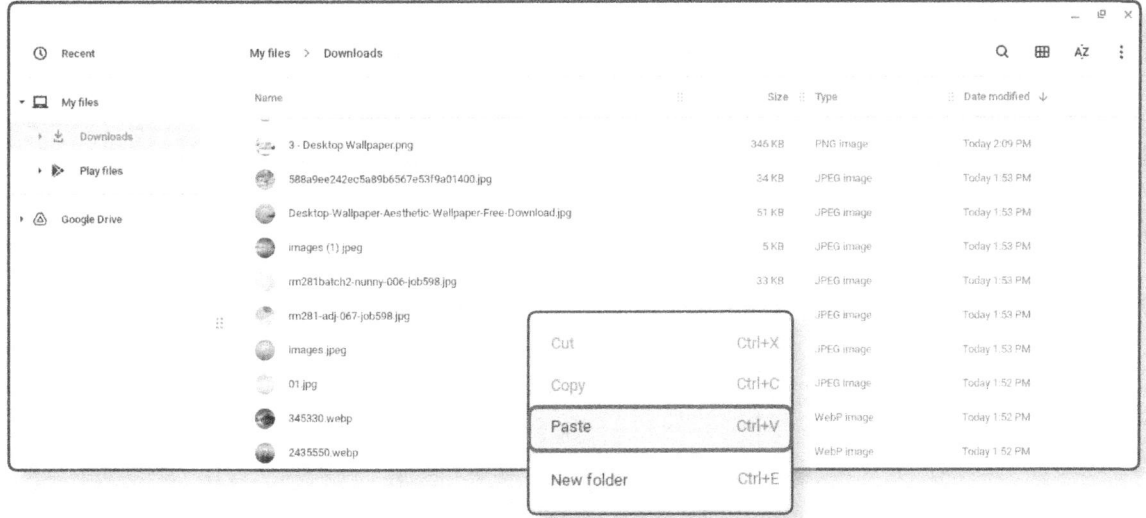

## COPYING USING TOUCHSCREEN

Using a touchscreen is almost the same as using the touchpad. The following steps will take you there:

1. Highlight the file you need to move by long pressing on it.

2. Select **Copy** or **Cut**.

3. Go to the desired destination and long press and **Paste**.

## RENAMING FILES

You need to rename your files to desired names for convenience. Renaming files might seem hard but there are two ways you can rename files easily on your Chromebook. You can do this by right-clicking or using keys. Let us go through these methods for you to have a better experience with your device.

### RENAMING THROUGH RIGHT CLICKING.

1. The first step is to open the **Files folder** on your Chromebook.

2. Open the folder that contains the file you need to rename.

3. Click only once on the selected file for renaming. Note that if you double-click the file, you will be opening it.

# CHAPTER 3

4. When using a mouse, right-click on the selected file. When using a touchpad, tapping with two fingers does the same as right-clicking.

5. Select **Rename** from the list and the text on the name of the file will turn blue.

6. Now you can type in the new text.

7. When you are done, press **Enter** and the changes will be saved.

 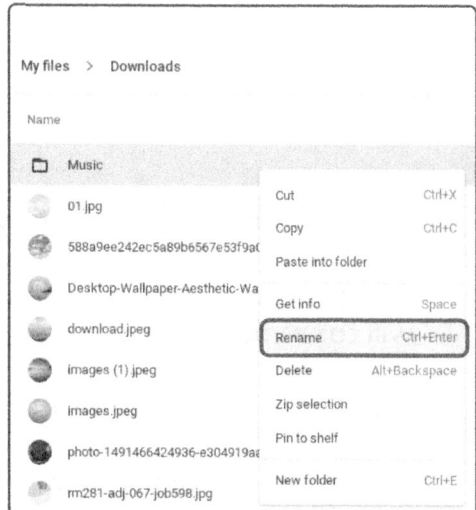

## RENAMING USING KEYS

The following instructions will make you fall in love with the use of keys for the renaming of files.

1. First open **Files** on your Chromebook.

2. Click on the file you want to rename once.

3. Press **Ctrl + Enter** keys simultaneously and the text will be highlighted in blue.

4. Type in the desired new name.

5. Press **Enter** to save the new file name.

The above-mentioned steps can be done to rename documents, images, videos, music, and several other files in your Chromebook.

# MANAGEMENT FILES IN CHROMEBOOK

## SORTING FILES

In your endeavor to organize your files on your Chromebook, you need to create several folders. Grouping the files accordingly will keep things in order and will ease access to them. This is done by moving files from the download folder to the appropriate folder. First, you need to create several folders with relevant different names and follow these steps.

1. Go to the **App Launcher app** icon which is in the bottom left corner and click it.

2. When the App Launcher appears, click it once and the files window separate from the Chrome browser opens.

3. Click on the file you intend to move and drag it to the destination folder. Considering that you are using a touchpad, click and hold the file while using another finger to drag the file to the desired destination folder.

4. Keep holding the file and move it onto the destination folder. The folder will be highlighted and you can release it to drop the file into the folder.

You may need to move several files at once. Get into the Files application window, press, and hold the **Ctrl** key. Click on the files you need to move and the files will be highlighted. Click any part of the selection, drag it to the desired folder, and drop-in.

## SEARCHING FILES

When using your Chromebook, you may need to use or view different files regularly. You do not necessarily need to dig the entire storage to locate the required file. You can search for the files easily by going through the following steps.

1. Click on the bottom left corner of the screen and click on the **Launcher** button.

2. The apps window will pop up from the bottom of the Chromebook screen and click on it.

3. Click on the **"up"** arrow which is just above the search field and you will see all the apps on your Chromebook.

4. Go to the Files app and click once to open it and on the left, you have to

# CHAPTER 3

choose the location of your file.

- To choose from the recently used files select **Recent**.

- To select from a list of files by type, select **Video, Image, or Audio**.

- As for Android App files, select **My Files** and go to play files. For more folders, select More in the top right and open **Show all Play folders**.

- For files saved in your cloud, select this folder for example Google Drive.

5. When you have found your file, double click it to open.

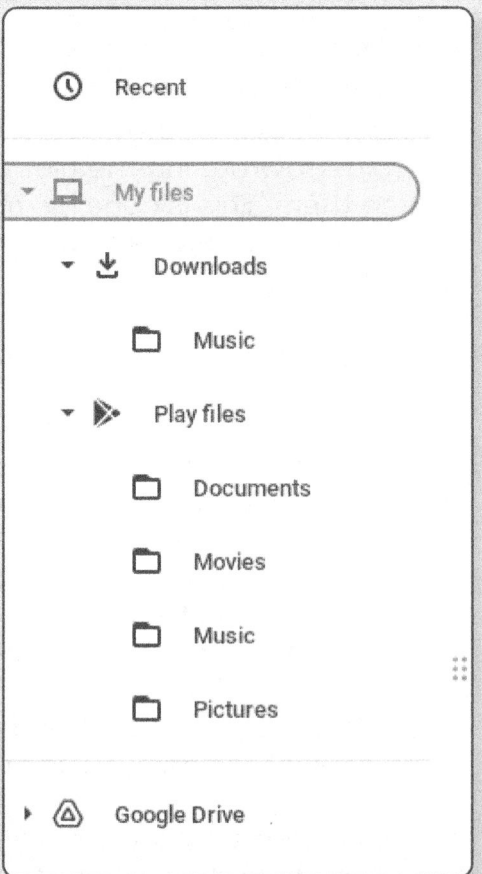

When you have searched and found the file you needed, you can now share it with others, move it to the desired destination, edit it, or even delete it if necessary.

## EXTERNAL DRIVERS

Chromebooks are different from laptops in the sense that they do not have large storage capacity, considering that they rely on the cloud for saving files. However, you can use an external hard drive or an SD card on your Chromebook. You can connect the external memory drive by plugging it into the Chromebook's USB ports.

Some Chromebooks have SD card slots so simply insert your card and the Chromebook will automatically detect the device, thereby making them available for browsing within **Files**. To find your external storage device, select it from the left side of the **Files** window. Open it to view its contents and you can add or move files from within the external drive.

Given that you need to move files from the drive to your Chromebook, drag them to the **Downloads folder** that is under Files on the left side of the Files window. Open the destination folder by hovering over it and drop the files or folders on the right of the Files window. You can also copy or move files and folders from the Chromebook to the

## MANAGEMENT FILES IN CHROMEBOOK

external drive using the same method.

When you are done, click the **Eject button** which is located near the name of the device on the left side of the Files window. Once done, the device will disappear from the Files window and it will be safe to remove from your Chromebook.

### FORMATTING EXTERNAL DRIVES

In the event that you want to do away with files that are in your external drive before using it, you will need to format them. This way you do not have to delete one item at a time but wipe out everything in one go. Here are the steps to formatting the external drive:

1. Go to the **Files app**, open it, and select the drive.

2. Now, right-click the drive and select **Format Device**.

3. The next step is to go to the pop-up window and rename your device using the keyboard and select a file type. There are three options which are FAT32, exFAT, and NTFS. If you intend to use the drive on windows as well, select **NTFS**.

4. Click **Erase and Format** to continue.

## NEARBY SHARE

A Chromebook allows you to share images, text, files, or web pages with Android and Chromebook devices that are close to you. The nearby share function is off by default, so to start sharing, you need to turn it on.

1. Go to the bottom right of your Chromebook screen and select **Settings**.

2. Select **Connected devices**, which will be on the left.

3. Select **Set-up**, which is next to "Nearby Share".

4. Now, name your device and click **Done**.

5. Set up your device visibility to others. There are three options you can choose from which are:

# CHAPTER 3

- **All contacts:** In this case, your device will be visible to contacts that are close while the screen is on and unlocked.

- **Some contacts:** When your screen is on and unlocked, your device will be visible to nearby contacts you select.

- **Hidden:** In this case, you only make your device visible when you need to share content with someone.

- Select **Confirm**.

When you want to turn Sharing off, go to **Settings**, select **Connected devices** and then turn off **Nearby Share**.

*Settings > Connected Device > Set up*

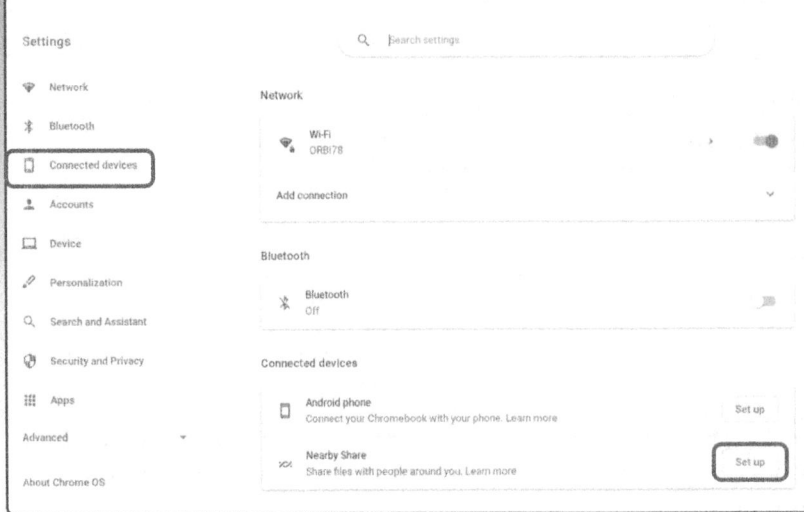
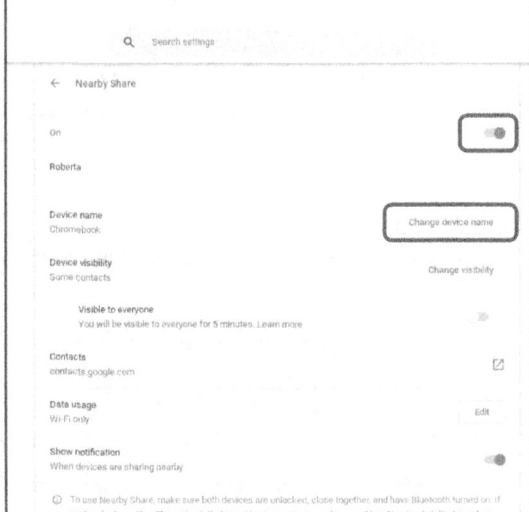

## SHARING CONTENT WITH OTHER DEVICES

1. Open **Files** on your Chromebook

2. Now, go to the file you want to share, right-click, select **Shar**e, and go to **Nearby Share**. When intending to share multiple files, press **Ctrl + click** the files you want to share and select **Share** which leads you to **Nearby Share**.

3. Select the device you need to share the files with and select **Share**. The receiver has to confirm the sharing and once done, the files are sent.

# MANAGEMENT FILES IN CHROMEBOOK

## RECEIVING CONTENT FROM SOMEONE

Make sure that your device is visible to the other device. To turn your visibility on, go to Device name and **Device visibility** and select **Turn on**. When visibility is turned on, a notification that someone wants to share files with you pops up. To receive the content, select **Accept**.

## NEARBY SHARE USING ANDROID

On your android device, make sure your Bluetooth and location are turned on and follow the steps listed below.

1. Open the **Settings** app.
2. Tap **Google**, click **Devices and Sharing**. Now, go to **Nearby Share**.
3. Turn **Nearby Share** on.

When this is done, your device will be ready to share files with others. To send a file to contact follow these steps.

1. Open the file, which could be an image, document, or video.
2. Tap **Share** and go to **Nearby Share**. Bear in mind that you may need to tap **Turn on** when prompted.
3. Make sure that your android device is close to your friend's device.
4. On the nearby devices list, tap your friend's device.
5. As soon as sending is done, tap **Done**.

## SCREEN CAPTURE

The 21st century has brought technological advancements that are making life even easier for everyone, including seniors. You no longer need to grab a camera and start recording certain activities that are happening on your screen. With screen capture, you can share with others a clear image or video of the on-screen activities. Screen captures are also done for security reasons for instance when making a huge payment online. In case you encounter a mistake or problem during the transaction, you can refer back to them.

# CHAPTER 3

There are two types of screen captures. We have screenshots, which are images of your screen contents and screen recordings that come in the form of a video.

## CHROMEBOOK SCREENSHOTS

You can take a screenshot of your Chromebook's screen. These screenshots are automatically saved to your clipboard. Let us take a look at how you can take a screenshot of your device.

1. Press **Shift + Ctrl + Show windows**.

2. Select **Screenshot** in the menu at the bottom.

3. Now choose one from the three options that appear on your Chromebook screen which are:

    - Take a full screenshot.

    - Take a partial screenshot.

    - Take a window screenshot.

You can also capture a screenshot from the bottom right menu. All you need is to select **Time** and click on **Screen capture** and you are done.

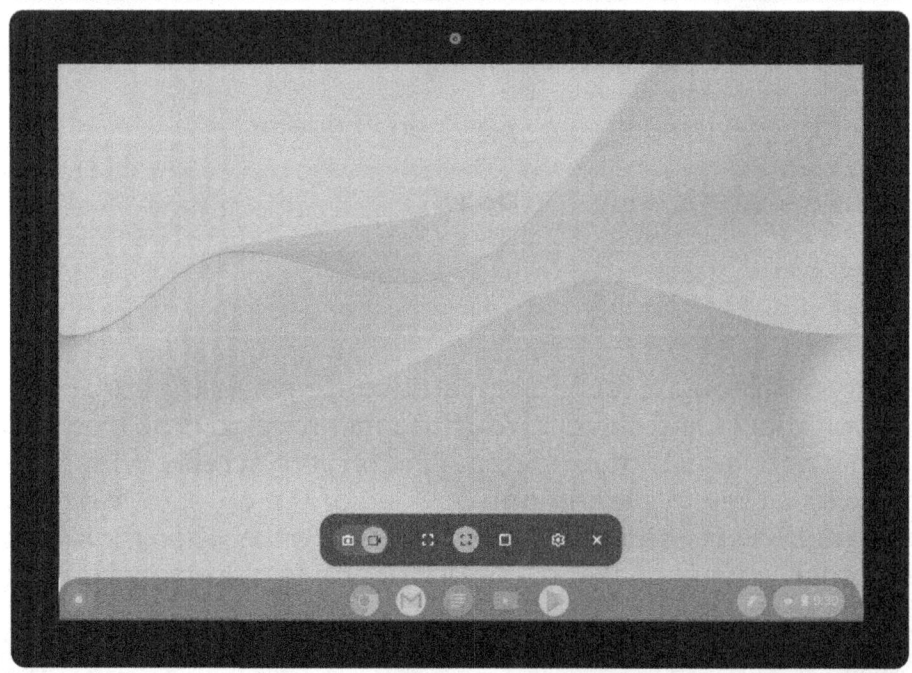

## MANAGEMENT FILES IN CHROMEBOOK

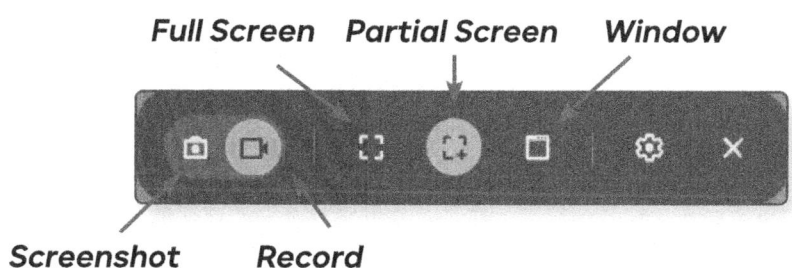
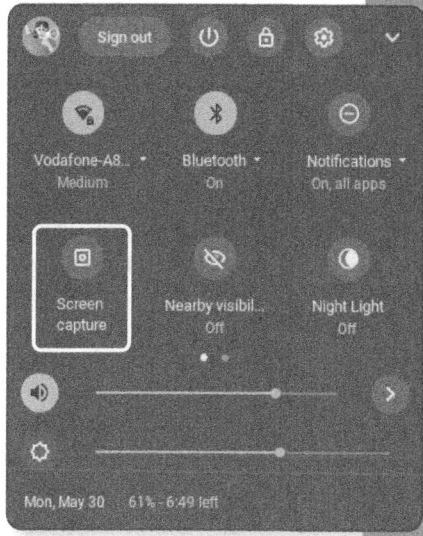

### RECORD THE SCREEN

A screen record comes in the form of a video containing the exact activities that you will be doing on your Chromebook screen. Here are the steps to screen recording.

1. Press **Shift Ctrl + Show windows**.

2. Select **screen record** from the menu at the bottom of your screen.

3. Choose one from the three options that appear on your screen to suit your desired and the appropriate type of recording. The three options are:

   - Record the full screen.
   
   - Record a partial screen.
   
   - Record a window.

Your screen recordings will be saved and will be ready for viewing later. They can also be shared via Nearby share.

### TALK TO YOUR CHROMEBOOK

You can talk to your device through the Google assistant function. First, you need to make sure the function is activated.

# CHAPTER 3

1. Go to the bottom right of your screen and select the time.

2. Select **Settings**.

3. To the left, select **Search and Assistant** and go to **Google Assistant**.

4. Turn on **Google Assistant**.

5. For you to use voice assistant, turn on "**Hey Google**."

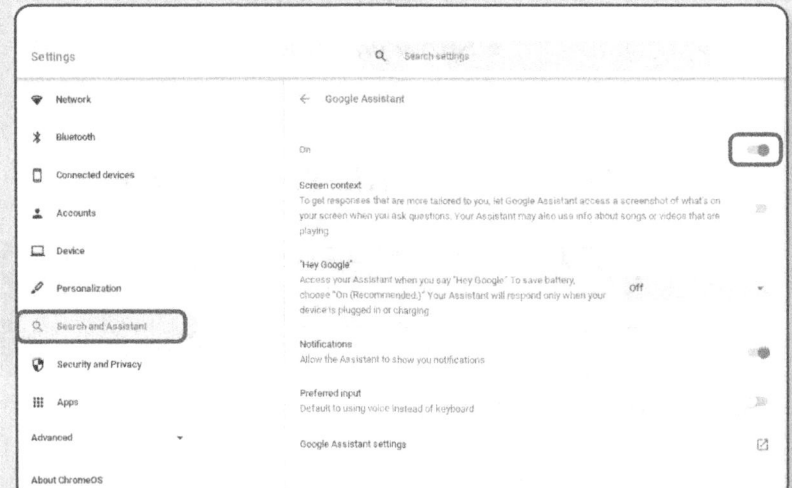

Now, you have to teach Google Assistant to recognize your voice. Here are the steps to voice assistant setup.

1. Make sure **Hey Google** is turned on and select the time.

2. Select **Settings**.

3. Go to **Search Assistant**, which is on the left, and select **Google Assistant**.

4. Under "**Hey Google**," which is next to Voice match, select **Retrain**.

5. Follow the on-screen steps to finish the setup.

When you no longer need the services of the voice assistant, you can turn it off by going through the following steps.

1. At the bottom right of the screen, select the time.

2. Select **Settings**.

3. Select **Search and Assistant** on the left and go to **Google Assistant**.

4. Now, turn off **Google Assistant**.

# Chapter 4: Using Chrome Apps

Chrome apps are web-based apps that are installed on Chrome OS. When installed, you can launch the apps from your desktop and use them to perform the tasks that they are meant for.

These apps can be downloaded and installed directly onto your device from the Google Play Store. They can be updated to newer versions for improved performance. However, when you no longer need a particular app on your device, you can uninstall it using easy methods that we will explore in this chapter.

## BROWSING CHROME APP STORE

The Chrome App Store has a wide coverage of apps that you need for different purposes on your Chromebook. As a senior citizen or beginner, some apps may prove to be quite difficult to use.

Fortunately, the Chrome App Store has alternative apps that you will find interesting and user-friendly. The following steps will lead you to the Chrome web store on Chrome OS.

1. First, click on the **Launcher icon** which is in the bottom left corner of your screen.

2. Search **"Chrome Web Store"** in the search box or click to view all apps.

3. Now, you can open the **Chrome Web Store** from the App list.

Considering that your browser supports the installation of Chrome extensions, going to the Chrome Web Store URL is an alternative.

# CHAPTER 4

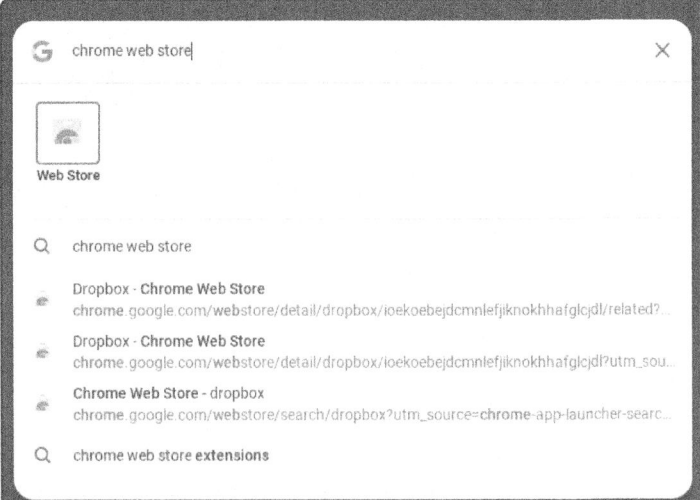

## SEARCHING THE STORE

You may need to add more apps to your Chromebook from time to time. As you continue using your Chromebook, you come across the need to have several apps to perform certain tasks. Let us look at how you can search for apps on the Play Store.

1. Go to the launcher and open the **Play Store**.

2. You can now browse the apps easily since they are grouped by category. You can also find your desired apps by searching them through the search box.

3. When you find the App that you want to download, click on it to install.

4. The app will download automatically and install on your Chromebook. It will also automatically appear on the Launcher.

## REMOVING CHROME EXTENSIONS

When you come across the need to remove or disable an extension, follow these steps.

1. Go to **Chrome** and open it.

2. Move to the options and select **More**. Click **More tools** and go to **Extensions**.

## USING CHROME APPS

3. Select the extension that you want to remove and click **Remove**.

You can also remove an extension using a button on the browser toolbar. Right-click that button and select **Remove from Chrome**. Bear in mind that it is also possible to disable an extension without deleting it. The following steps will enable you to disable an extension so that you temporarily stop using it.

1. Go to **Chrome** and open it.

2. Select **More**, go to **More tools**, and click **Extensions**.

3. Select the extension you want to disable and turn it off.

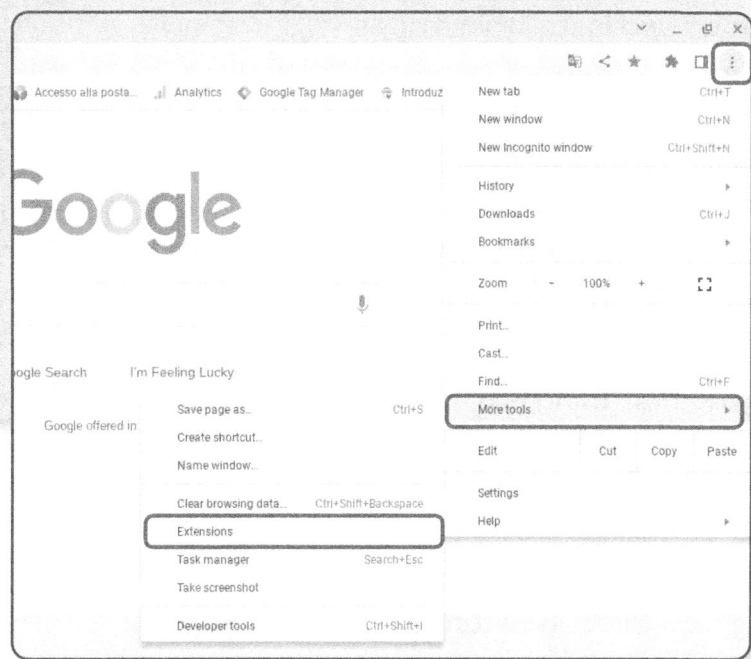

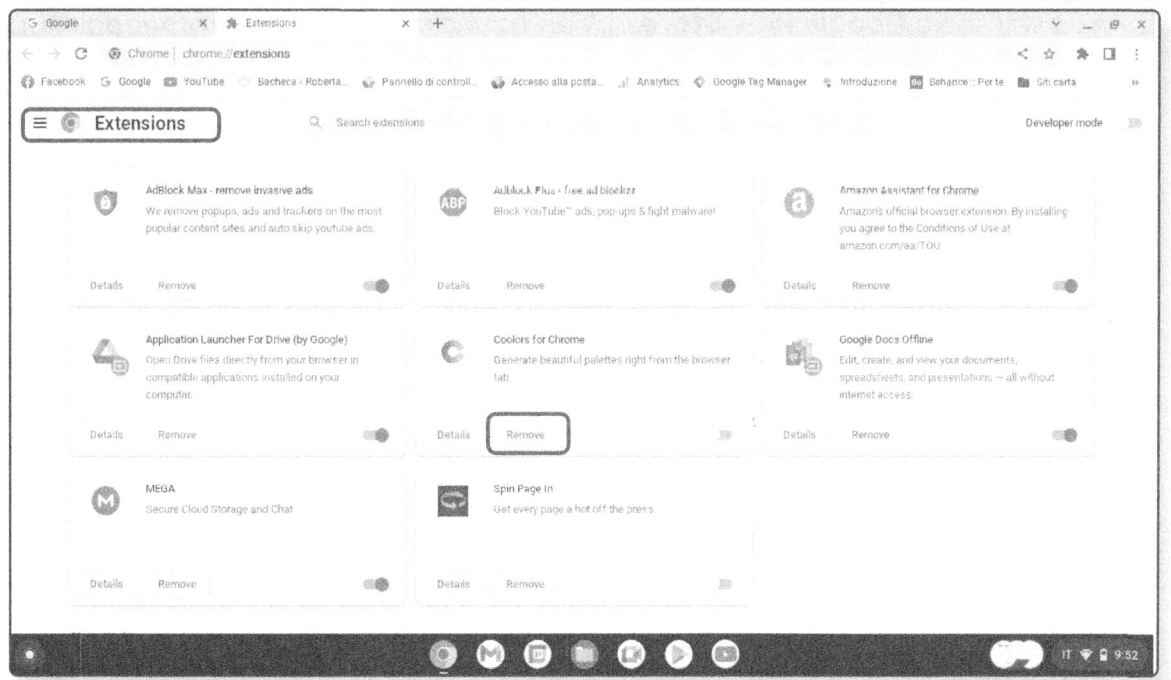

# CHAPTER 4

## USEFUL ONLINE APPS FOR YOUR CHROMEBOOK

There are a variety of apps you may need to install on your Chromebook. The introduction of the Google Play Store on Chrome OS has increased its efficiency, possibly even more efficient than the Chrome app store. Some of the best Chromebook apps include Adobe Lightroom, Google Drive, Gmail, MediaMonkey, Libre Office, and Gimp Image Editor. Later on in this chapter, we shall get into detail on how you can download and install these apps.

## ANDROID APPS ON CHROMEBOOKS

Chrome OS apps are cloud-based, meaning that they store their items in the cloud. However recent versions of Chromebooks support Android apps that can be downloaded through Google Play Store. These apps have made the use of Chromebooks more interesting. Let us get you started with Android apps on Chrome OS.

The first thing is to check whether your device is compatible with Android apps. The following steps will guide you in checking if your Chromebook supports the Google Play Store.

1. Go to the bottom right corner of the screen and click on the time.

2. Click on **Settings** and select **Apps**.

3. You will see a **Google Play Store** option to show that your Chromebook supports Google Play Store.

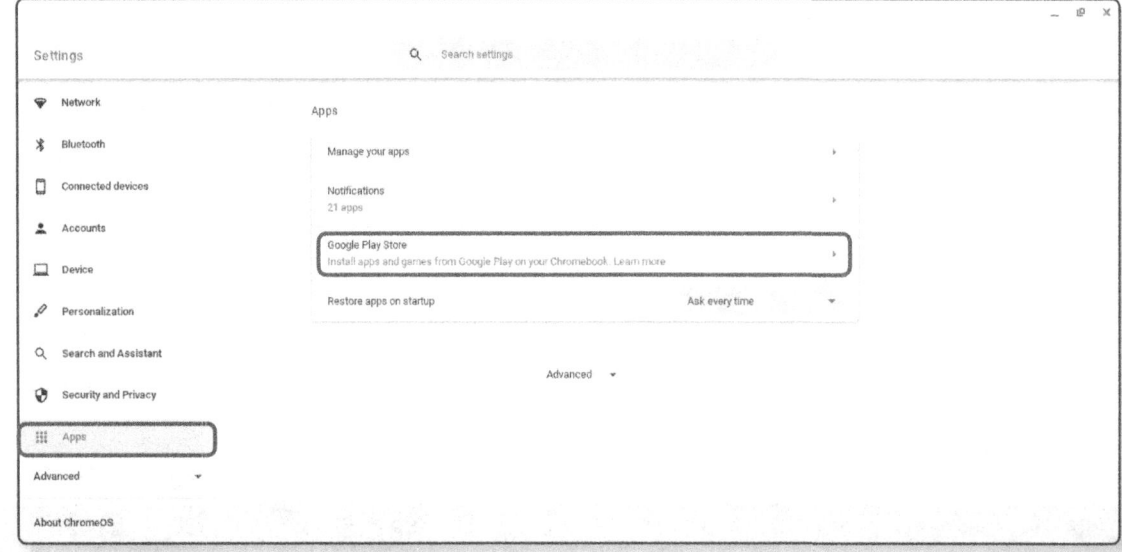

## USING CHROME APPS

If your Chromebook does not have Android support, it is possible to enable it via an update. Follow this guide to update your device's Android App compatibility.

1. Turn on your Chromebook and log in.
2. Connect to WiFi.
3. Go to the bottom right corner and click on the time.
4. Go to **Settings** cog.
5. Select the **About Chrome OS** option.
6. Select **Check for Updates** and follow the given instructions to complete the update.

## ENABLE GOOGLE PLAY STORE

Now that you have Google Play Store on your device, you need to enable it for use. The steps that are outlined below will lead you through.

1. The bottom right side of your Chromebook screen has a **Quick Settings Panel** which you should open.
2. Click on the **Settings** icon.
3. Scroll down and get to **Google Play Store**.
4. Click **Turn on**.
5. Read through the terms of service and select "**Accept**."

By following these steps, you have successfully enabled Google Play on your device and you now have access to the wide coverage of apps you may need on your Chromebook.

## SEARCHING, BROWSING, AND DOWNLOADING APPS

As a new Chromebook user, you may need knowledge on how you can search, browse, and download apps to your device. Bear in mind that some apps are more user-friend-

# CHAPTER 4

ly and so they display increased convenience more than others. This way there is a need to download the appropriate apps to suit your needs. The following steps will show you how you can find, download, and install apps from the **Google Play Store**.

1. Turn on your Chromebook and log in.

2. Open the app drawer and click on the **Launcher icon**, or swipe from the bottom to find the Google Play Store app.

3. Select the **Google Play Store** app and open it.

4. Search for your desired app via the search panel or browse the listed apps.

5. When you find the app you need, click and install it.

6. Wait for the app to install and it will be visible in the app drawer automatically.

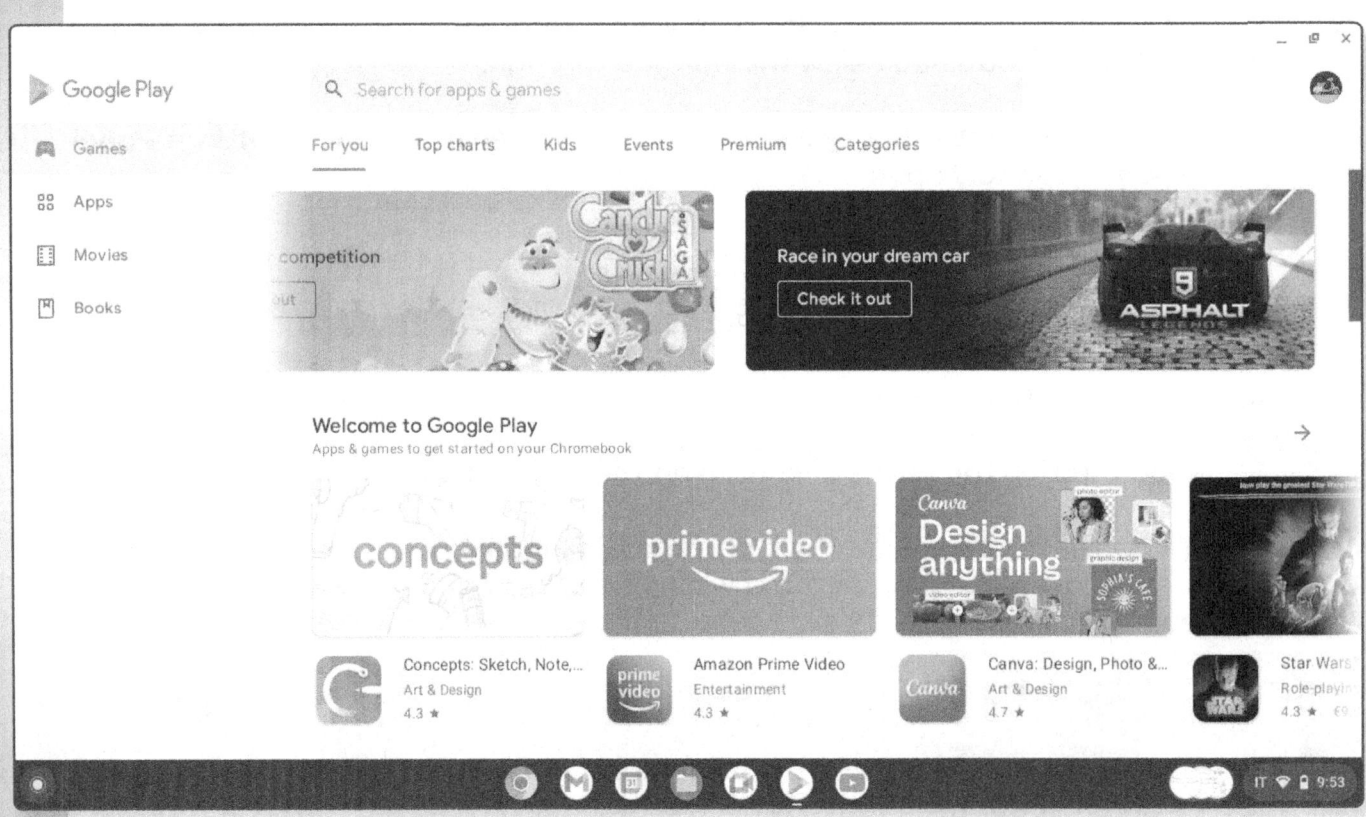

## USING CHROME APPS

## MANAGING APPS

The management of apps is important in keeping your Chromebook sorted and easy to use. App management includes sorting files into folders, managing app notifications, as well as removing, and disabling apps when the need arises.

## REMOVING APPS

Given that you no longer need an app that is installed on your Chromebook, the following steps will be helpful for uninstalling it.

1. Select the **Launcher** which is in the corner of your screen and click the Up arrow.

2. Select the app you want to remove and right-click on it. When using the keyboard, press **Shift + Search + Increase volume** or press **Shift + Launcher + Increase Volume**.

3. Now, select **Uninstall** or **Remove** from Chrome.

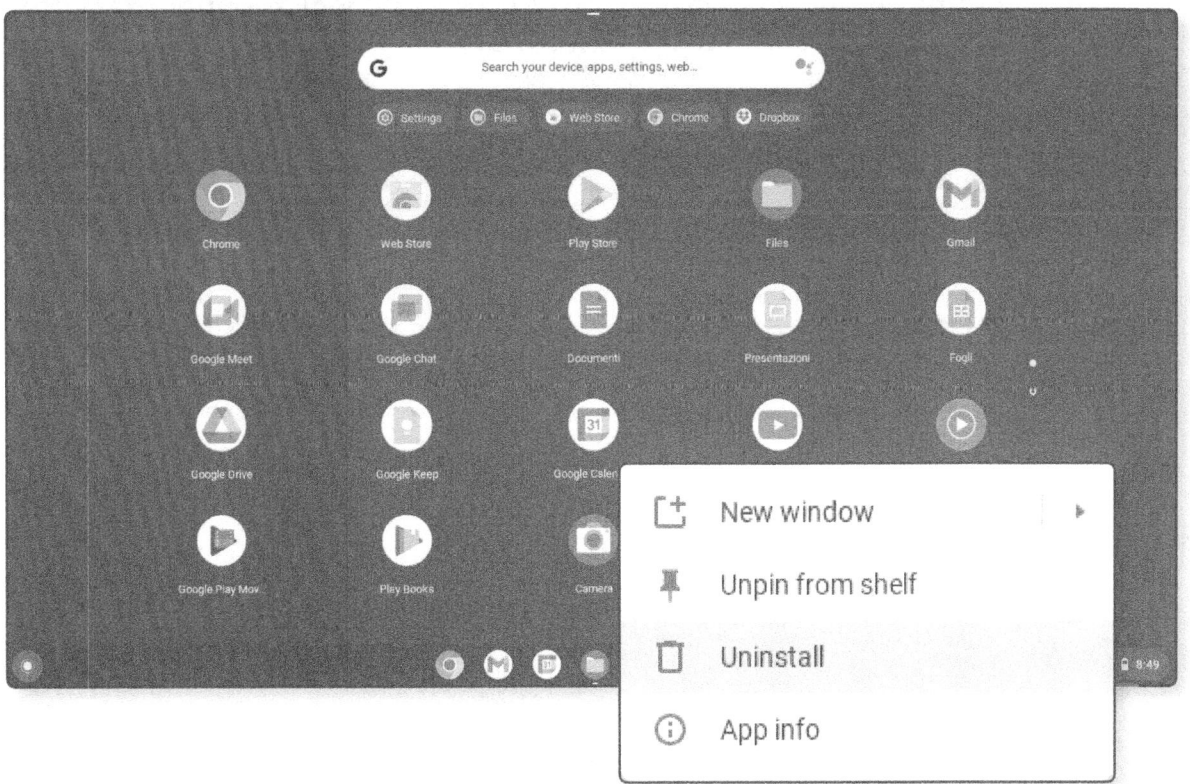

# CHAPTER 4

## USING LINUX APPS

The use of Linux apps on your Chromebook opens up several interesting options since they can expand your device's capabilities. Linux operating system is free and open. Chrome OS and Android also have Linux-based technology within them. Given that your Chromebook does all you expect from it, there may not be any need for introducing Linux apps to it. Linux is used to fill in the gaps that cannot be accomplished by using a general Chromebook.

The Linux app can support Photoshop caliber image editing software or robust audio and video editing software on your Chromebook. It exceeds the capabilities that are offered by Android-based or web-based tools in performing their functions. To use Linux, your device must be compatible with the technology. The underlisted steps will help you in checking whether your device is Linux-compatible or not.

1. Open the **Settings** app.

2. Select **About Chrome OS** in the left navigation pane.

3. Under the Google Chrome OS option, check your Chrome OS version.

4. If the Chrome OS version is less than 69, click the **Check for updates** button which is at the right of the version information.

5. Now you have to wait for the update to download and complete before restarting the Chromebook when prompted.

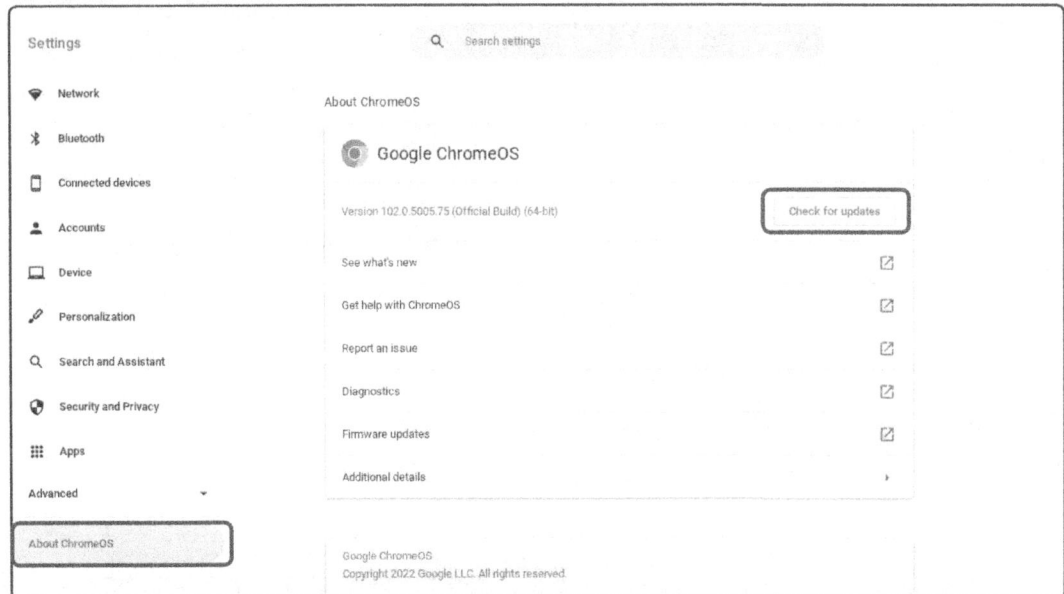

## USING CHROME APPS

## HOW TO TURN ON LINUX?

Linux is always off by default. When you need it, you can turn it on from the Chromebook settings by going through the following steps.

1. Go to the bottom right side of your Chromebook screen and select the time.

2. Select **Settings**, click **Advanced,** and go to **Developer**.

3. Next to **"Linux development environment"** select **Turn On**.

4. Now, you need to be patient and follow the on-screen instructions. The setup can take about 10 minutes or more.

5. A terminal window opens and you have a Debian 10 (Buster) environment. Now, you can install more tools via the APT package manager, and also run Linux commands.

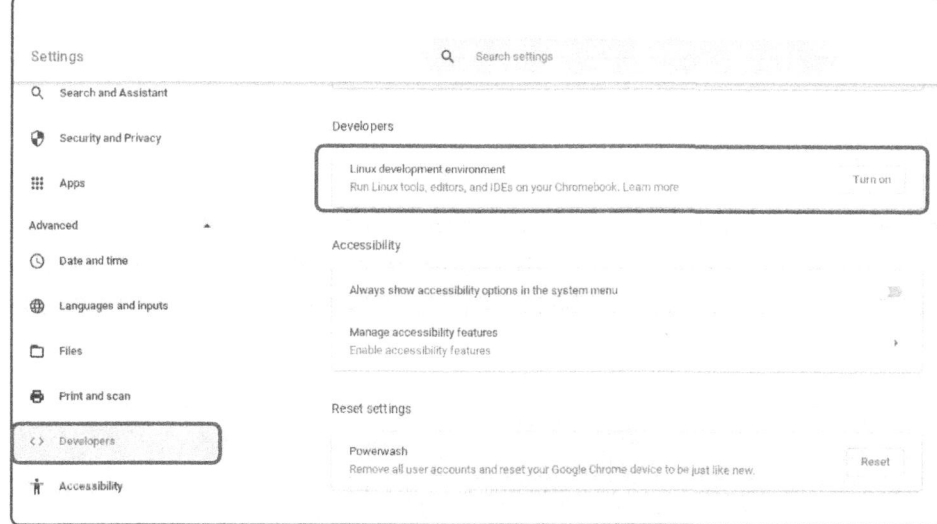

## TURNING LINUX OFF

1. Select the time, at the bottom right of the screen.

2. Select **Settings**, go to **Advanced**, and click **Developers** which will further lead you to the **Linux development environment**.

3. Under Remove Linux development environment select **Remove**.

# CHAPTER 4

By following the above-stated steps, you have successfully turned off Linux and its features. Remember you can still turn it on whenever the need arises.

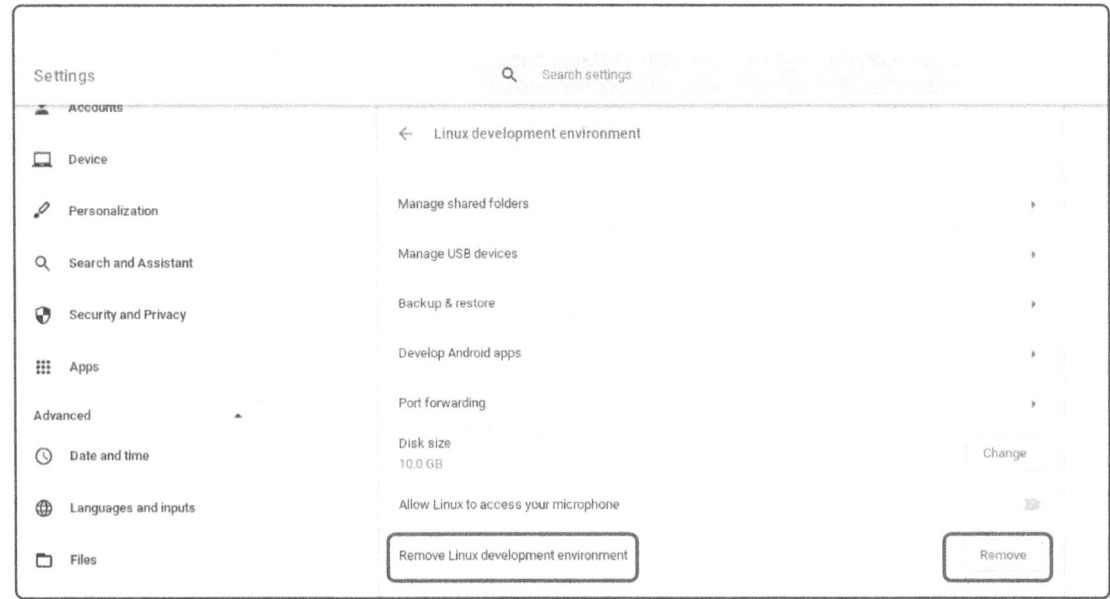

## INSTALLING LINUX APPS

When you choose to use Linux apps, make sure that your device is running smoothly. Update your packages by entering "**sudo apt – get update && sudo apt- get update – y**" into the terminal window, prior to pressing **Enter**. Once this is done, you can start downloading Linux apps on your device.

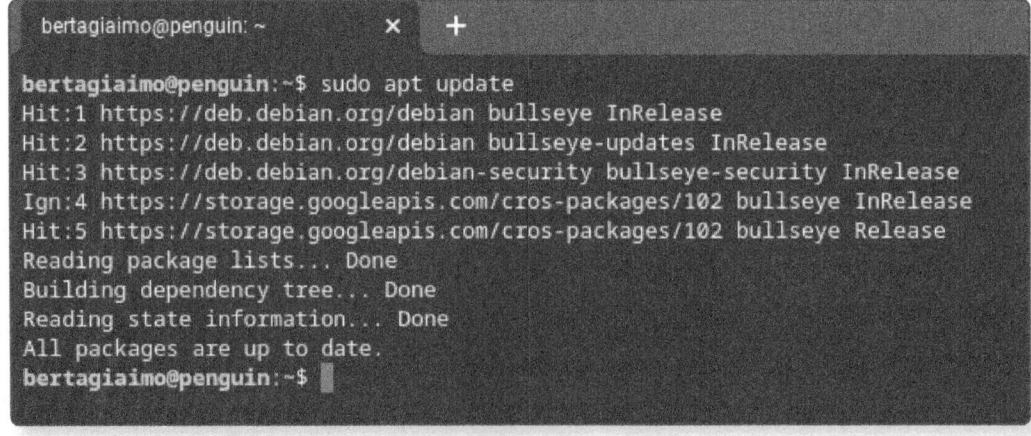

**Command: sudo apt - get update**

## USING CHROME APPS

### Installing Linux Apps via Terminal

Type in the command "**sudo apt- get install app name -y**" and be sure to change the "app name" part with the exact name of the app you want to download. Press **Enter**. You will see many text lines in the terminal as the app is being downloaded and installed. When the app is installed, the terminal will remain idle. You can now search for the installed app in the Chromebook to open it.

### Installing Linux Apps via the .deb File.

In this method, you can download the .deb Linux installer files directly from the internet for some apps. Once the download is finished, you can find the app in your Chromebook's Downloads folder. Copy the file by pressing **Ctrl+C** or **right-click** and Copy and paste it into the Linux folder on the left navigation pane. Double click the downloaded file to run.

An installation window appears and you must click **Install**. When the installation is done, click **Ok** to close the window.

## HOW TO INSTALL FILEZILLA FTP?

**FileZilla** is an app that can be installed on your Chrome OS for file transfer to and from a remote computer using a method known as File Transfer Protocol (FTP). FTP is a very fast and secure means of file transfer that can be used to upload files to a web server or access files from a remote site such as your home directory.

# CHAPTER 4

Installing **FileZilla** on your Chromebook is quite easy. Ensure that Linux is installed and running on your device before attempting to install FileZilla. Let us go through this detailed guide for a better understanding.

1. Go to the top left corner of the Chrome OS interface and click on the circle-shaped icon.

2. When the Terminal is running, you need to check the software for any updates.

3. If the Chrome OS system states that there are updates that you can install, just follow the on-screen instructions to go on with the process.

4. Type in or copy the following commands "**sudo apt – getupdate or sudo apt-get upgrade**" into the Terminal.

5. Now, enter the command "**sudo apt - get install FileZilla**" onto the Terminal to initiate FileZilla and this will prompt the installation to begin.

6. After a brief pause, this program will ask you for confirmation regarding the download. Press **Enter** and the download will commence.

7. When the download is done, go to the Chromebook Launcher and find FileZilla in the Linux apps folder.

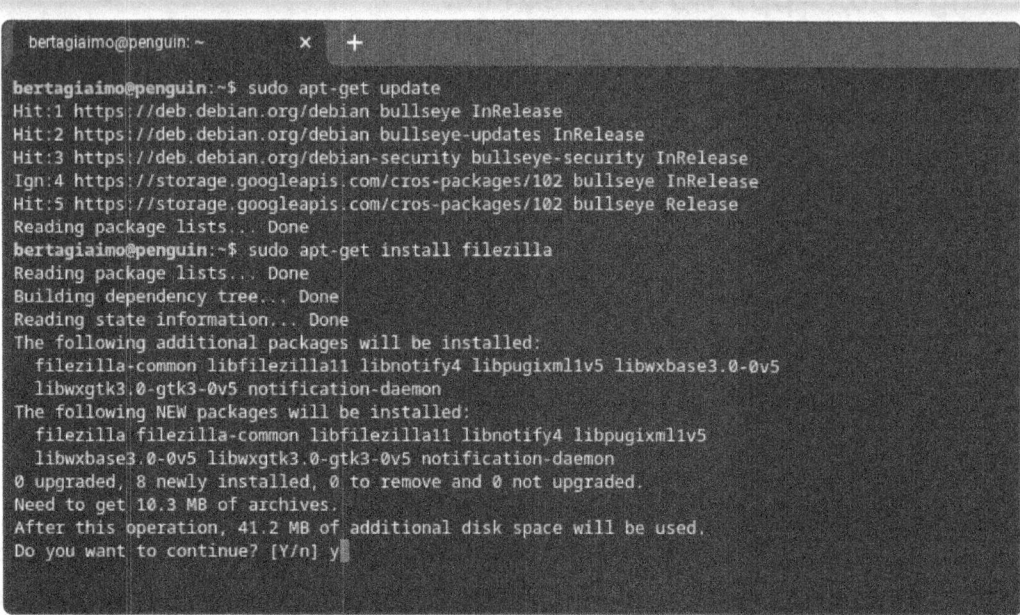

**Command: sudo apt - get update**

## USING CHROME APPS

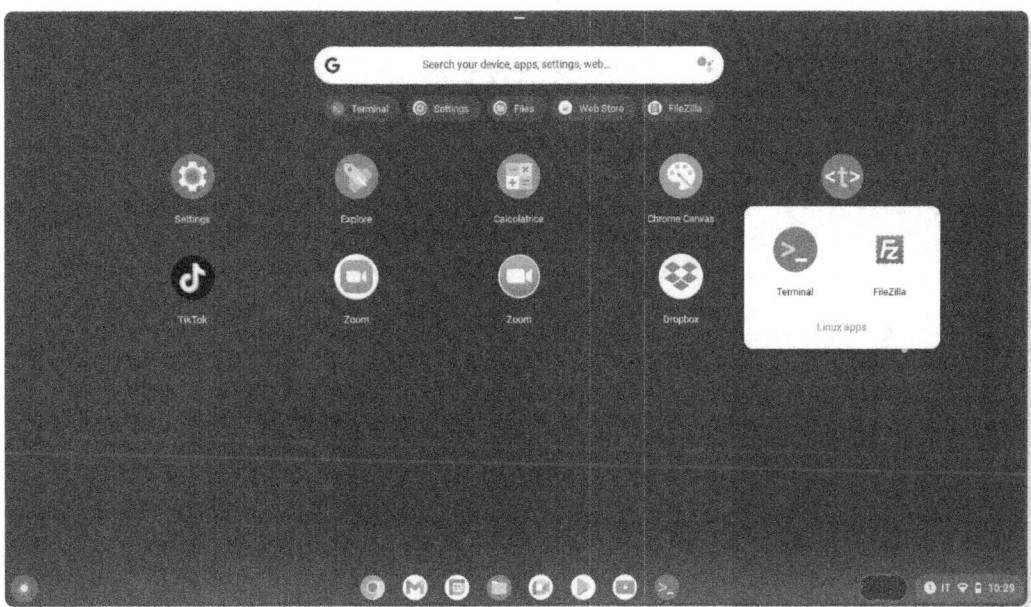

## HOW TO INSTALL AUDACITY ON CHROMEBOOK?

Audacity is a free app that is easy to use. It is a multi-track audio editor as well as recorder which is compatible with Linux, Windows, macOS, and other operating systems. Audacity can be used to record live audio, cut, copy, mix sounds, and convert records and tapes into CDs or digital recordings. If you are a music lover, this app is for you.

Listed below are steps you need to go through for you to successfully install audacity on your Chrome OS.

1. Turn on Linux support and click the time on your taskbar and go to **Settings** cog.

2. Search for '**Linux**' and enable it. This will take around five minutes so you need to be patient.

3. The terminal console will appear on the screen and now type in the command "**sudo apt – get install audacity**". You will be asked if you want to install many things and you need to type '**Y**' to agree and press **Enter**.

4. Your screen will fill with texts you cannot understand. This is just Linux installing programs and libraries and Audacity v2.2.2 will be installed this way.

# CHAPTER 4

5. The Audacity icon will appear in your Launcher ready for use.

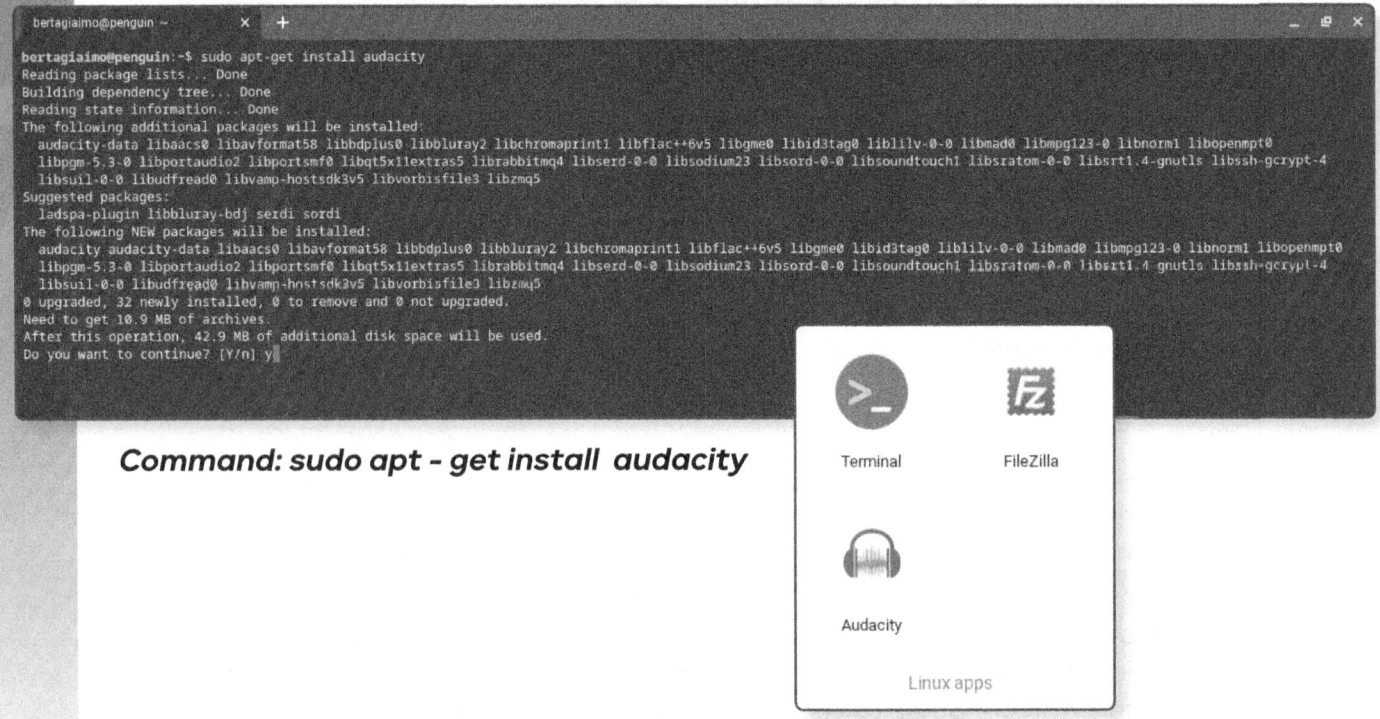

*Command: sudo apt - get install audacity*

## INSTALL GIMP IMAGE EDITOR

Gimp Image Editor is used for tasks that include photo retouching, image composition, and image authoring. It is also used for image editing, photo retouching, and image format converter. If you are a photo lover, try it on your Chromebook.

Installing Gimp on your Chromebook is very easy. The first thing is to activate Linux on your device. Follow this tutorial to download and install Gimp on your Chromebook.

1. Open the Linux Terminal on your Chromebook.

2. When the Linux Terminal is up and running, type in "**sudo apt- get update**" to make sure no other update is in line for this software.

3. After this is done, enter the command "**sudo apt- get install gimp**" into the Terminal to start the installation of GIMP.

## USING CHROME APPS

4. Press **Enter** to confirm and start downloading the files needed for setting up GIMP.

5. After installing the app, locate the Gimp application within the Linux apps folder on the Chromebook launcher.

6. The final step is to launch the app and start enjoying it.

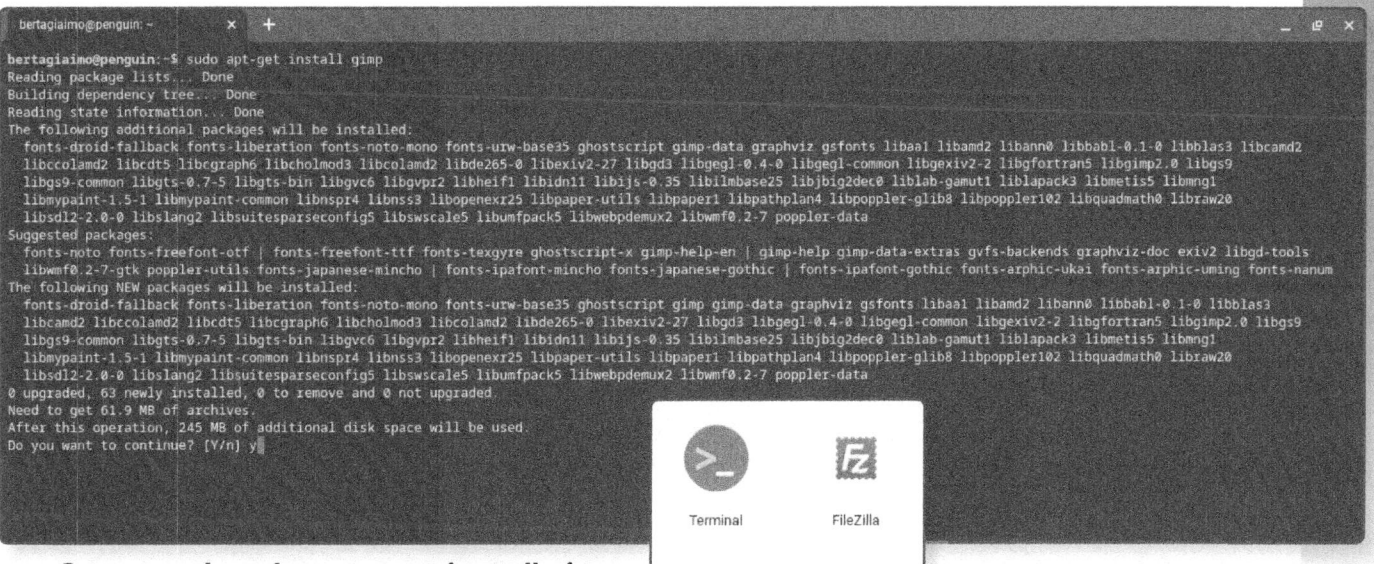

**Command: sudo apt - get install gimp**

## INSTALL LIBREOFFICE ON CHROMEBOOK

LibreOffice is a Linux-based office suite that can be used on your Chromebook. It gives you access to local programs and is ideal for the use of a spreadsheet or word processor when there is no internet connection.

Here are a few Terminal commands you need to execute to successfully download the LibreOffice on your Chromebook. If you have an older version of LibreOffice on your device, you need to remove it first. If you had installed it from the Terminal, remove it by typing in the command **"sudo apt remove libreoffice"** and press **Enter**.

## CHAPTER 4

The current version of the Libreoffice will need a 64-bit Linux (deb) file. If you do not have it, you should download it and move it from your Download folder to the Linux folder. This file contains all the Debian packages needed to install LibreOffice. The following steps will lead you through the LibreOffice download process.

1. Enter the command **'ls'** into the Linux terminal to confirm that the file is in the proper place.

2. Enter "**sudo tar -xf LibreOffice_6.4.1_Linux_x86-64_deb.tar.gz**" to unpack the tar.gz file. Make sure that the filename matches the one you downloaded.

3. A new folder named **LibreOffice_6.4.1.2_Linux_x86-64_deb** will appear inside your Linex folder. This folder has a readme folder inside as well as a DEBS folder that has all the Debian packages necessary for the installation of the LibreOffice.

4. Entering this command, "**cd LibreOffice_6.4.1.2_Linux_x86-64_deb cd DEBS**" will point the terminal to the **DEBS** folder, thereby beginning the process.

5. Now, install all the Debian packages for the LibreOffice with a single command "**sudo dpkg -I *.deb**." The Debian packages are a suite of applications that makes the process take a few minutes.

Despite this process being quite long, after finishing the installation, you will enjoy the latest versions of all LibreOffice applications.

## USING CHROME APPS

# INSTALL PYTHON ON YOUR CHROMEBOOK

Python is a very popular and widely used programming software. It is used for web and software development. You can also use Python for data analytics, design, and even machine learning. Installing Python may prove to be difficult for beginners. Follow these steps to start using Python on your Chromebook to clear the air around this matter.

1. Make sure that your Google Chrome OS is updated to the latest version. Given that your Chrome OS is up to date, go to the next step.

2. Ensure that the Linux app is installed and enabled.

3. Upgrade your Chromebook's Apt-Get-Manager by pasting or typing "**sudo apt – get update**" in Linux Terminal and pressing **Enter** to start downloading and installing the update.

4. To install Python, you need IDLE3 which is good enough to run it. Type in the command "**sudo apt – get install idle3**" in the terminal and IDLE3 will start installing in your OS.

5. Type in the command "**sudo apt install python3 – pip.**" And Python3 will start installing.

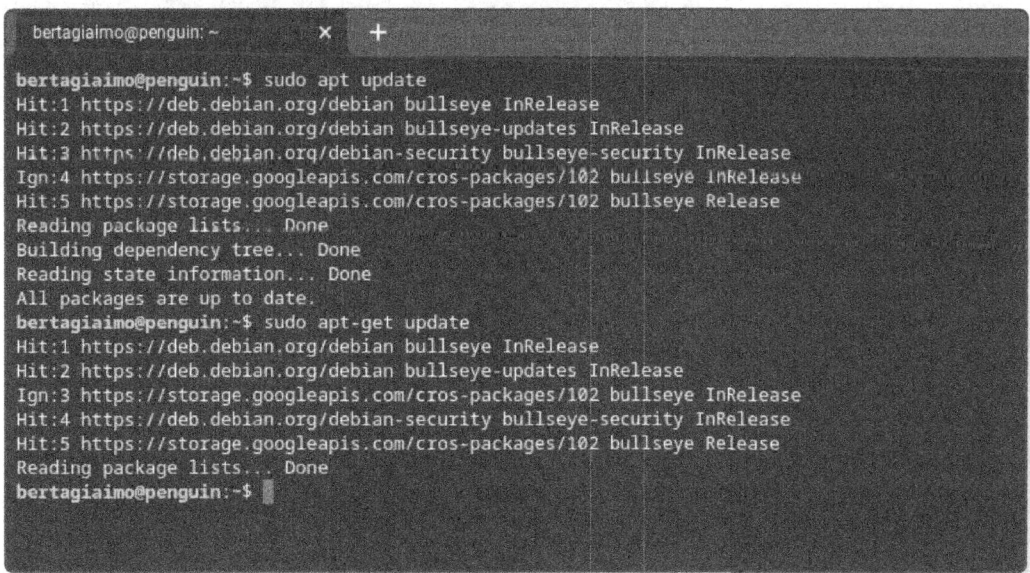

*Command: sudo apt – get update*

# CHAPTER 4

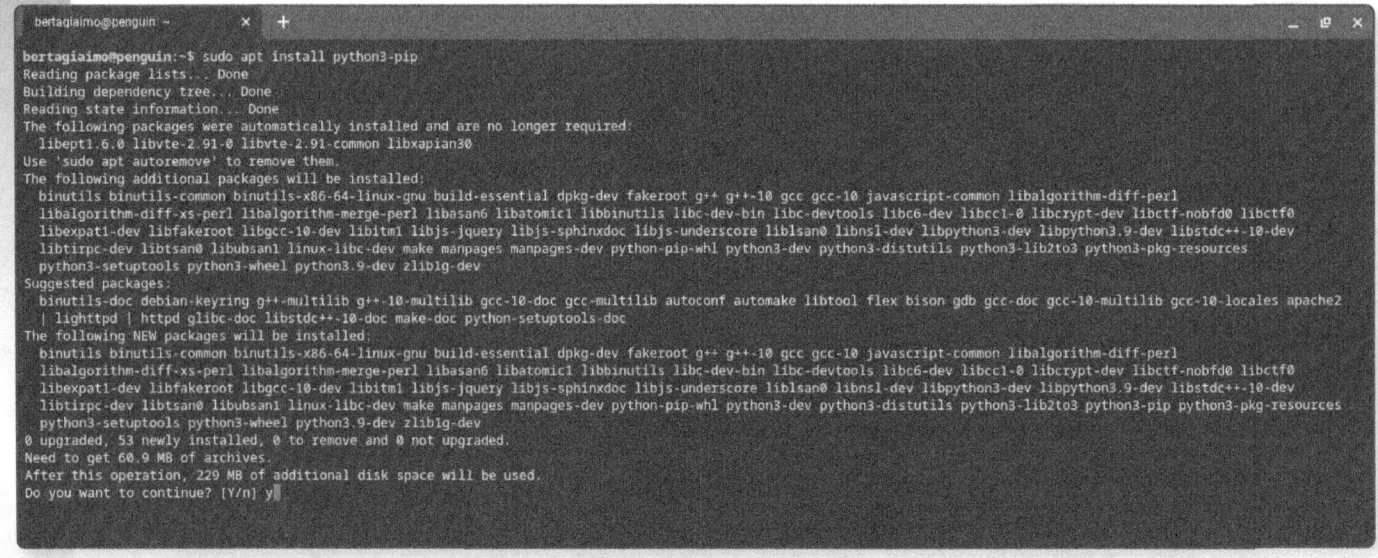

*Command: sudo apt - get install idle3*

*Command: sudo apt - get install python3*

After installing Python, you can check if it is working by clicking on the **IDLE3 icon** which you will find on the menu bar. Type **2+2** and if the result is 4 then you have successfully installed Python on your device.

## USING CHROME APPS

```
File  Edit  Shell  Debug  Options  Window  Help
Python 3.9.2 (default, Feb 28 2021, 17:03:44)
[GCC 10.2.1 20210110] on linux
Type "help", "copyright", "credits" or "license()" for more information.
>>> 2+2
4
>>> |
```

## REMOVING LINUX APPS

To search for the app that you need to remove from your Chromebook, Run the command "**dpkg –list**"and all the packages installed in the Linux container will be listed. Press **Enter** to move the list down one by one. You can also use the spacebar to move one page at a time.

When you have found the package you want, press **Ctrl + C** to go back to the command prompt. To remove the package together with the configuration files that came with it, you can use the "**do the washing up and remove**" commands. Enter "**sudo apt – get --purge remove app name**" in the Terminal and when prompted, press '**Y**' and then **Enter** to confirm.

***Command: dpkg-list***

# CHAPTER 4

Bear in mind that on the app name part, you need to enter the name of the app you need to uninstall. By following these steps, the app will be uninstalled from your Chrome OS.

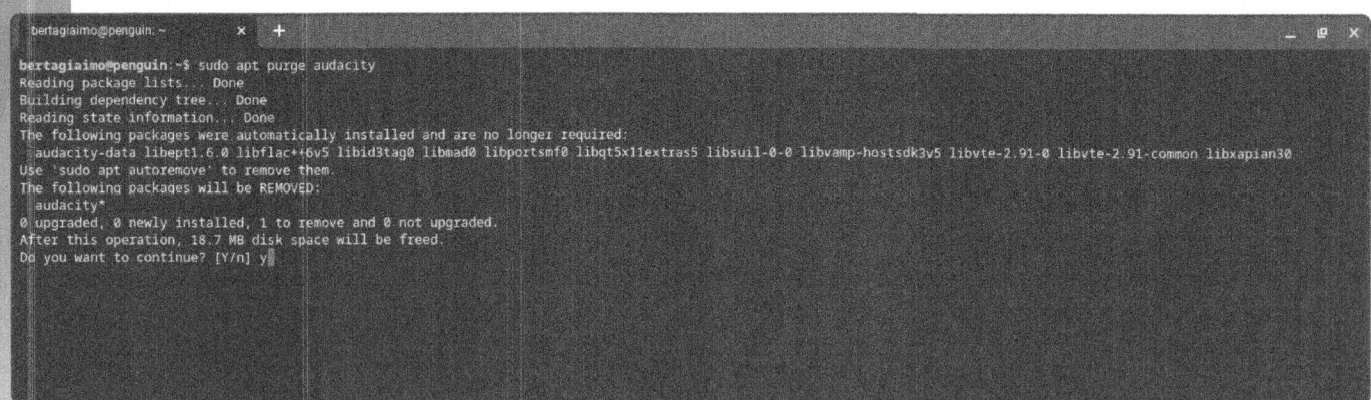

**Command: sudo apt purge audacity**

# Chapter 5: Web, Email, and Communication

Due to reasons such as the Covid 19 pandemic, online communication has become a necessity. Applications that include Google Chrome, Gmail, and Google Meet have become resourceful, be it on social or business grounds. This chapter will elucidate more on how to use the applications. Greater emphasis will be given to the various tasks that you can do using these apps and more in this chapter.

## GOOGLE CHROME

Google created the free web browser and named it Google Chrome. This browser has become popular worldwide because of its unique design and advanced features. This section will outline some of the features that are found in Google Chrome.

# CHAPTER 5

## BROWSER TABS

When using the Google Chrome browser, it is possible for you to open numerous tabs. These tabs can be viewed, switched, and organized as well. To open a new tab on the Chrome browser, go to the top of your window on the right side, then tap **New tab**. To group your tabs, right-click a tab, prior to selecting **Add to new group**. By right-clicking the colored circle, you can assign a name, add extra tabs, or remove the group.

*New Tab*

## BROWSE INCOGNITO

If you want your browsing information to be private, you can activate the Incognito mode (Lewis, 2022).

This specially applies to when you are not the only user on the Chromebook that you use. By activating this mode, your browsing history will not be saved. Your cookies and browser cache will be cleared once you close the window.

To activate the incognito mode, go to the top-right part of your screen and tap on the **Three dots**. Select **New incognito window**. If you prefer to always be in the incognito mode, you can activate the default settings in Google Chrome so that you will browse in private.

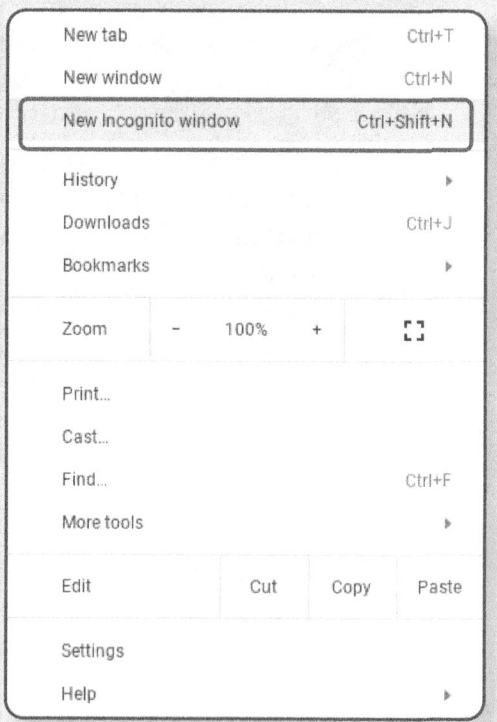

Bear in mind that when this mode is active, and you open a new tab, a message will appear in the middle of your screen which says "You've gone incognito."

# WEB, EMAIL, AND COMMUNICATION

## BROWSING HISTORY

To see your Browsing History, click on the three dots that are located at the top right part of your screen. You should then click History, then History again. By clicking these options, you will be able to see the information about your browsing history, including the links and time of access.

If for any reason, you wish to delete your browsing history, click the **three dots** at the top right. Tap on **History**, then **History** again. Afterward, you should check the boxes that are next to the items that you wish to remove. Go to the top right and tap **Delete**. After that, confirm the action by tapping on **Remove**.

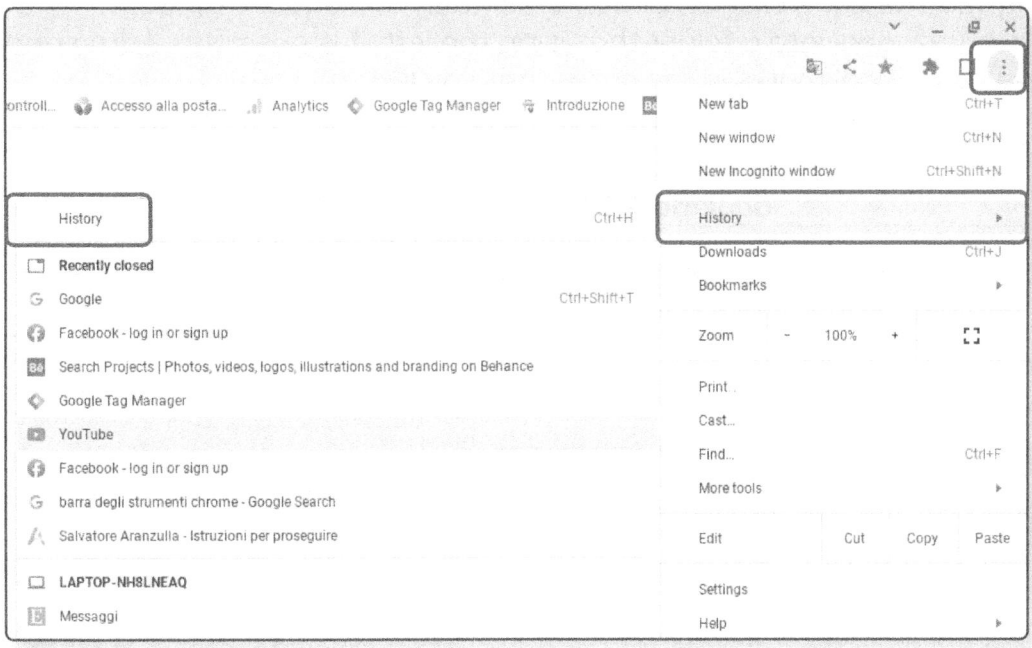

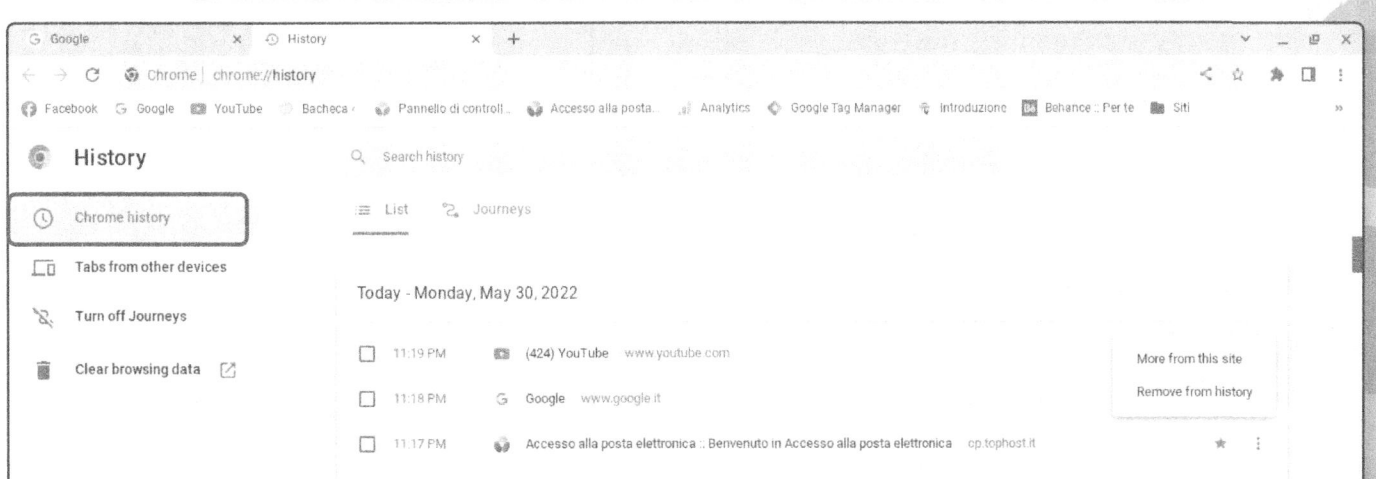

# CHAPTER 5

## BOOKMAKING A SITE

Bookmarking a site will help you find it quickly when you want to revisit it. To add a bookmark to a site, open your Chrome browser. After opening it, go to the site that you would like to visit again in the future. Tap the **Star** which is at the right of the desired address bar.

## BOOKMARK FOLDERS

Sometimes your bookmarks may become numerous such that they become difficult to manage. In that case, it is wise to create a folder for your bookmarks. To arrange your bookmarks into a folder, open Google Chrome and tap the **Three dots** at the upper right. After that, click on **Bookmarks**, then **Bookmark manager**. Next, you can drag the bookmarks into a folder that is on the left. It is possible to drag and drop or copy and paste bookmarks in the order that you like.

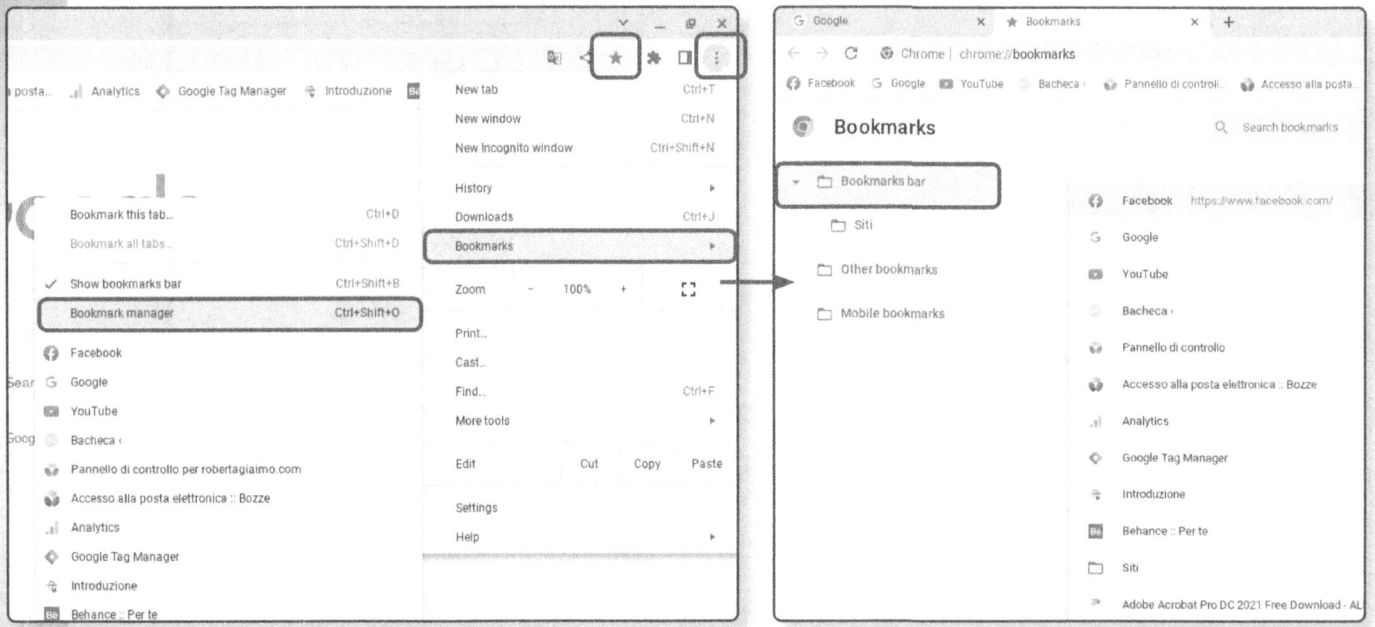

*Tap the Star to add a bookmark to a site*

## SITE SHORTCUTS

You can always create an efficient way to access your favorite websites. This can be done by creating a **Desktop Shortcut** that allows you to instantly open a page.

## WEB, EMAIL, AND COMMUNICATION

To create the shortcut, visit your website of choice and tap on the **three dots** that are on the upper right of your browser's window. Next, click on **More tools**, then **Create shortcut**. Last, assign a name to your shortcut, then tap **Create**.

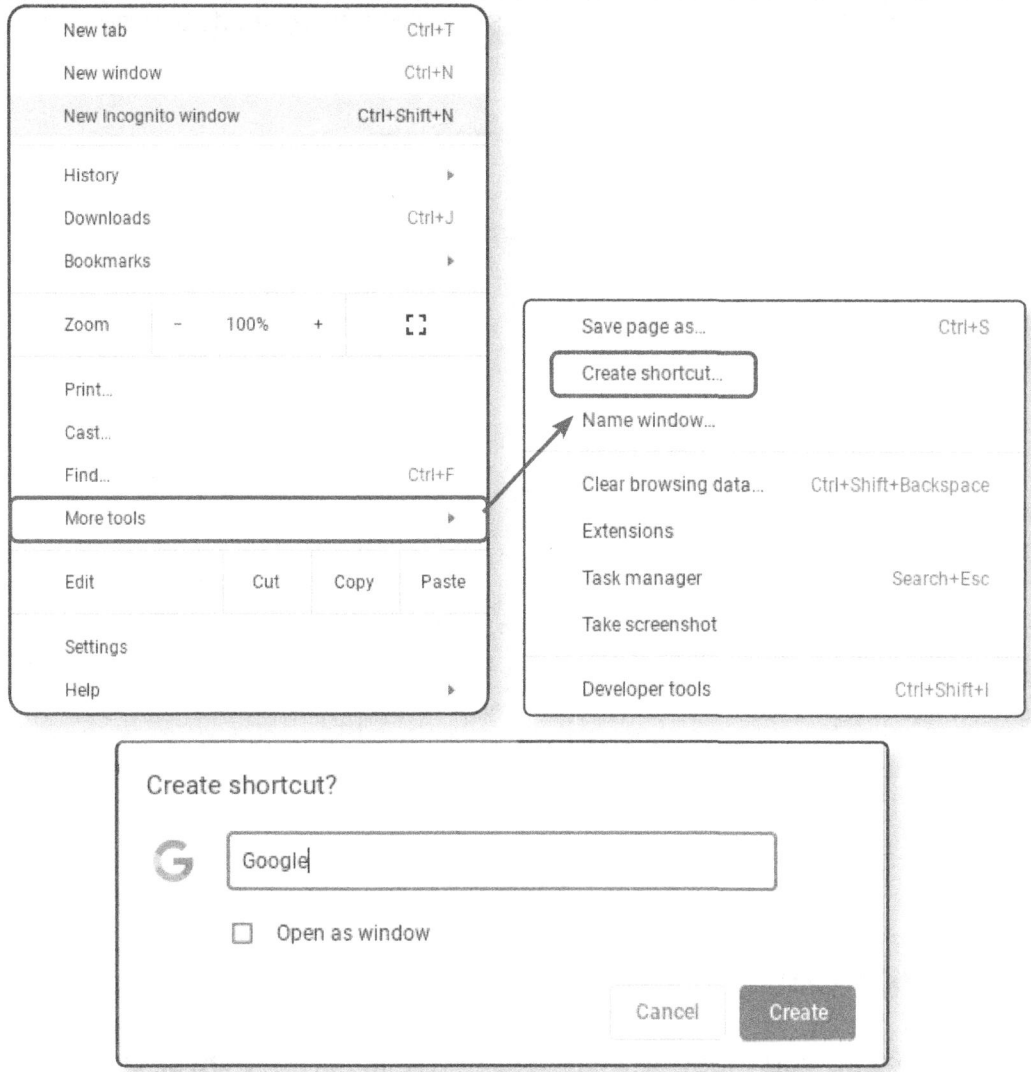

## DOWNLOADS

You can download different types of files on your Chromebook. For most files, visit the webpage for which you wish to download a file. Afterward, you should tap on the **Download link** or do a right-clicking action on the file and select Save as. If it is an image that you want to download, right-click on it, then select **Save image as**. For videos, point your cursor to the video, then tap **Download**. In some cases, this action

# CHAPTER 5

cannot be executed because the video's owner may have activated settings for preventing downloads. If it is a PDF, you can right-click on the file, then select **Save link as.** When you want to download a webpage, go to the top right and tap the **Three dots**. Next, choose **More tools**, then **Save page as**. When the download is complete, it will appear at the bottom of your browser's window. To open it, tap on the file name.

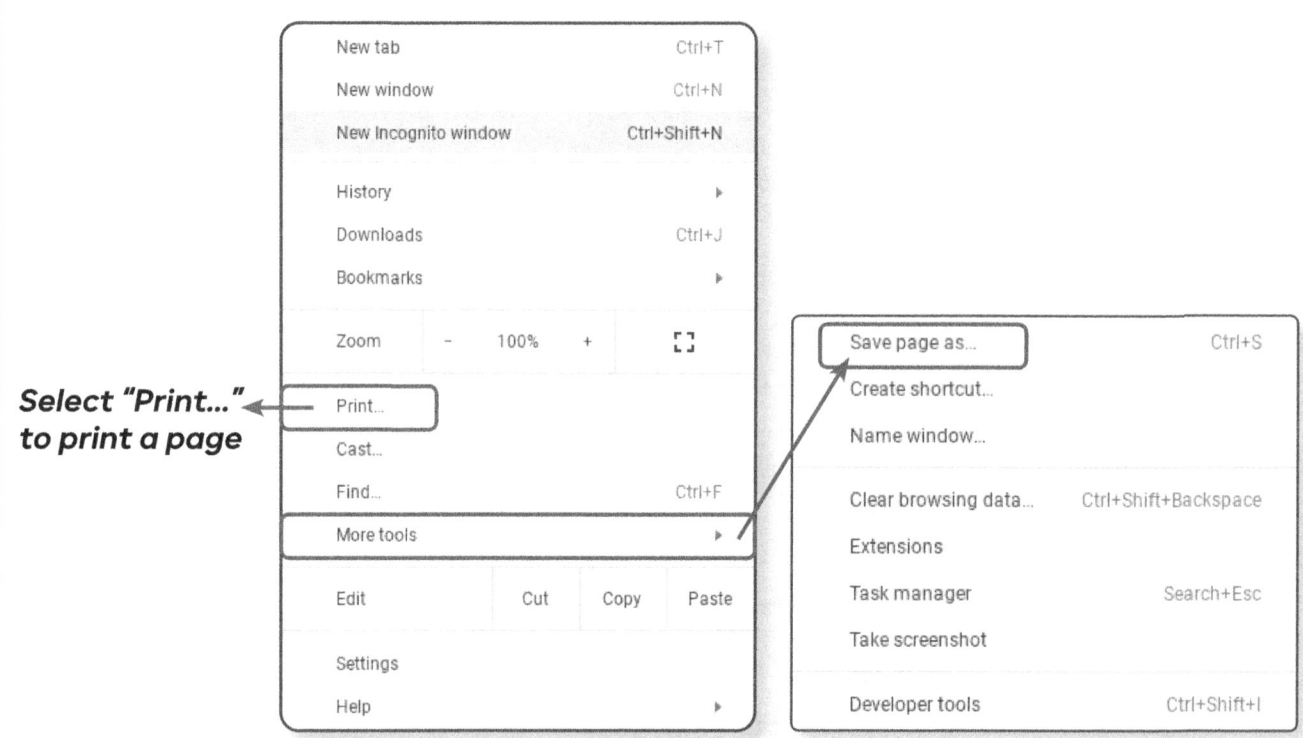

## PRINTING A WEBPAGE

To print a web page, you must first open it, then click on the **Three dots** on the upper right of the window. Tap **Print** and enter your desired settings such as page orientation and pages to be included. Once you are satisfied with the settings, select **Print**.

## SAVING PASSWORDS

To save a password, click on the **three dots** at the top right corner. After that, tap **Settings**, then **Autofill**. Click on the arrow to the right of the Passwords option. Afterward, activate the option which says **Offer to save passwords**.

# WEB, EMAIL, AND COMMUNICATION

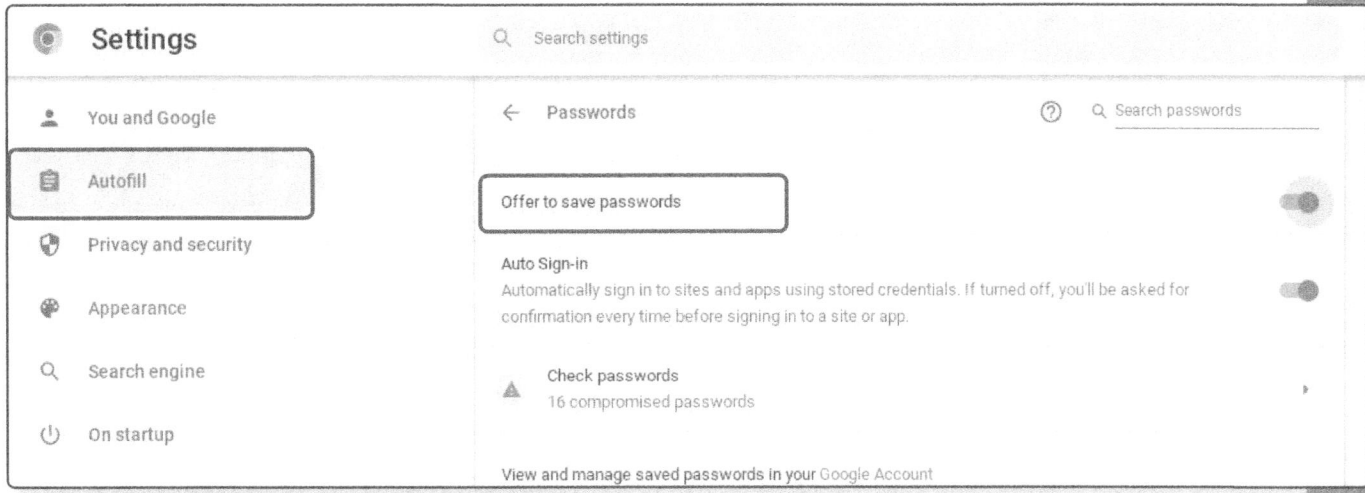

## MANAGING PASSWORDS

To manage passwords in Google Chrome, go to the browser menu and click on the **Three dots** that are on the top-right of your browser's screen. Scroll down to the bottom until you find the Settings option. Click on **Settings**, then **Advanced**. Afterward, click on **Passwords** and forms before clicking on **Manage saved passwords**.

### Generate Automatic Strong Passwords

If you want to generate a strong password with Google Chrome, open your browser and go to the top-right corner, where you have to tap on your profile. A menu will appear from which you should click on the option that says **Passwords**. On the passwords page, tap on **Offer to save passwords**. Afterward, open the website for which you wish to generate a strong word. Upon launching the website, Chrome will provide a password suggestion in the password field.

If for some reason, the password is not automatically suggested by the browser, go to the password field and right-click on it, then tap on **Suggested password**. If you desire to use the suggested password, there will be a pop-up that will ask you to keep the log in authorizations or details in the Password manager.

## CHROME SECURITY

The Chrome browser helps to notify you whenever you are at risk of malware and phishing sites. If you want to alter your Safe browsing settings, select the **Three dots** at the upper right of your browser window, then tap on **Settings**. After that, click on **Privacy and Security**, then **Safe browsing**. Afterward, you should then select a protection level that you desire from **Enhanced**, **Standard**, and **No protection**.

# CHAPTER 5

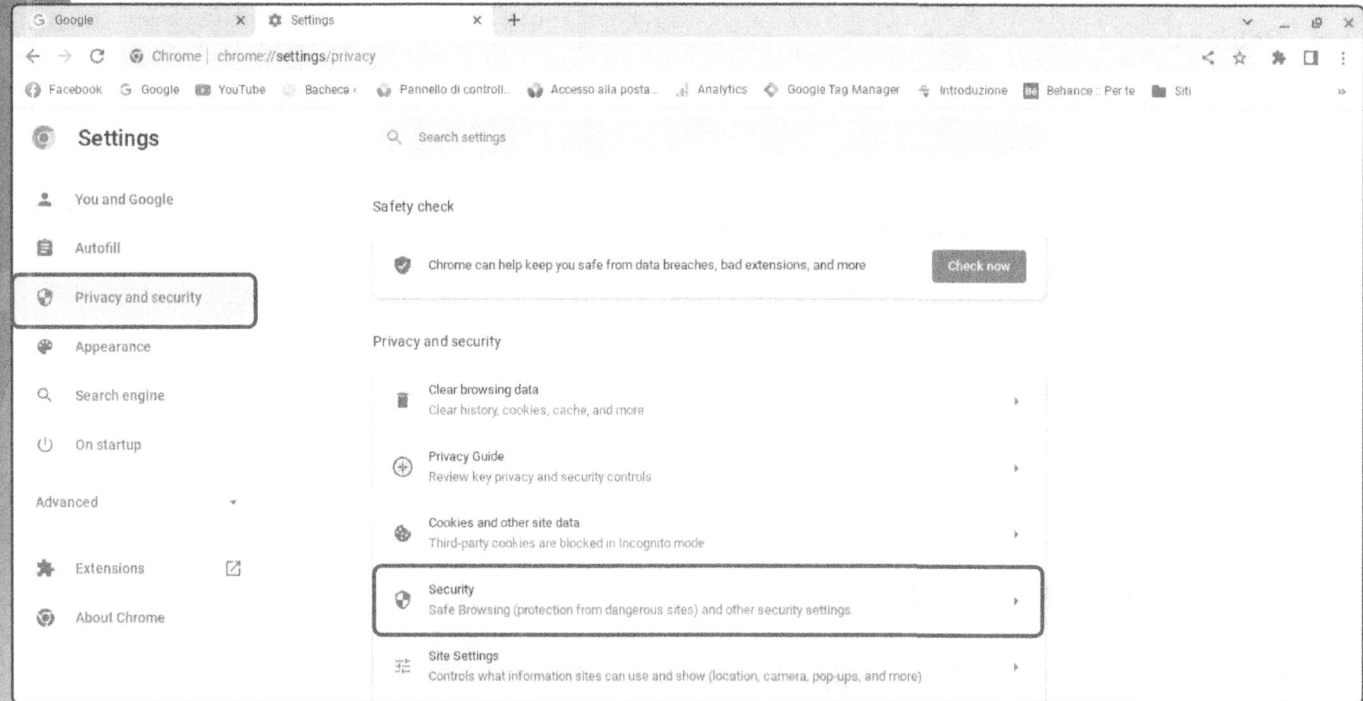

## GMAIL APP

When you have the Gmail app, you can easily access your email online. With this app, you can read messages that have been sent to you and you may as well respond to them with great ease. Let's discuss how to use the app in this section.

### READING EMAIL

The inbox of your Gmail contains mail that has been sent to you. Your inbox will contain the mails in an organized manner, with the recent mails on the top. As you scroll down, you will find your older emails. If you want to read an email that has been sent to you, simply click on it and it will open.

### REPLY AN EMAIL

In case you desire to respond to a mail, you have to first open the message by tapping on it. After that, tap on the **Reply arrow**. When you click on the reply arrow, a preview pane will appear. The pane will contain the name of the individual that you want to send a reply in the field labeled **To**. Next, type your response and click on **Send**.

# WEB, EMAIL, AND COMMUNICATION

## WRITING A NEW MESSAGE

When you want to write a new message, tap the **Compose** button which is located on the top part of your left. A New Message window will appear, which will allow you to enter the email address of your recipient in the **To field**. There is also a **Subject field** underneath in which you can write about the reason why you are writing the email. If you are interested in sending copies of the same message to other people, you can add Cc or Bcc. The next step is to write your message, then tap on **Send** when you are finished.

*Click to open and reading the email*

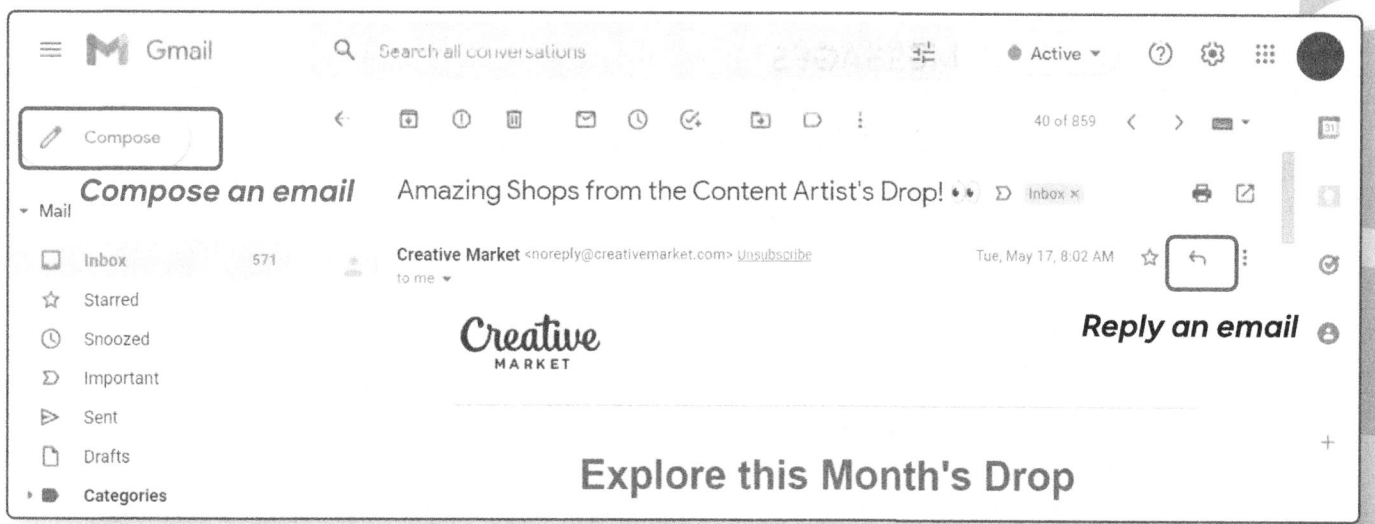

*Compose an email*

*Reply an email*

# CHAPTER 5

**Add Attachments**

## ADDING ATTACHMENTS

To add attachments to your Gmail, click on the app to open it. Afterward, tap **Compose**, then write your message, if need be. Go to the **Attach files paperclip icon**, at the bottom of the message and click on it. A dialogue box, which is labeled **Open** will appear from which you have to select after choosing the file or files that you wish to attach to your email. After adding the attachments, you can click on **Send** when ready.

## RECOVER DELETED MESSAGES

Please note that when you delete a message on Gmail, it will not be gone at that instant. There is a grace period of approximately 30 days for which you are able to recover your message before it is lost forever (Johnson, 2021). Let's get more details about how you can recover your deleted messages.

To recover deleted messages on your Gmail, go to the left side of the page. Afterward, scroll down your labels and tap **More**, then click on **Trash**. Select each of the emails that you want to recover by clicking on the checkbox. After that, go to the top of the message list and tap on **Move to**, prior to choosing a location to which the messages should be recovered.

# WEB, EMAIL, AND COMMUNICATION

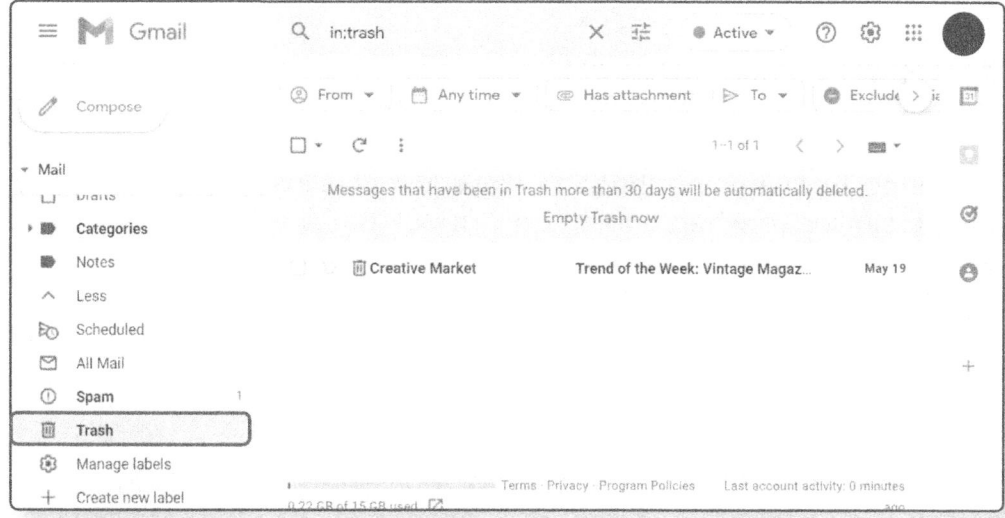

## SEARCH MESSAGGES

If you want to search for a certain email, you can just scroll down your emails so that you can find the one that you are looking for. However, sometimes you may not have the time to scroll through multiple emails. The easiest way to go about it is to search by using the search bar. This involves typing your search term.

To search for an email, open your Gmail prior to typing a search item into your **Search Bar**. For example, if you are looking for an email concerning your business proposal, simply type in "Business proposal" in your search bar. After typing in your search term, a list will appear on your screen that will show recent emails relating to your search term. When you see your desired email, simply open it by clicking. In case you do not see the email that you are looking for from the list, tap on **More search results** so that you see all the other emails that relate to your search term. Afterward, scroll down to find the right one. Sometimes the list may still be too long. In that case, use a search operator, for example, type in "from:susan" if you want to search for messuges sent from Susan.

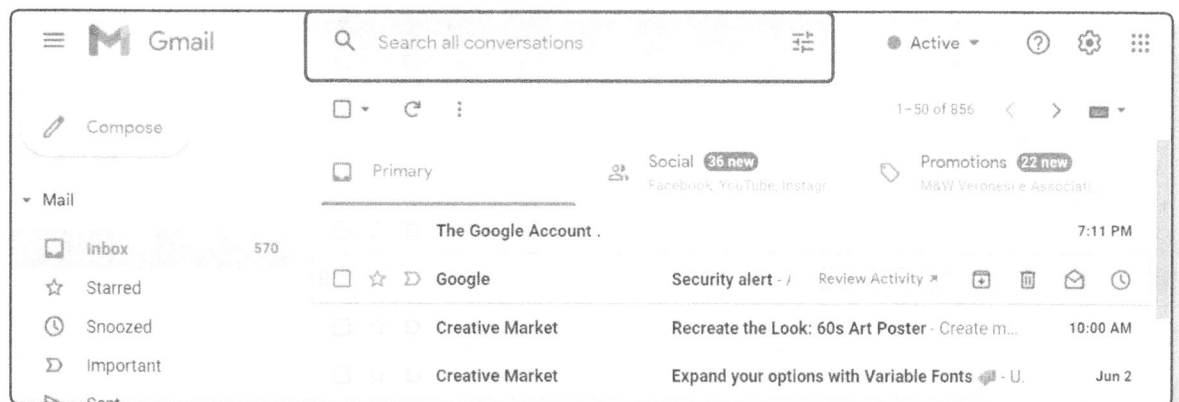

# CHAPTER 5

## ADDING OTHER EMAIL ACCOUNTS

It is possible to add other email accounts to your Gmail, be it another one from Gmail, Outlook, or Yahoo. Bear in mind that the steps involved in adding a Yahoo account to your Gmail are similar to when adding an Outlook one. Let's discuss how to add another Gmail as well as a Yahoo account to Gmail.

You may wish to add another Gmail account. To do this, open your account and go to the top-right corner. After that, tap on your profile picture before you click on **Add account**. You should then log in to the Gmail that you wish to add.

To add a Yahoo account to Gmail, sign in to your Gmail account and click **Settings**. Afterward, tap the **Accounts and Import** or **Accounts** option. There is a section that says **Check mail from other accounts**. On this option, select **Add** a mail account. You should then put down the Yahoo email address that you wish to link prior to tapping **Next**. Choose the option which says **Link account with Gmail** before clicking **Next**. Afterward, follow the on-screen instructions, then click **Sign in** or **Next**.

## CALENDAR APP

With your calendar app on your Chromebook, you can view the date and time at a quick glance. This app is advantageous because it can work offline. By using this application, you can get information about what time it is elsewhere in the world. In addition to this, you can easily manage your tasks, documents, and meetings. The calendar app also allows you to create and see various tasks and meetings. You can sync the tasks and meetings with your Outlook and Google calendars as well.

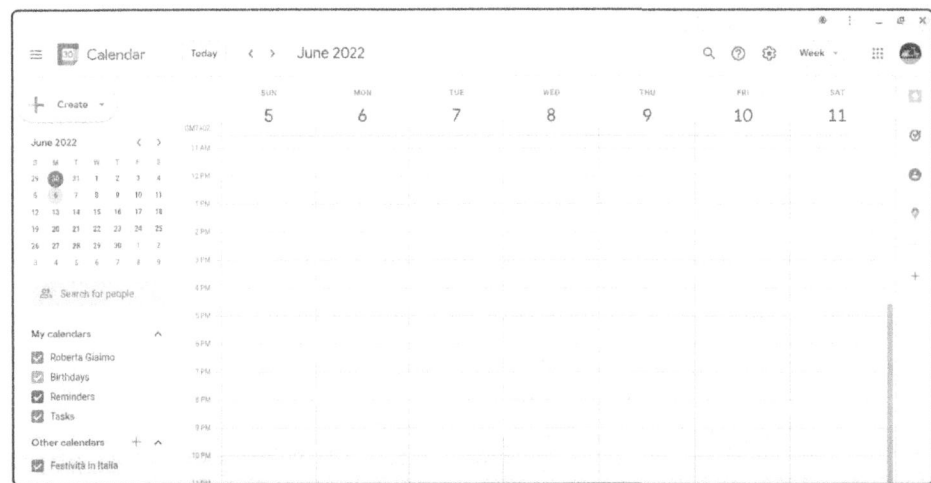

## WEB, EMAIL, AND COMMUNICATION

## ADDING EVENTS

To add an event, start by opening the Calendar app, then click on **Create Event**. After that, swipe up so that you can alter the event details such as **Title** and **Location**. The last step is to click on **Save**.

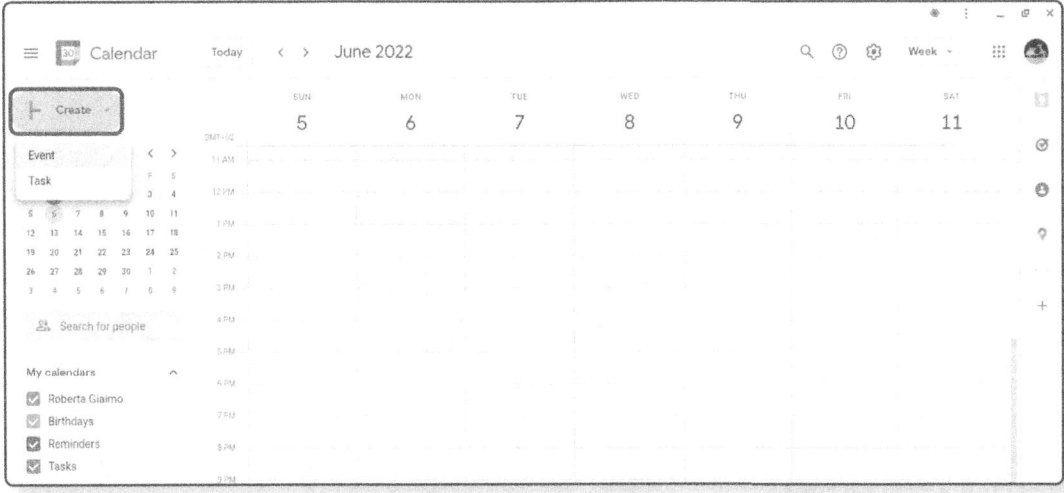

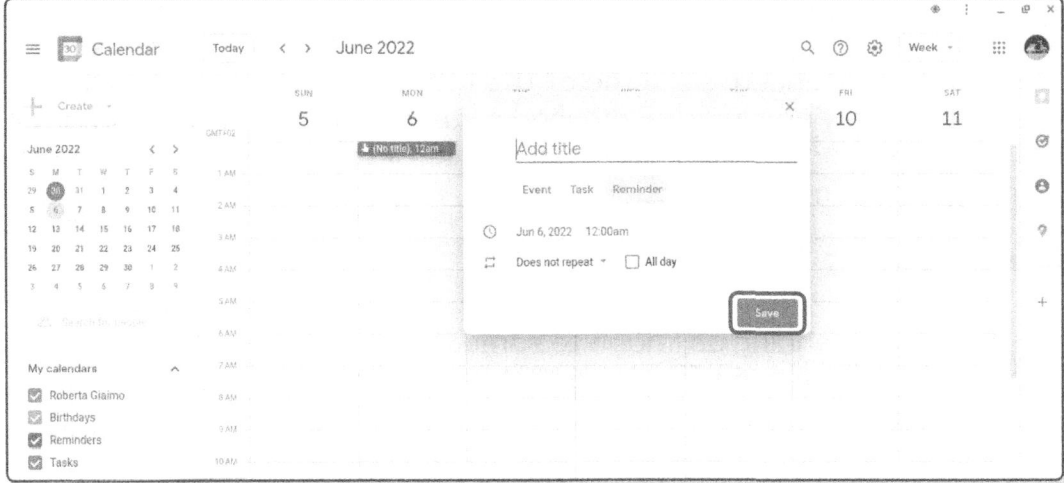

## ADDING REMINDERS

If you want to add a reminder, open your Calendar app and go to the lower right of your screen. Click on **Create**, then **Reminder**. Afterward, you should then select a suggestion or type in your reminder. Next, put down information relating to frequency, time, and date. Go to the top right and click on **Save**.

# CHAPTER 5

## ADDING TASKS

To add a task, open your Google Calendar app and click on **Add**, then **Task**. Afterward, assign a title and description. Next, select a date, frequency, and time. Go to the top right part of your screen and click on **Save**. Once you save, your tasks will be visible in the Google Calendar app. Please note that finished tasks will stay on your calendar but crossed out.

## ADD A GOAL

To create a goal on your Chromebook, go ahead and open the Google Calendar app. Click on **Create** at the lower right of your screen. Click on **Goal** and select your desired category such as **Friends**, **Family**, or **Exercise**. If you wish to create a custom goal, choose your preferred category, and afterward, click **Custom**. Follow the on-screen instructions to create your goal, then select **Done**. Beginning with the first four weeks, sessions will be added to your calendar. At any given time, it is possible to adjust the length or time of these set goals.

# GMAIL ON THE WEB

When you are using Gmail on the web, you will be able to carry out various tasks as far as communication is concerned. Some of the tasks that you can do include reading mail, writing, and replying to a new message. Furthermore, you can add other email accounts and add attachments when using Gmail. Details of carrying out these tasks have been shared in an earlier section.

## INSERTING IMAGES

If you are thinking of sending an image to someone, you can do it by inserting it as an attachment or in the body of the message that you want to send (New Tricks, 2018). Begin by clicking on **Compose in your Gmail**.

If you prefer that the image appears below the text, start by writing your message. Afterward, point your cursor to where you want your image to appear, then tap **Insert image**. Upon tapping on the insert image option that is at the bottom of the screen, options such as **Photos**, **Albums**, **Web address**, and **Upload** will appear from which you have to choose your desired one. For an image on the web, simply enter its URL.

Select the image that you want to insert. After that, you can choose to insert the image inline or as an attachment. It is possible to change the size of the image by selecting options such as **Best fit**, **Original size**, or **Small**.

## WEB, EMAIL, AND COMMUNICATION

## CONTACTS WEB APP

You will find the contacts web app on the dropdown list that appears after clicking on your Google apps button. With the contacts web app, you can easily back up and sync your web and mobile contacts. In addition to that, you can organize and update your contacts.

### VIEW CONTACT DETAILS

To view contact details, go to your web browser and open Gmail. Afterward, click on the **Google apps button** and select **Contacts** from the dropdown menu. By doing this, your contact list will be launched so that you can find the person that you are looking for.

### ADD NEW CONTACTS

To add new contacts to your Gmail, start by opening your account. Tap on the **Google apps** button in the upper right corner of your screen. Afterward, choose **Contacts** from the provided menu, then click on **Create contact** in the top left part of the screen. When prompted, tap **Create a contact** and enter the necessary contact details such as name, email address, and phone number. In case you wish to add more information, tap Show more so that extra slots are revealed. When you are done, click **Save**.

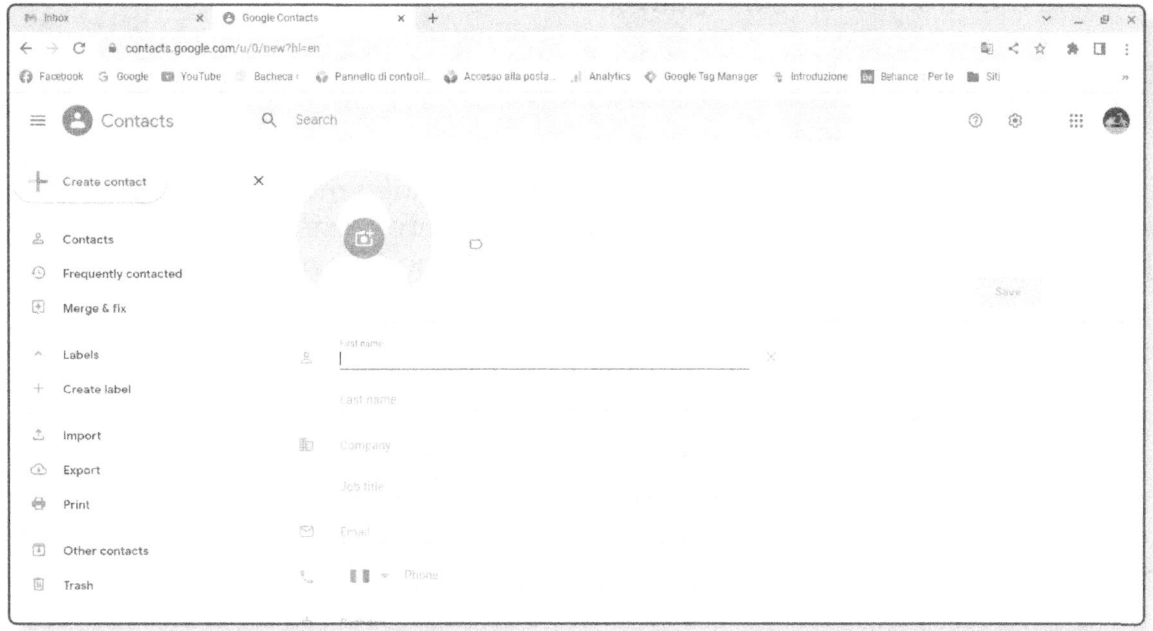

# CHAPTER 5

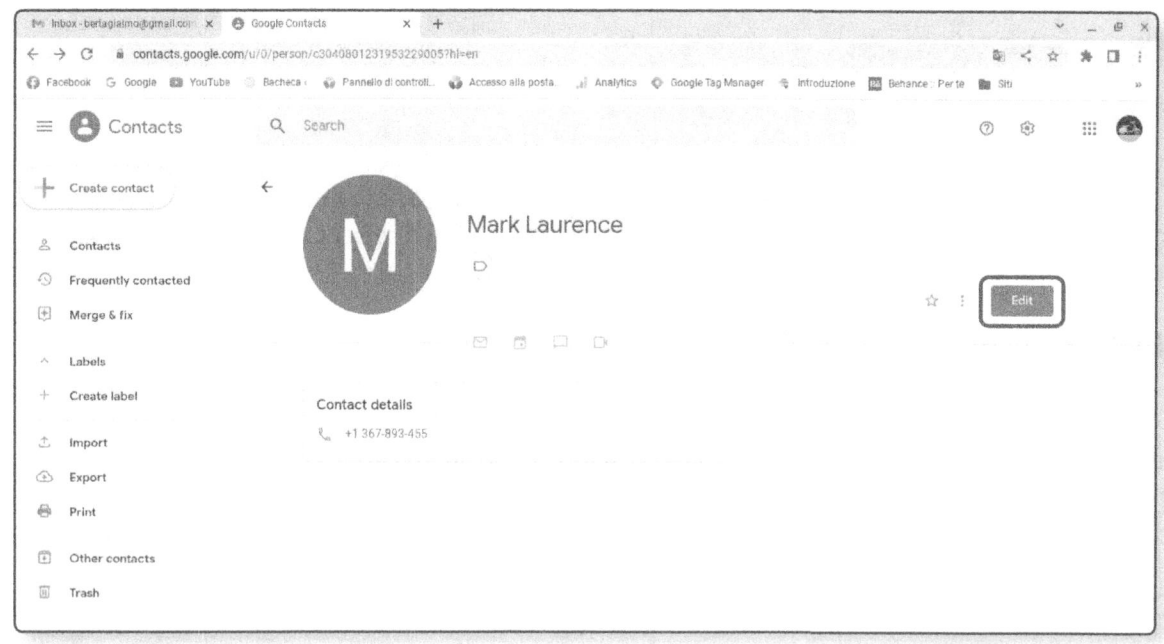

## ADD A CONTACT FROM MESSAGE

To add a contact from messages, proceed by opening the message from the sender. At the upper part of the email, move your cursor over the name of the sender. Afterward, a pop-up pane will appear, from which you should tap **Add to contacts**. If you need to add more details pertaining to this contact, click **Edit contact**. When you finish adding the information, select **Save**.

## GOOGLE MEET

Consider using Google Meet for efficient and quick video meetings. Google Meet is one of the best software for video conferencing. This software contains special features that will accommodate more advanced users.

### STARTING A GOOGLE MEET

To start a Google Meet, you will need internet access and a Google account. If you are using Gmail, select **Start a meeting** which you will find on the menu on your left side. In case of a browser, visit *https://meet.google.com* and tap **New meeting**.

After that, you can follow the on-screen instructions. A link is generated when you start a meeting. You can then send the link to other participants so that they can immediately join the meeting.

# WEB, EMAIL, AND COMMUNICATION

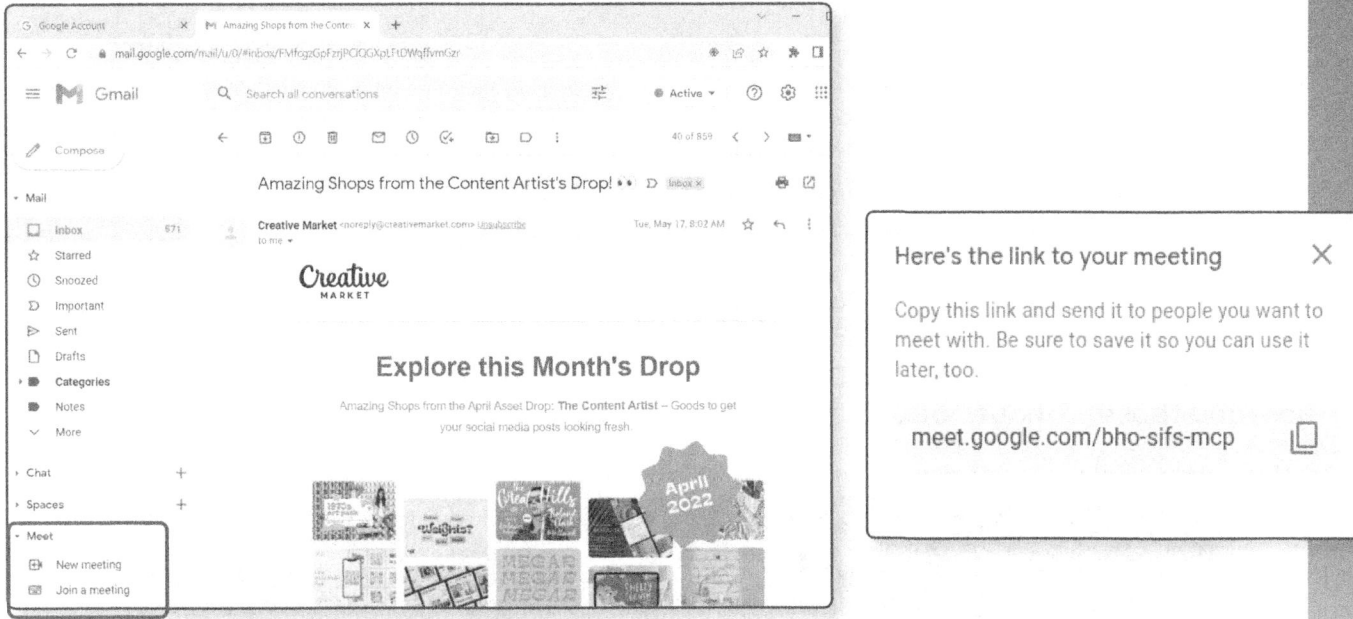

*Select New meeting or Join a meeting*

## CREATING A MEETING FOR LATER

There are times when your schedule gets very busy. In times like these, you may prefer to do some of the things in the present moment for later use. An example is when you want to create a meeting for later. If you want to create a meeting for later, go to **Google Meet** and tap **New meeting**. Afterward, select **Create a meeting for later**. You can then share the meeting details with the participants.

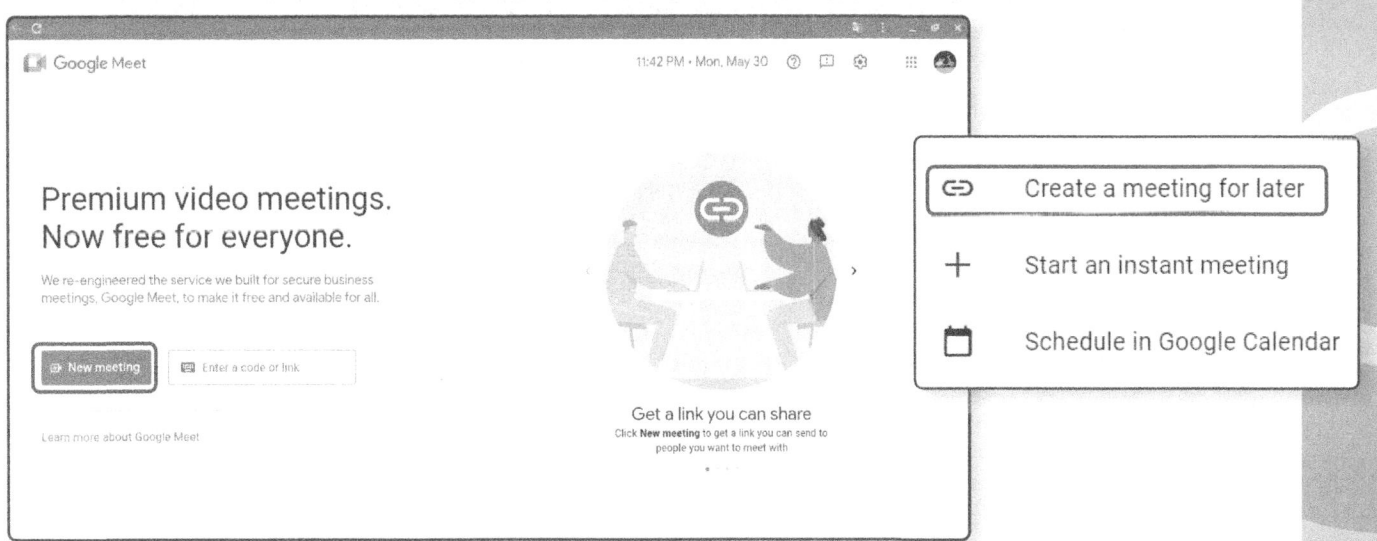

*https://meet.google.com*

# CHAPTER 5

## START INSTANT MEETING

If you wish, it is possible to instantly start a meeting. To proceed tap on **New meeting**, then from the menu, click **Start an instant meeting**. Next, you must tap **Allow** to accept the usage of your camera, microphone, and notifications.

To add participants you can **Copy joining info** that you will send to them in order for them to join the meeting, or **Add people**. If you have finished carrying out these steps, you can click to **Admit** or **Deny** entry in order to allow people with invitations to join and those without not to join.

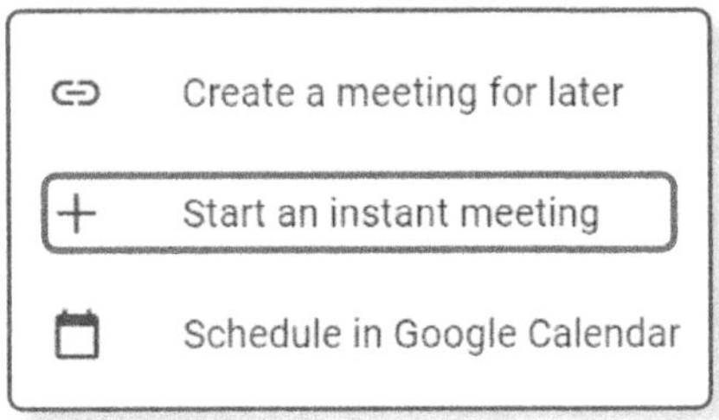

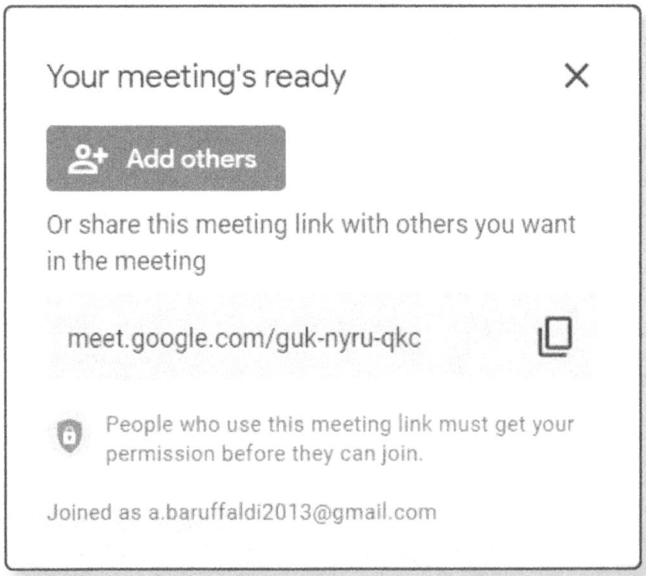

## WEB, EMAIL, AND COMMUNICATION

### SCHEDULE MEETING IN THE CALENDAR

The Calendar app that is part of Google apps is unique. This is because it can allow you to schedule a meeting up to five years from the present moment, with 250 participants, at no cost. Let's get more details in this section.

To schedule a meeting, open your Gmail and tap **Google Apps**. Go to **Google Calendar**, then click **Create**. Afterward, a dropdown window will appear, and from there, tap on **Event**. After tapping on Event, you should click **Add**, then schedule the meeting.

Next, click on the **Clipboard icon** so that you can share the link to the meeting. Go to the Add guests field and send invites by typing their email addresses. Last, verify your meeting details and tap **Save**.

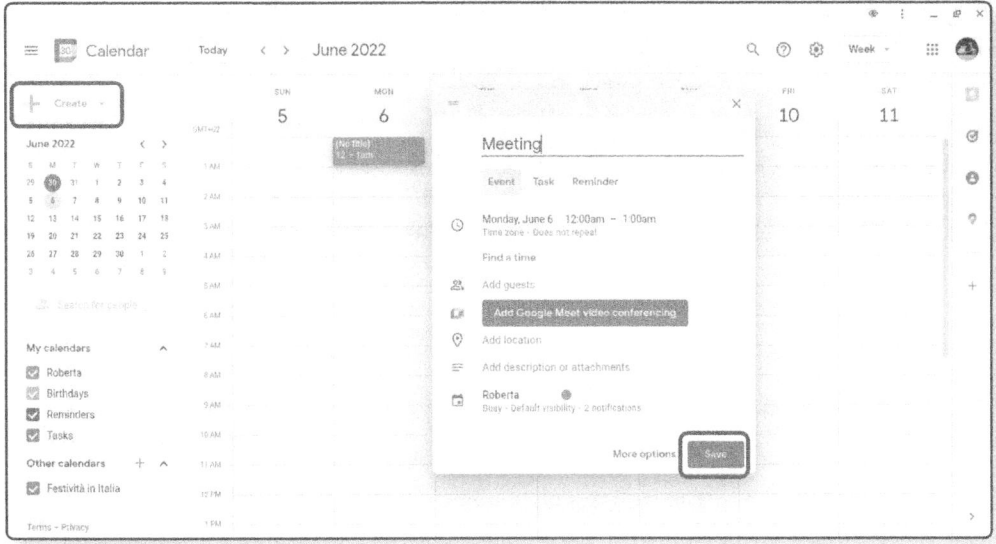

### JOINING A MEETING

To join a meeting, go to Gmail and click **Join Meeting** from the menu, on your left. Next, enter the meeting code or click the link that has been sent to you by the host of the meeting. You could also visit *https://meet.google.com*, then tap on **Join meeting**. Afterward, click the link or enter the meeting code so that you join the meeting.

### IN-CALL OPTIONS

It is possible to change video and audio settings during a Google meeting. To change the settings, click on the **three dots**, then **Settings**. Go to the left of your screen and

# CHAPTER 5

tap **Video**, then **Camera**. Afterward, choose a setting and tap **Close** in the upper right. To change audio settings, click on the **three dots**, then **Settings and Audio**, after that, choose a setting that you prefer to change. When you finish, click **Done**.

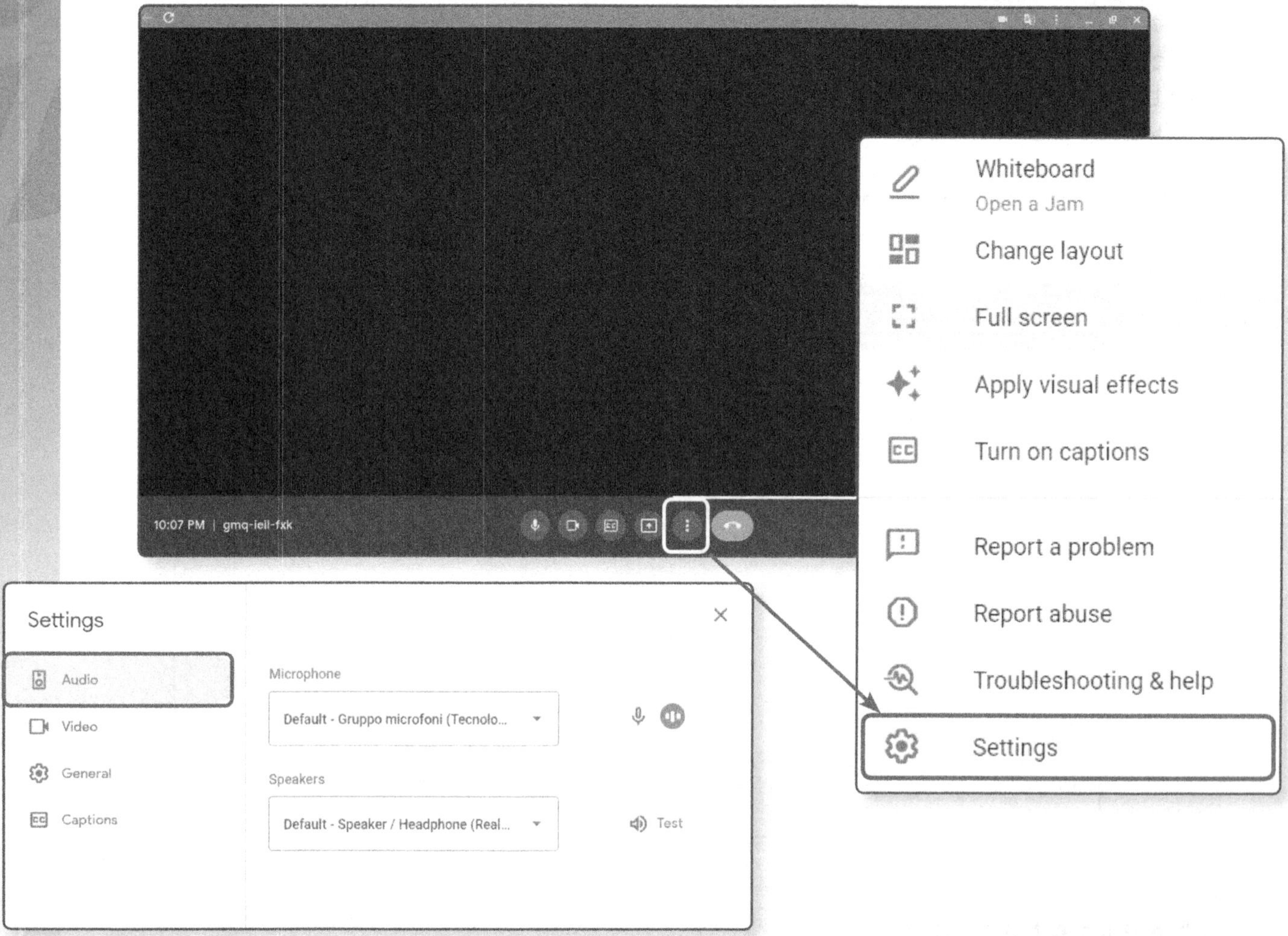

## PRESENT AND SHARE DESKTOPS

When presenting something in video meetings, you may want to show specific details to your audience. To share your desktop, go to the lower part of your screen and tap **Present now**. Depending on what you want to show, it is up to you to select the entire screen, Chrome tab, or a single window. In case you want to show a different Chrome tab, simply go to the bottom of the page and tap **Change source**. If you want to stop sharing, click on **Stop presenting**.

## WEB, EMAIL, AND COMMUNICATION

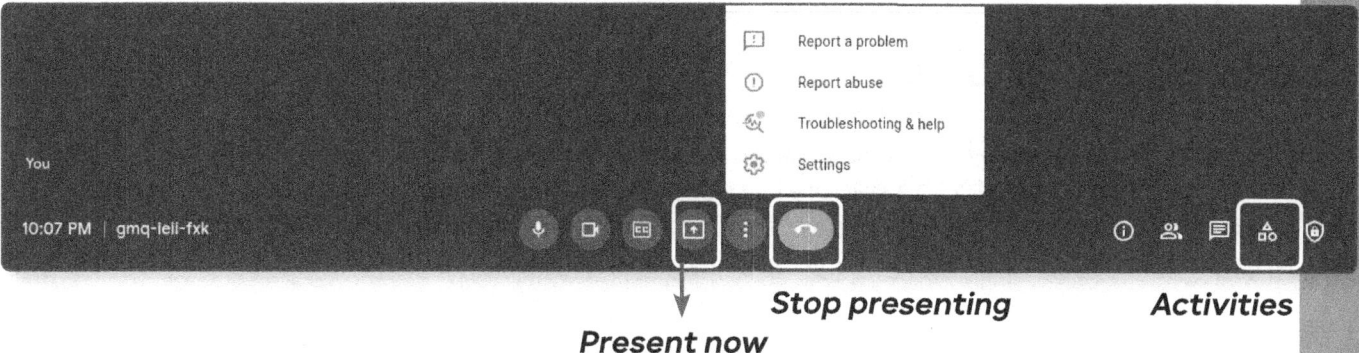

*Present now* — *Stop presenting* — *Activities*

## WHITEBOARD

Consider a situation in which you are in a Live classroom and would like to demonstrate something. The Whiteboard is a tool that allows you to demonstrate certain concepts to your audience. In some cases, the whiteboard may act as a tool that allows interaction between both the host and attendees. Tools such as Canvas and Jamboard are compatible with Google Meet and efficiently help when it comes to a demonstration.

To utilize a whiteboard in Google Meet after joining or starting a meeting, go to the bottom right and tap **Activities**.

After that, click on **Whiteboarding**. You will then have to select **Start a new whiteboard** in order to create a new Jamboard. However, if you want to open an already existing Jamboard from your computer, drive, or shared drives tap on **Choose from Drive**.

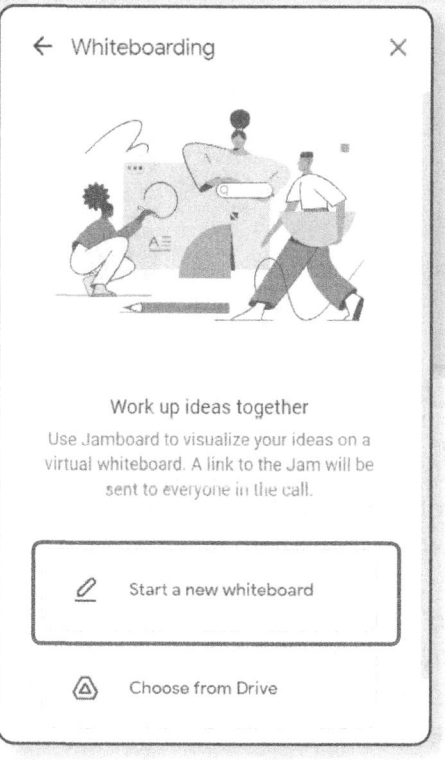

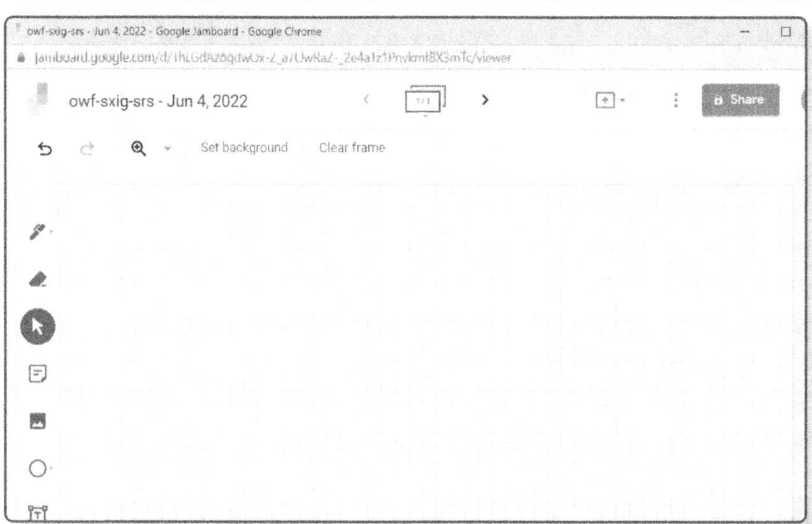

# CHAPTER 5

## CHANGE BACKGROUND

Bear in mind that you have the choice of changing your background if you think that it may be distracting to the people in the meeting. To alter your background, start by clicking the icon with **three dots** so that you can access **More options**. After that, tap **Apply** visual effects to activate your background of choice.

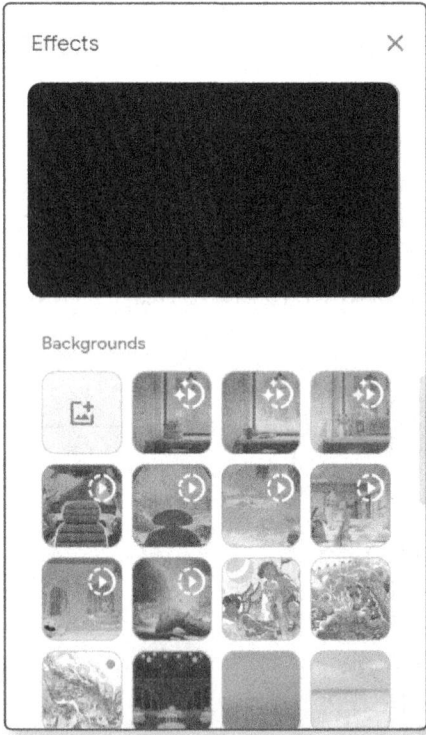
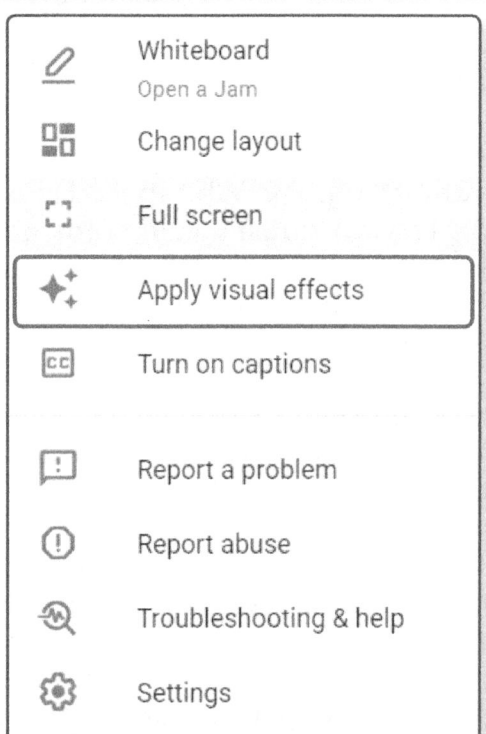

## CAPTIONS

When you are using video calls on Google Meet, live captions come in handy. They help in making sure that you understand what is being said in cases where you are experiencing difficulties in hearing.

To activate captions, tap the **three dots** at the bottom of your window and choose **Captions**. Afterward, you will notice captions being displayed at the screen's bottom as the participants of the meeting speak. An alternative way is to turn on captions in Settings. Go ahead and tap on the **three dots** and select **Settings**. Afterward, click on **Captions** prior to enabling the toggle at the upper part. Captions will then show on the lower part of the screen as the meeting participants speak.

# WEB, EMAIL, AND COMMUNICATION

*Turn on Captions*

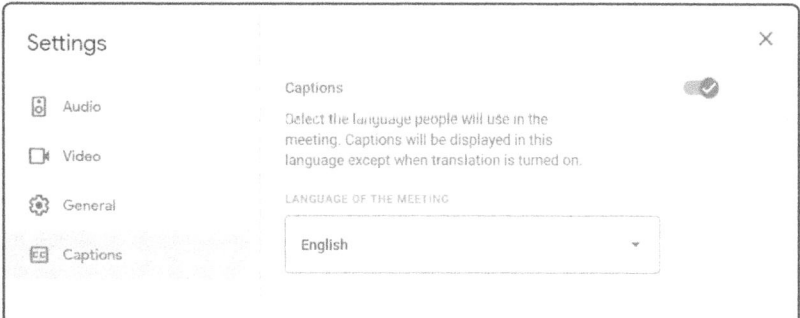

*Settings Captions*

## GOOGLE CHAT

**Google Chat** makes it possible for people to hold chat sessions, be it on a formal or informal basis. With Google Chat, you can ask questions, make virtual spaces for team projects, and do group chats. Let's discuss more pertaining to this application in this section.

### STARTING GOOGLE CHAT

To start Google Chat, you should open your Gmail account, then go to **Settings**, in the top right corner. Afterward, tap **See all settings** prior to selecting **Chat and meet**. From the available options, click on **Google chat**. Tap on the **Plus sign** in the corner of the Chat box so that a drop-down menu appears. If you desire to chat with a certain individual, type their name in the field provided at the top. Once you do this, a small pop-up chat box will appear. That will allow you to start chatting.

### GROUP CONVERSATION

For group conversations, go to your Gmail settings and select **See all settings**, then **Chat and meet**. Choose **Google chat** from the list and click on the **Plus sign** that is at the corner of the chat box. Next, tap **Start group conversation** and list the names of the people that you wish to chat with.

# CHAPTER 5

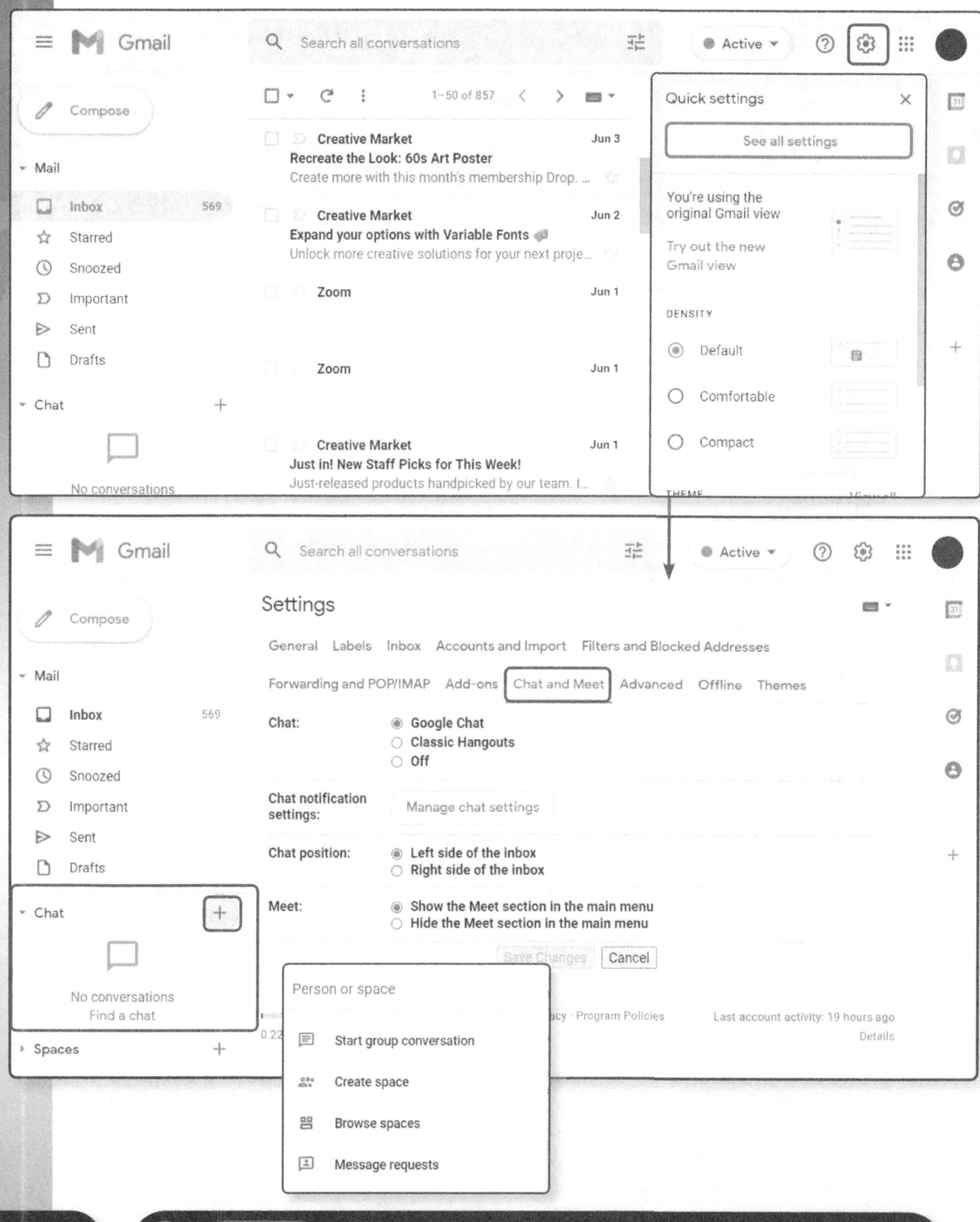

## WEB, EMAIL, AND COMMUNICATION

### CHAT ROOMS

Google Chat consists of Chat rooms, which mainly focus on threads. Each conversation is put into a thread, for which users can choose which conversations to join. This means that each person gets to see information that is applicable to them.

If you have something that you want to share, you can open a **Chat room** that you want. After that, go to the bottom center and tap **New thread**. After doing that, you can then post your new message. If you want to reply to an old message, you can pull up the thread and send a direct reply to someone.

### CREATING A ROOM AND CHATTING

If you have a project that you want to start, you have to create your own room. To do this, go to the upper-left corner of Chat and tap **Find people, rooms, bots bar**. Click on **Create room**, then assign a name to the new room. To add people to your new room, select anyone from the list, or search for people by typing names or emails. If you still need to add more people, simply refer to them in a Chat message. By doing this, Chat will then offer to invite them to your room. To chat in this newly created room, tap **New thread**, then post your message.

### SHARE FILES ON GOOGLE CHAT

The Google Drive icon is clearly visible in the **New conversation** and **Reply boxes**. You can tap on each of the options if you want to share a document from your Google Drive. As an alternative, if you already have a link to Sheets, Google Docs, Drive, or Slides that you want to share, simply preview it. This can be done by pasting the link into the reply box or thread.

### ASSIGN A TASK

To assign a task, open your Google Chat app and select **Spaces**, then **Space** on the bottom. Go to the top and tap the **Tasks** option, then **New task**. Afterward, enter the title for the task. It is possible to add a description, date, time, or name of the person to which the task is assigned. After that, select **Save**.

## GOOGLE DUO

Google Duo is a video calling application. This application uses your phone's contact numbers thereby making it easy to call someone if they use Duo and are in your contacts list. This means that with this app, there is no

# CHAPTER 5

need to know someone's email address.

## STARTING GOOGLE DUO

To begin using Google Duo, download the app on your Android or iOS device. Next, agree to Google's privacy policy and terms of service. Afterward, provide information on whether or not Duo can send notifications to you or access your camera and microphone. Afterward, you should verify your number and enter the verification code that is sent to you via SMS. Once you do that, you will see the app's main interface.

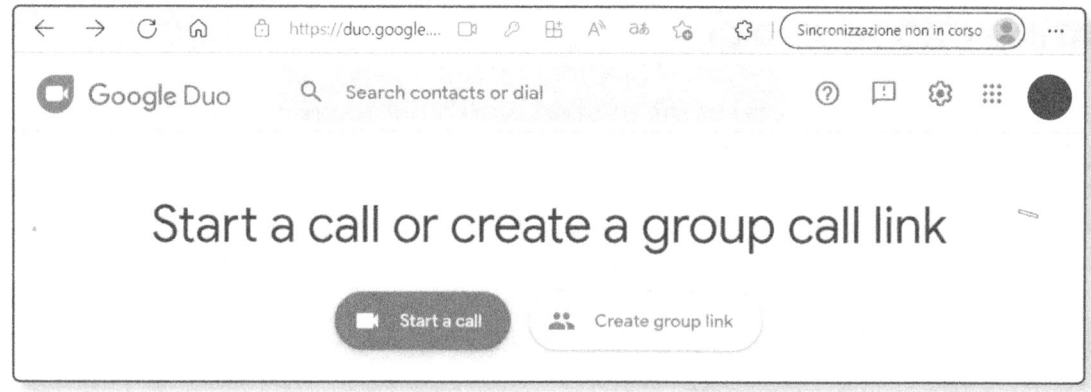

## SETUP

The main interface of Google Duo is characterized by a split-screen. The top half will be showing what the camera sees while the other one offers your contacts or groups. At the top, there is a search bar as well as a menu that allows you to access settings.

## START A CONVERSATION ON GOOGLE DUO

To start a conversation on Google Duo, tap a contact. Three options will appear on your screen from which you have to choose the one you prefer. The list includes **Video call**, **Voice call**, or **Message**. Apart from the video call, you can do a voice call or send a message. When you choose how you want to call them, they can choose to pick up or not. In case they choose not to pick up. You can always leave a message.

## GROUP CONVERSATION ON GOOGLE DUO

Not only does Duo allow you to make one-to-one calls, but it is also possible to do group conversations. These group conversations can accommodate a total of 12 people. To start a group conversation, you should click on **Create group** above your

# WEB, EMAIL, AND COMMUNICATION

contact list. Go ahead and add 11 people, then begin a video call with all of them.

Please note that upon creating the group, Duo will ask you to name it so that it can be saved. After doing this, the group will appear as one of your contacts in Duo.

This means that when you want to start a conversation with this group, it becomes easier in the future. When you receive a Duo call, you can swipe down to reject it or swipe up to answer.

## INVITE A FRIEND ON GOOGLE DUO

You may be interested in inviting someone on Google Duo. Follow the instructions to invite a friend to Google Duo. The first step is to open **Duo** on your tablet or Android phone. Afterward, tap **Video call** and look for the contact you want to invite. Upon finding the contact, click on **Invite**. After that, tap **Send** on your SMS app that contains a pre-loaded invitation. The recipient will then receive the invitation and can directly reply to the notification or download the app.

Alternatively, open **Duo** on your tablet or Android phone. Afterward, tap the option that is above your contact list, which says **Invite friends**. You should then select the **Share** invite link option. Afterward, invite the contact by tapping Invite.

# Chapter 6: Entertainment

People who engage in enjoyable activities for the sake of entertainment are less likely to become depressed. Chromebooks offer platforms that can be used for entertainment purposes. Forms of entertainment available on Chromebook include movies, TV shows, books, fun pictures, and videos. You can also actually get vacation destination ideas from the photos and videos shared on the internet by others. This chapter will explore the nitty-gritty of using some of the entertainment features on your Chromebook.

## GOOGLE PHOTOS

When it comes to using a Chromebook and Google Photos, Google is so close to bridging the gap. When Google removed the sync between Photos and Drive, it completely ruined the slightly-confusing procedure that allowed Chromebook users to view their Google Photos straight from the Chrome OS Files app. When synchronizing Photos with Drive was still possible, users could scroll their Google Photos in Drive files to find a photo to upload or add to an app. When Google deactivated the sync feature, they also deactivated many users' workflows.

What we're seeing from the Google Photos app right now isn't a complete fix, but it's a step closer to the full integration we'd like to see in future Chrome OS updates. This method currently only works when using an Android app on your Chromebook, but you'll notice that using the Files app on its own or as a file picker for a web-based application will not offer you this option.

All you have to do now is download the latest version of the Google Photos Android app and sign in. You can access some other Android apps such as Instagram and choose a picture from your Google Photos library for use. Google Photos would then show up as an option in the Files app when you've agreed to sign in and your Google Photos account is fully operational.

## ENTERTAINMENT

By selecting the **Photos** option on the left, you'll be taken to a new window where you can search through all of your Google Photos to find the exact image you're looking for. Currently, the interface that appears when you do this is identical to what you want to see on an Android phone when you do so.

### PHOTOS IN CHROME OS: VIEWING AND EDITING

Let's take a look at how to view digital photos on your Chromebook first. You can view photos locally on your Chromebook's long-term storage, memory card in your camera, USB drive, or an external hard drive. It is also possible to view them online via a cloud-based storage service or photo-sharing service.

### VIEW LOCAL PHOTOS

The Files app allows you to access photos that are stored on your Chromebook or any connected storage device through the following steps:

1. Open the Launcher panel by clicking the **Launcher icon**.
2. To open the Apps panel, click **All Apps**.
3. To open the Files app, click the **Files icon**.
4. Select the device or folder containing the photos. Click **Downloads** if the photos are on your Chromebook.
5. To see thumbnails of the stored photos, click the **thumbnail view** button.
6. Choose the picture that you want to view.
7. Select the **Open** option from the drop-down menu so that the photo is enlarged to fill the entire screen.
8. To see the navigation controls, move your mouse over the photo.
9. Use the right and left arrows or keys on your keyboard to move to the next or previous photos.
10. To go straight to another picture in this folder, click the thumbnail for that picture.
11. Click the **Mosaic View** button to see all of the photos in this folder as a

# CHAPTER 6

mosaic.

12. Click the **Slideshow** button to see all of the photos in this folder in a slideshow.

13. Click the **Print** button to print the photo of your choice.

14. Click the **Delete** button to remove a photo.

15. Click the **X** in the top-right corner to close the photo-viewing screen.

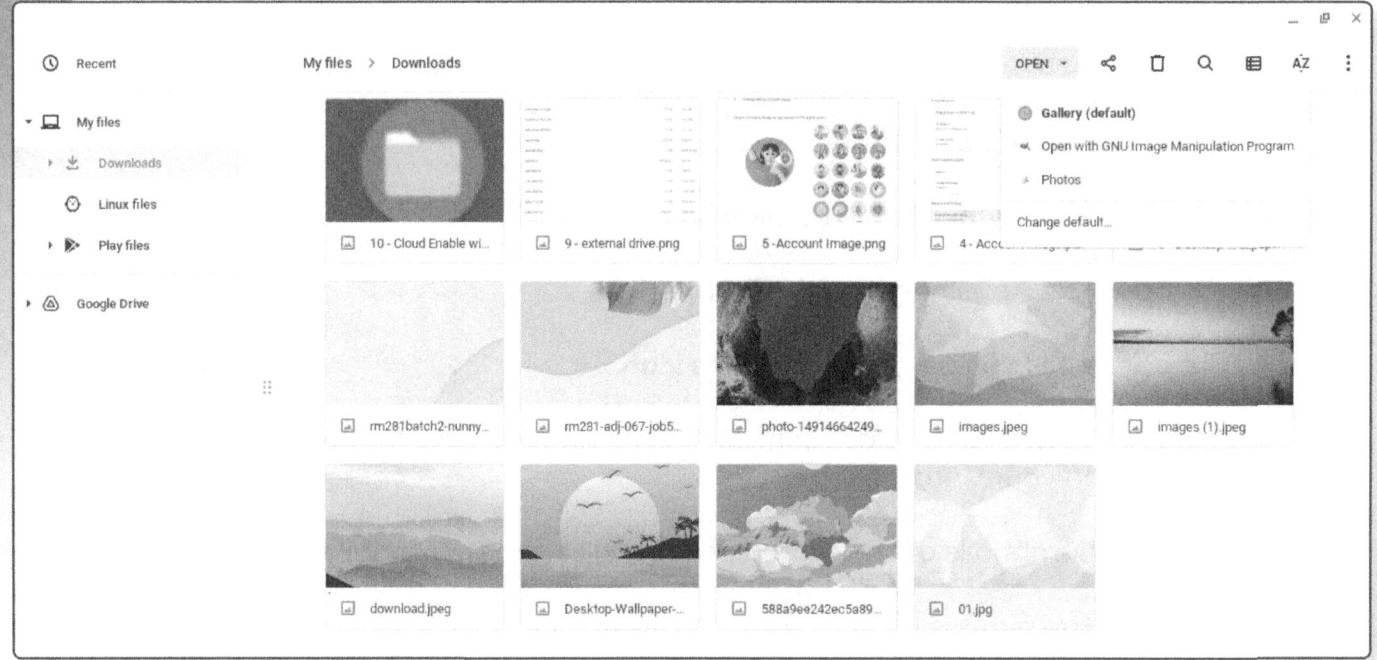

## ROTATE A PHOTOGRAPH

When a photograph appears to be sideways, it can be rotated. You can do this with the Photoshop Express Editor through a few simple steps.

1. Make sure **Edit** is selected, then go to the Basic section in the left panel and click **Crop & Rotate**.

2. Click the **Rotate Left** button in the Rotate & Flip section to rotate the image 90 degrees counterclockwise.

# ENTERTAINMENT

3. To rotate the image 90 degrees clockwise, click the **Rotate Right** button.

4. Click the **Done** button when the photo appears the way you want.

# CHAPTER 6

## ZOOM

Zooming in on a photo allows you to see small details (such as red eyes) more clearly. The Zoom slider will appear if you press the Zoom button that is at the bottom of the display. Drag the slider up or down to zoom in or out on the picture.

## USE THE AUTO-CORRECT FEATURE.

Color, brightness, and contrast can all be tweaked slightly in some photos. Use the Auto-Correct control in **Photoshop Express Editor** to apply an automatic fix to these elements.

1. Make sure **Edit** is selected, then click **Auto-Correct** in the Basic section of the left panel.

2. At the top of the editing window, there is now a thumbnail selection. Choose the thumbnail that appeals to you the most.

3. Click **Done**.

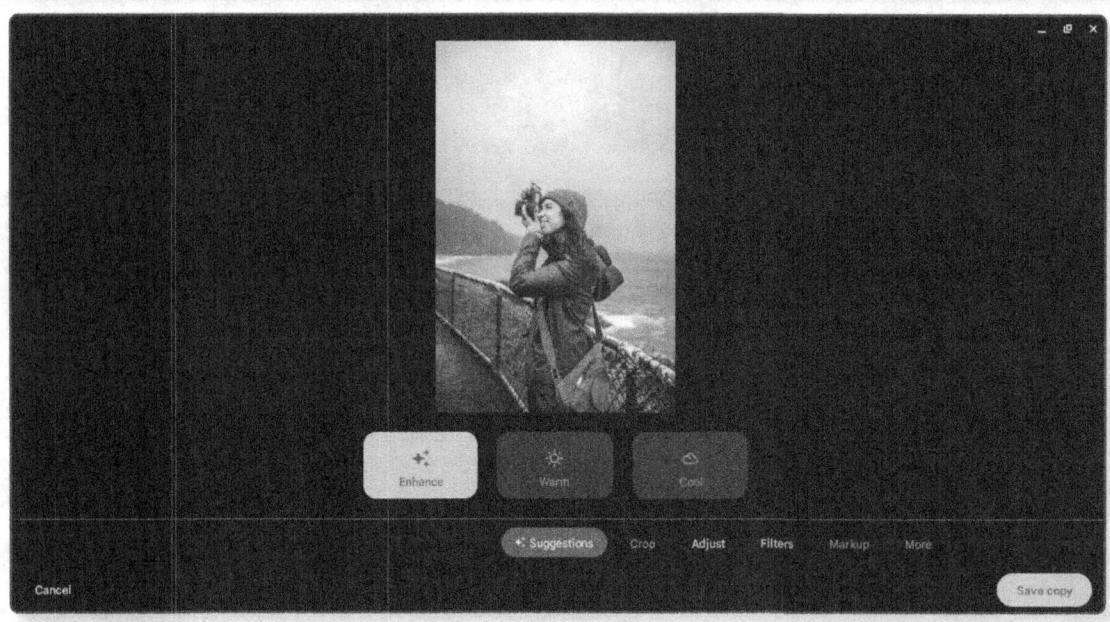

## MAKE ADJUSTMENTS TO THE EXPOSURE

A photograph that is underexposed appears too dark. When a photograph is overexposed, the image appears too light as well. Within the **Photoshop Express Editor**, you

# ENTERTAINMENT

can adjust the exposure of any image. To do this

1. Make sure **Edit** is selected, then click **Exposure** in the Basic section of the left panel.

2. At the top of the editing window, you'll see a selection of thumbnails ranging from dark to light. Darker thumbnails have a lower exposure, while lighter thumbnails have higher exposure. Choose the thumbnail that appeals to you the most.

3. Click the **Done** button.

## COLOR SATURATION CAN BE ADJUSTED

The color saturation of a photo can be adjusted in **Photoshop Express Editor**, ranging from no color (black and white) to too much color.

1. Make sure **Edit** is selected, then choose Saturation in the Basic section of the left panel.

2. At the top of the editing window, you'll see a selection of thumbnails ranging from undersaturated to oversaturated. Choose the thumbnail that appeals to you the most.

3. Select the **Done** button.

# CHAPTER 6

## APPLY ADVANCED MODIFICATIONS

Professional photographers will appreciate the advanced adjustments that are included in Adobe Photoshop Express Editor. White balance, highlight, fill light, dodge, burn, sharpen, and soft-focus settings can all be tweaked to match your desires.

1. With **Edit** selected in **Photoshop Express Editor**, go to the **Adjustments** section in the left panel and select the adjustment you want to apply.

2. Some adjustments display a series of thumbnails representing various levels of the adjustment. Select the desired thumbnail by clicking on it.

3. Each adjustment has its own set of controls. To apply the effect, use the controls.

4. Click the **Done** button.

## CROPPING AND ROTATION

Three tabs are available in the editing pane. The first allows you to apply a variety of filters to your image. The second is for in-depth editing. The third option makes it possible for you to crop and rotate your image. Select the **Crop & Rotate** tab after opening the image for editing. Select the desired aspect ratio, such as Square or 16:9, by clicking the **Aspect Ratio** button. Drag the crop handles around until you're satisfied with the outcome. To rotate the image 90 degrees counterclockwise, click the **Rotate** button. To rotate the image in more discrete increments, click and drag the **Rotate slider**. When you're happy, click **Done**.

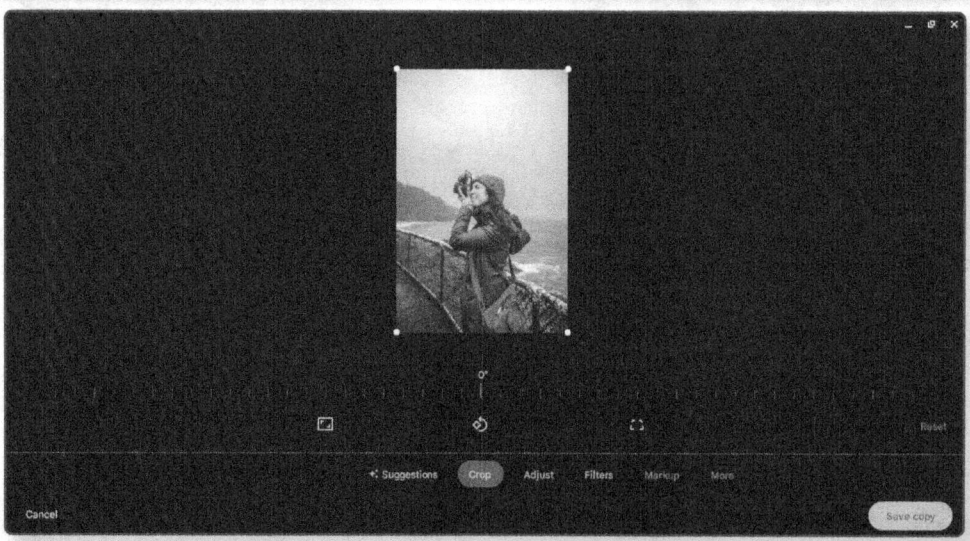

ENTERTAINMENT

## MUSIC ENJOYMENT

Chrome comes with its own media player, which you can use to listen to music and watch videos. Your Chromebook's storage limitations make it difficult to store large numbers of music files internally, just as they do when viewing photos. Transferring the desired music files to a USB memory device and then inserting that device into your Chromebook is a better option. The files on the USB device can then be listened to using Chrome's Media Player.

Note that not all types of music files are supported by Chrome's Media Player. It supports the MP3 audio format, but not Apple's .aac or Microsoft's .wma. To listen to your files on your Chromebook, you'll need to convert them to MP3 format if they're in an iTunes library.

### LISTENING TO MUSIC

In this section, we'll assume that you already have your favorite MP3 files copied to a USB memory device. On your Chromebook, you'll use that device to play music.

1. Connect your external storage device to Chromebook.

2. Open the **External Storage** folder in **File Manager** and locate the folder where the MP3 file is saved.

3. Double-click the music file you'd like to listen to. You can also select the file and then press the **Play** button in the Preview pane to play it.

4. The Media Player will open and playback will begin. Click the **Pause** button to pause playback; click the **Play** button to resume playback.

5. To adjust the volume of the playback, click the **Volume** button to bring up the Volume slider. Alternatively, you can use the Chromebook keyboard's Volume Up and Volume Down buttons.

6. Click the **X** in the upper-right corner to close the Media Player.

### PLAYING A SONG FROM A PLAYLIST

A playlist of multiple tracks can also be played back using the Media Player. This allows you to program music for a long period of time.

# CHAPTER 6

1. Connect your Chromebook to the external storage device.

2. Open the **External Storage** folder in File Manager and browse to the folder where the MP3 file is saved.

3. Choose the files you want to add to the playlist. To select multiple files, hold down the **Ctrl and Shift** keys.

4. In the Preview pane, click the **Enqueue** button.

5. The Media Player will open, and the first song in the playlist will begin to play. Click the **Pause** and **Play** buttons to pause and resume playback, respectively.

6. Choose the **Playlist** button to see the entire playlist.

7. In the Media Playlist pane, click a song to switch to the next one in the playlist.

## LISTENING TO MUSIC STREAMING SERVICES

Music fans used to purchase albums and singles on vinyl. They began purchasing digital compact discs around the mid-1980s. Then, around the turn of the century, another shift occurred, with the introduction of digital music downloads via the Internet.

Another shift is taking place right now. Instead of purchasing music one track or al-

# ENTERTAINMENT

bum at a time, an increasing number of people are signing up for online music services that allow them to listen to as many songs as they want for free or for a low monthly fee. Pandora and Spotify, for example, stream music to your Chromebook in real-time over the Internet; there's no need to download or store it on your computer, and it's all completely lawful.

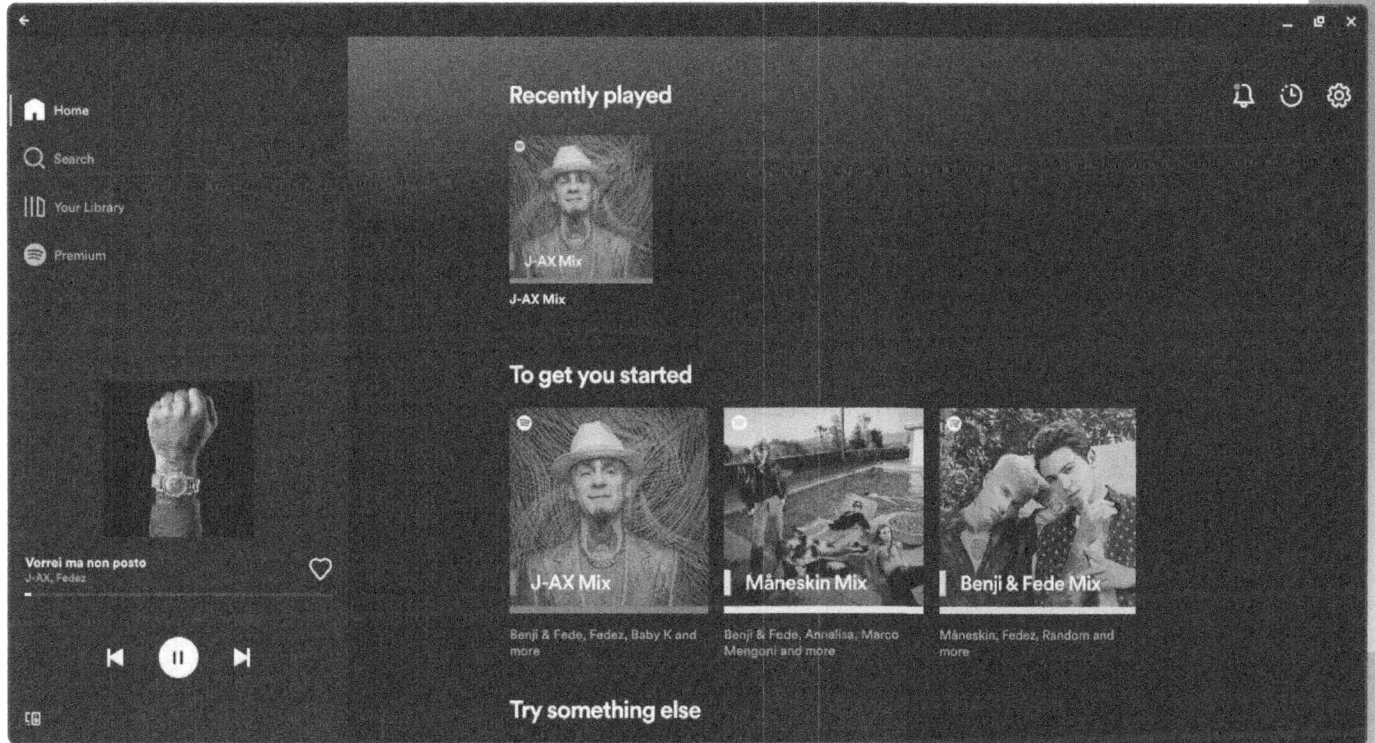

## USING SPOTIFY TO LISTEN TO MUSIC

Spotify's web player is used to listen to music. A traditional software-based player is also available, but it cannot be used on a Chromebook. The Spotify app, available from Google's Web Store, is the simplest way to access Spotify's web player. A $9.99 per month subscription is required to remove commercials as well as access on-demand music on your mobile devices. Basic access, which is accompanied by lots of commercials, comes for free. To use Spotify,

1. Click the **Launcher** button on the shelf to open the Apps panel after installing the Spotify app from Google's Web Store.

2. In the Chrome browser, click the **Spotify** icon to launch the Spotify web player.

# CHAPTER 6

3. In the left sidebar, select **Browse**.

4. To browse by musical genre, go to **Genres & Moods** and select genres

5. Hover over a genre tile to see music of that genre.

6. To find a specific song, album, or artist, go to the left sidebar and click **Search**, then type your query.

7. To see all the songs in a playlist, album, or artist, click the specific name.

8. To listen to all the songs in the playlist, album, or by that artist, click the green **Play** button.

9. To play a specific song, double-click its title.

10. A new pane on the right will display playback controls. Use these controls to pause, rewind, or fast-forward playback, or to raise or lower the volume.

## VIDEO STREAMING

You can watch movies, TV shows, and home movies on Chrome's Media Player as long as each video file format is approved and fits on a USB storage device or memory card. Chrome currently supports mp4, mpv, mov, webm video files, as well as Ogg Vorbis video files.

### WEBM

**Google is promoting WebM. Chrome Media Player can view all supported videos.** You can watch movies on full screen or in the Media Player window.

1. Connect an external storage device to your Chromebook

2. Open **File Manager** and navigate to the folder in which the video file is stored in the External Storage folder.

3. Select the video file that you would like to watch by double-clicking it. Alternatively, in the Preview pane, select the video file, and press the **Play** button.

4. In the Media Player window, the video starts playing. Click the **Pause** button

# ENTERTAINMENT

to pause playback; click the **Play** button to resume playback.

5. Drag the slider to the right (forward) or left (reverse) to control the progress of your video.

6. Click the **Full-Screen** button for the video screenful-screen to fill the screen of your Chromebook.

7. Click the **Full-Screen** button once more to exit full-screen mode.

Not all popular video formats are supported by Chrome OS. You can't use it to watch movies in the avi and wmv formats, for example. Other file formats, such as mp4 and mov, are also sometimes problematic for Chromebooks (QuickTime). The WebM format is the most reliable file format for video playback, despite being one of the less-used video formats today.

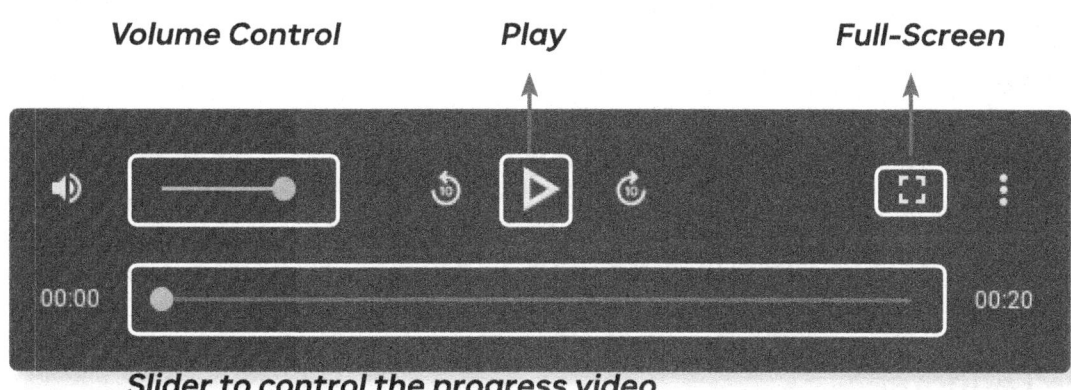

*Slider to control the progress video*

## USING ONLINE VIDEO STREAMING SERVICES

You can find a lot of programming on the Internet that you don't have to buy or download as large video files. This programming is available through a streaming video technology that is ideal for viewing on your Chromebook. It works by streaming the movie or TV show you want to watch in real-time from the Internet to your Chromebook, which you then watch in the Chrome browser. Hundreds of streaming video services offer tens of thousands of free and paid videos to watch.

All of the streaming video services mentioned in this chapter have their own Chrome or Android apps, which are available for free download from the Google Play Store. Simply download and install an app, then launch the streaming video service on your

# CHAPTER 6

Chromebook by clicking the app icon. Some services are free, but the majority require a monthly fee.

Amazon Prime Video, Hulu, and Netflix are the three most popular streaming video services, all of which have Chromebook apps. Each offers a free trial period so you can try them out before making a decision.

### Using Amazon Prime Video

Amazon Prime Video is an add-on to Amazon's Prime service, which includes free two-day shipping on a limited number of Amazon purchases. Your Amazon Prime Video subscription is free if you're a Prime member. Amazon Prime Video has a large selection of new as well as older movies and TV shows, though the selection is skewed toward the latter. Bosch, Forever, Good Omens, The Man in the High Castle, The Marvelous Mrs. Maisel, Tom Clancy's Jack Ryan, Sneaky Pete, and Transparent are among the Prime Originals. Amazon Prime Video also sells and rents a variety of movies and TV shows; once you've paid for something, you can stream it on your device.

### Netflix

With over 137 million subscribers worldwide, Netflix is the most popular streaming service today. Netflix, like Amazon Prime Video and Hulu, offers unlimited video streaming for a monthly fee. It began by focusing on movies but has since expanded to include a wide range of new and classic TV shows, as well as a wealth of original programming. It's a fairly comprehensive service.

### HDMI Adapter

Many Chromebooks include an HDMI port on the back or side of the device. Connect your Chromebook to a TV or audio/video receiver with this connector. It transmits both HD video and audio from your Chromebook.

### Chromecast

Chromecast is a Google-developed line of digital media players. The dongle-like devices can stream audio-visual content from the Internet to a high-definition television or home sound system. The user can control playback from a mobile device or a computer using Chromecast-compatible mobile and web apps, or by using Google Assistant to issue commands. Content can also be mirrored from a personal computer's Google Chrome web browser or through the screen of some Android devices.

## ENTERTAINMENT

## GOOGLE PLAY BOOKS

Google's ambition for books began with searching and cataloging them based on a full-text search and get-paid revenue from tailored advertising inside the search results. Books are now available in its digital multimedia distribution service. Dubbed Google Play, which includes options for purchasing digital downloads directly from Google or, in the case of books, from websites and others on The Kindle Store is a great place to get eBooks.

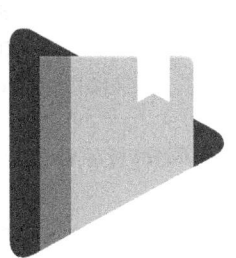

The Kindle Cloud Reader's main page lists all of the eBooks you've purchased and downloaded from Amazon. You can also buy new books for your Chromebook and other devices to read. If you want to download an ebook from the EBSCO database, first click the download button and then create an account. To sign in or create an account, go to **Sign In/Create Account**.

After that, you'll see a login screen with a link to set up an account at the bottom and through third-party online sites for purchasing printed books. You'll need to download Adobe Digital Editions from the Google Play Store after you've created an account.

Click the **download button** once more after logging in to your newly created EBSCO account and installing Adobe Digital Editions on your Chromebook. When the window appears, check the box indicating that Adobe Digital Editions (or equivalent) has been installed, and then click **Full Download**. A pop-up window will appear, indicating that your ebook has been downloaded and for how long you will have access to it. A download notification will also appear in the bottom-right corner of your browser

# CHAPTER 6

window. Select **'view in folder'** from the drop-down menu.

## LIBRARY

Libraries are InDesign documents that include elements. You can make a library by going to **File>New>Library**. The Library palette appears after you name the library. Libraries are initially created in the same way as documents—blank, with no elements. Objects from the InDesign page are transferred to the library by dragging them into the library. The library items are visible in the Library palette.

You can create personalized library entries by dragging objects into the library one at a time, or you can drag full pages into the library to create large library items. Using the instructions in the Library palette menu, you can also add items to a library:

- **Add Item** is a command that adds a selection to the library.

- **Add Items on Page** creates a single library entry for all of the items on the selected page.

- **Add Items on Page as Separate Object**s creates individual library entries for the page items.

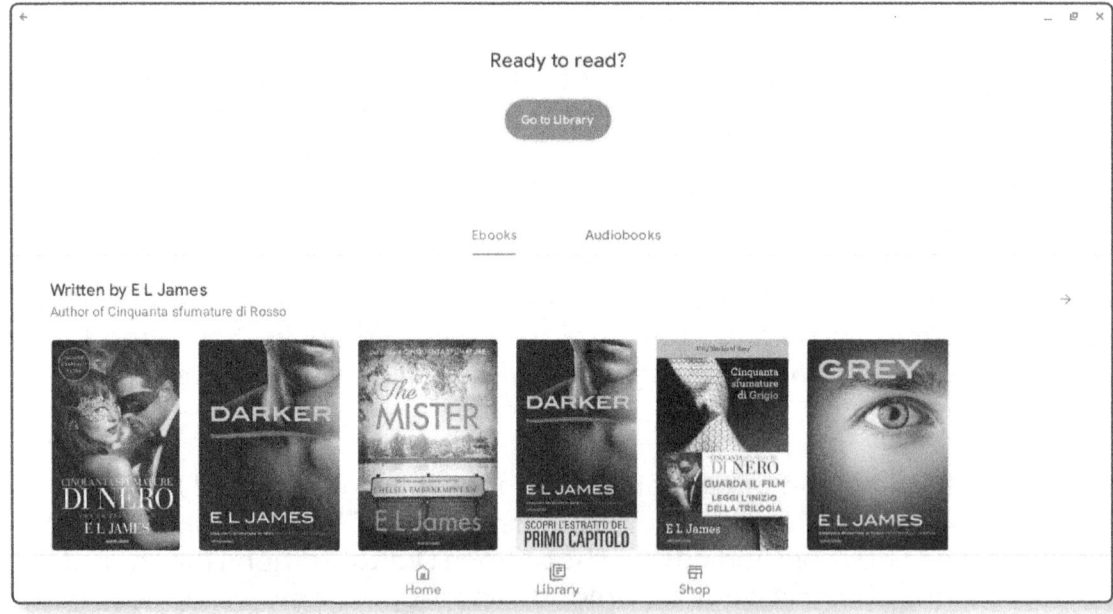

# ENTERTAINMENT

It's simple to add library items to a document once you've created one. Drag the thumbnail of a library item from the library onto the page. You can select multiple items in the library at once by holding down the **Shift key** and selecting a range of items, or you can select several individual items by holding down the **Command/Ctrl** key. Drag the library items to the desired location. You can also choose **Place Item(s) from the Library palette menu** after selecting the items you want to place. This returns the items to their original position when they were first added to the library. This works even if you put library items in separate documents because they are in the same relative position on the screen.

## SHARING FILES

Sharing files, photos, photo albums, music, or videos can be made easy through the use of an application called Nearby share, which you can download and install on your Chromebook. This is done in the same way as you share any other files as described earlier in this book.

# Chapter 7: Productivity with Google Suite

Google Suite was formerly known as Google Apps. It comprises web applications that are generated mostly for business people by Google so that your work becomes easier. **By using Google suite, you will have access to productive Google applications like Sheets, Docs, Calendar, and Hangouts.**

This suite has an advantage for small businesses as it makes your work easier by allowing you to save and share calendars, documents, and spreadsheets among your colleagues. In addition, the Google suite also facilitates the creation of video meetings using the Hangout application. You will be able to make decisions faster as you do not wait for someone to be physically available to conduct a meeting.

## GETTING AROUND GOOGLE DOCS

**Google Docs** is a word processor that is essential in making your document or text being unique. The Google Docs makes it possible for you to format, edit, and create documents online. Editing the document with someone else is also possible on Google docs.

You can also work with your colleagues on Google Docs through instant messaging and videos. Google docs does not have all the functions that are found in Microsoft Word but there is information to be learned about it.

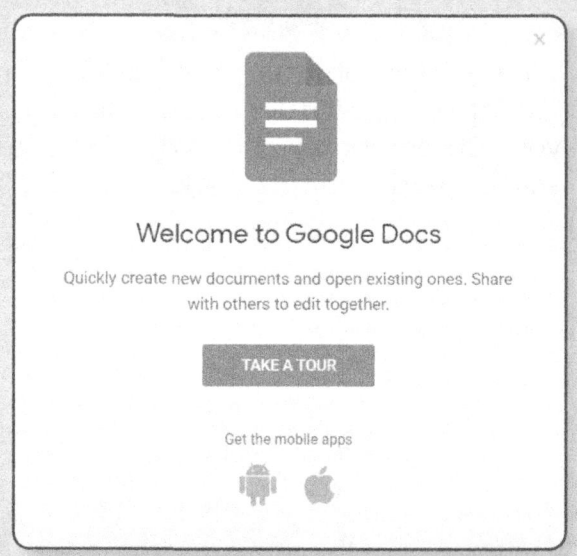

### USING PARAGRAPH STYLES

You can use the following paragraph styles to format and update your documents quickly and easily.

# PRODUCTIVITY WITH GOOGLE SUITE

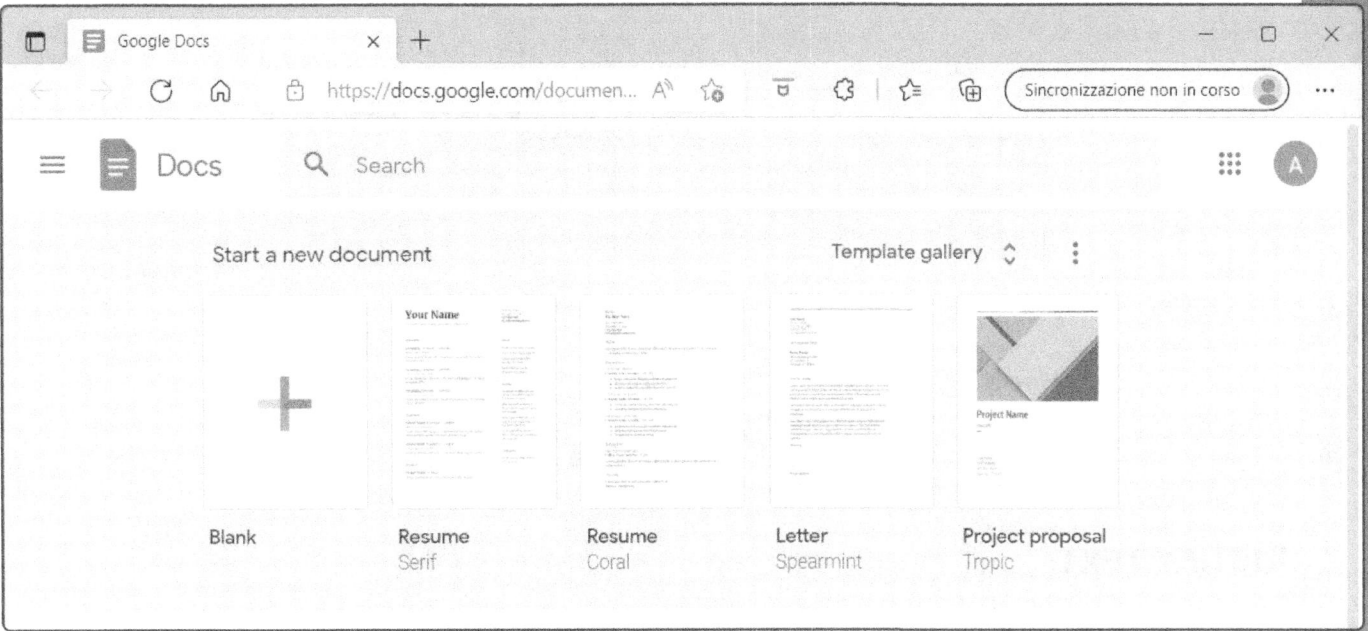

The paragraph styles are also used on titles, regular paragraphs, and headings.

- **Heading:** To change the text style on your heading, go to **Google Docs** and open the document you want to work on. Choose the text to be changed. Then **Click Format** and you will see the paragraph styles. The paragraph styles will be written **Normal text**, **Title**, **Subtitle**, and **Heading 1 up to** 6. Select the style you want and Click **Apply** and your heading will change to the style you have selected.

- **Bold, italic, and underlined:** Choose the text to be modified, then go to the shortcut toolbar. Click the **bold** (B), **italic** (I), or **underline** (U) buttons and you will visibly see the change as per your selection.

- **Changing fonts:** You need to highlight the text you want to apply the changes. Then go to the toolbar and click where it is written Font size. The list of all the font sizes will appear and you choose the one you want to use like 12 (GCF Global, n.d). Your text will change its size either to become bigger or smaller depending on your new selection.

- **Font color:** To change the font color, select the text to be altered first. Tap the **Text color** option from the toolbar and a menu of colors will appear as circles. Click on the circle with the color you want and it will be applied to your text. For example, if you choose the red circle, your selected text will automatically become red.

# CHAPTER 7

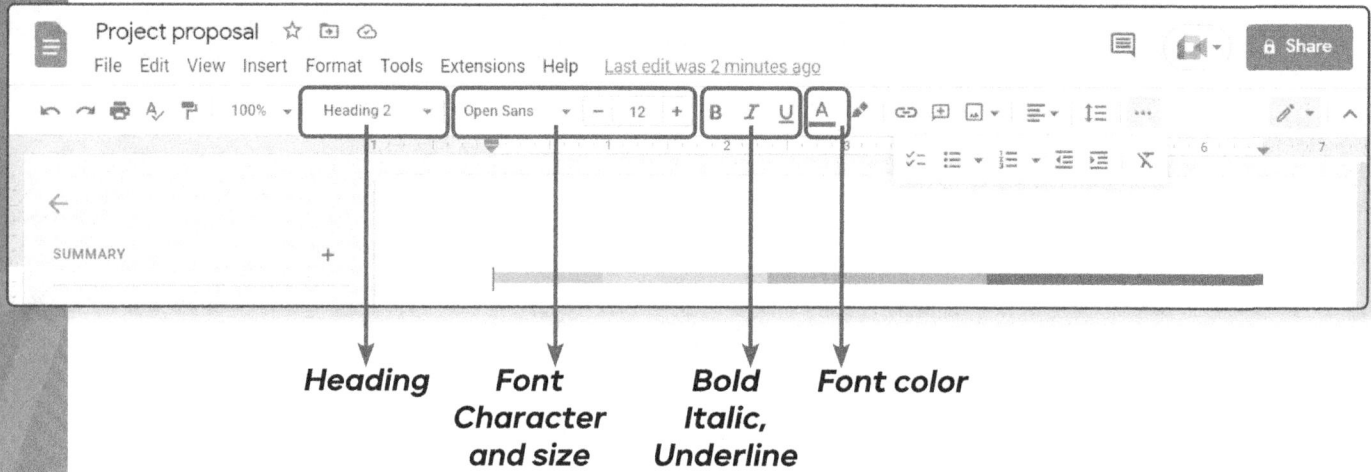

*Heading*  *Font Character and size*  *Bold Italic, Underline*  *Font color*

## JUSTIFY TEXT

Look for the four parallel lines of the same size on the task toolbar and tap on them. Once you select that symbol, all the text you are going to type will be justified. Your text will be evenly distributed between the margins and you will achieve a clean document (Silicon Dales Ltd, 2022). You can also justify a block of text. Highlight the block of text to be justified first and then do the procedure explained in this paragraph.

You can also justify the text using the shortcut. Press the **Ctrl + Shift + J** simultaneously and the text you selected will be justified.

*Justify text*

## BULLET LISTS

Open the document in Google Docs on your Chromebook and click the page or text you want to add the bullets. Check for three parallel lines with the dots at the beginning of each line on the toolbar. Once you click the symbol, you will have bullets that are like black dots. Click the arrow on that symbol for more suggestions on the types of bullets to use. Then click on the one you prefer and it will be created on your document.

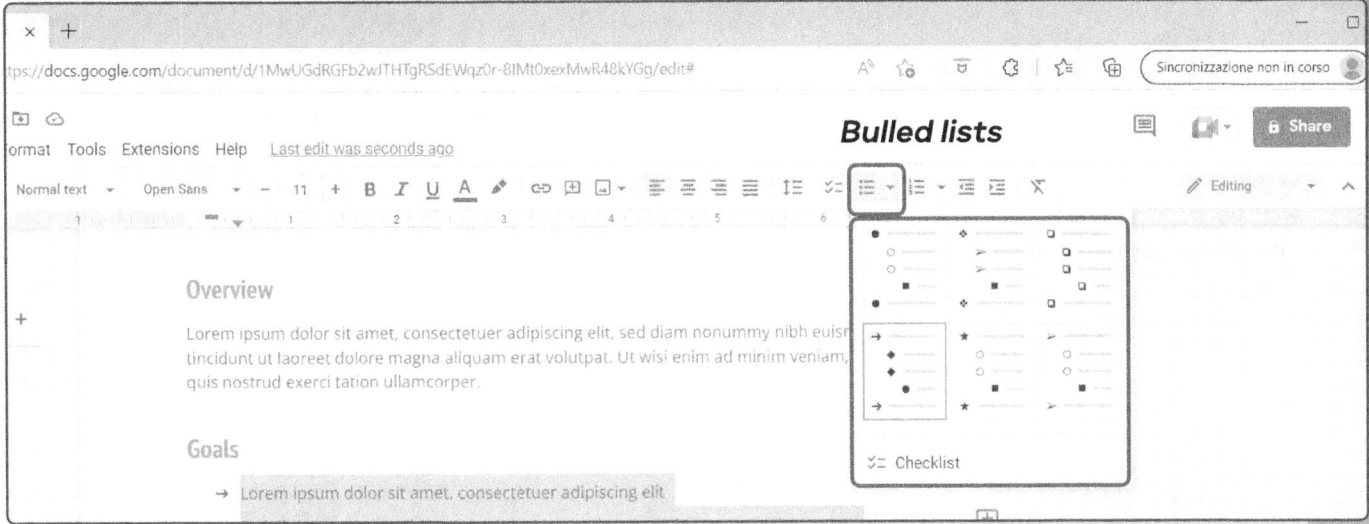

# NUMBERED LISTS

There is a symbol on the toolbar that has three numbered parallel lines. Go to that symbol and click on it. Your text or document will be numbered and for more numbering formats, click on the arrow besides the lines. Choose the numbering format you want and it will be applied to your document.

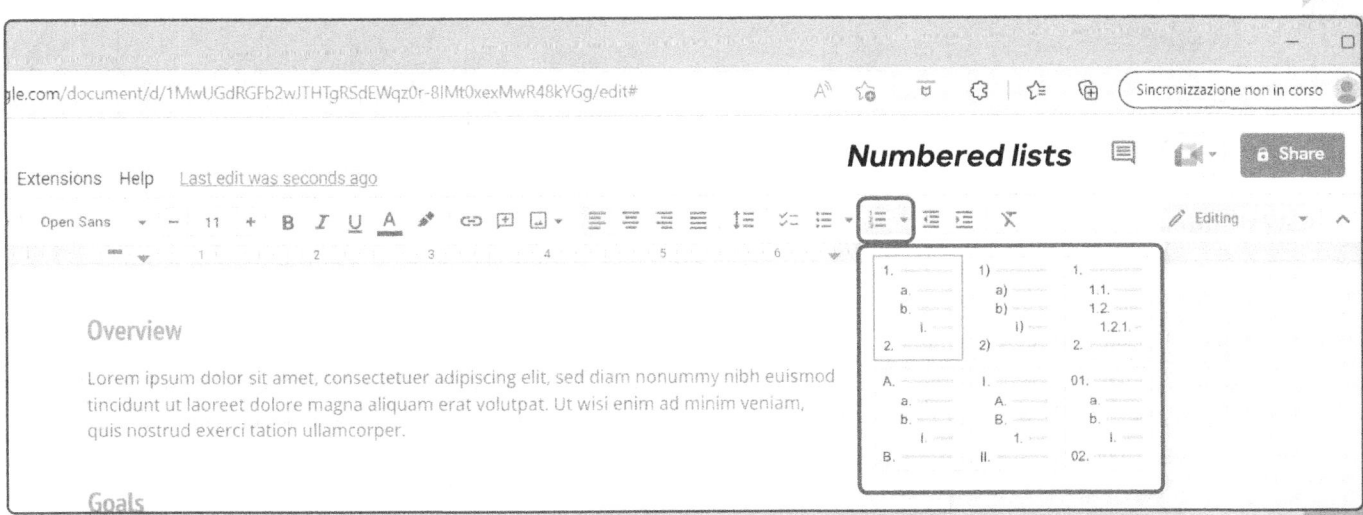

# CHAPTER 7

## CUT, COPY, AND PASTE

When copying or cutting text or document, you are saving it temporarily in a Clipboard until you paste it somewhere else where it will be used. Cutting is when removing the document from its original place to another and copying is making a duplicate.

So to cut or copy, highlight the text or the whole document you want. Click the **Edit** option on the toolbar and you will see the drop-down menu. Select **Copy** or **Cut** and the information will be stored shortly in the clipboard. Go to the page or document where you want to place the text and click **Edit** again. On the appearing menu, select **Paste** or press **Ctrl + V** on the keyboard at the same time. Your text will be placed in the new location.

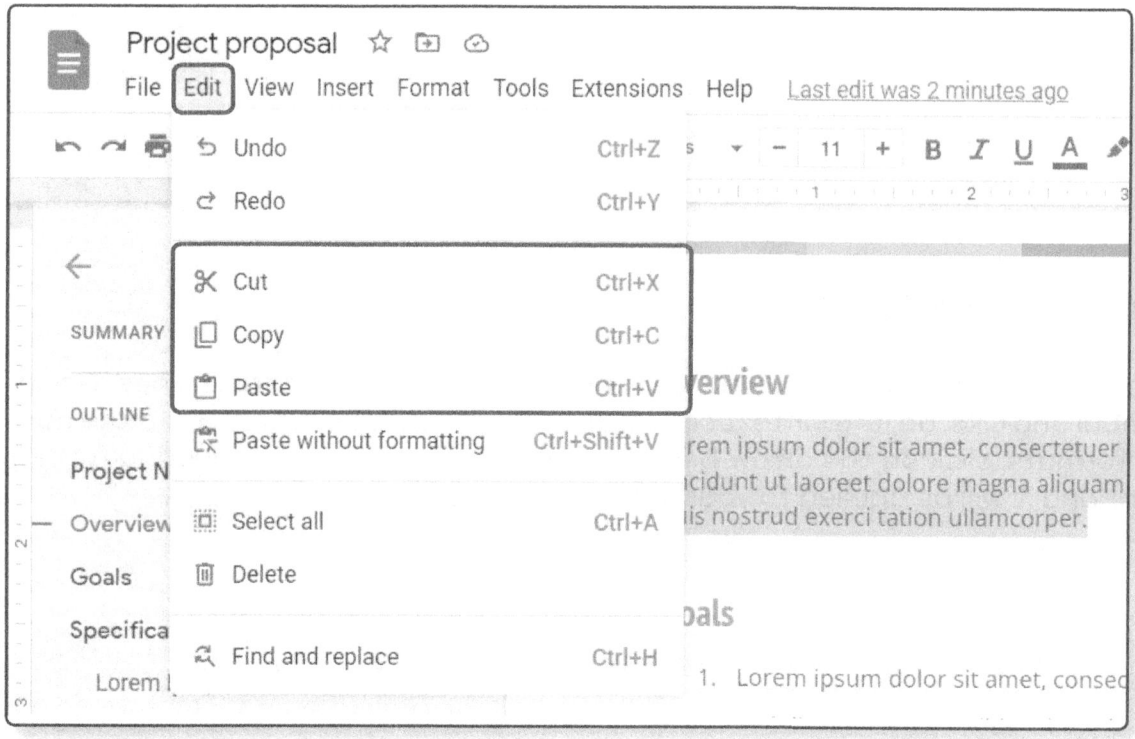

## ADDING IMAGES

Start by opening your presentation or document. Afterwards, click **Insert**, then on **Image**. More options on where to get the image will pop-up and you have to choose the right one. For example, there will be options like **Drive**, **upload from computer**, or **By URL**. Lastly, click on the insert or open option and your image will be placed where you want it to be.

# PRODUCTIVITY WITH GOOGLE SUITE

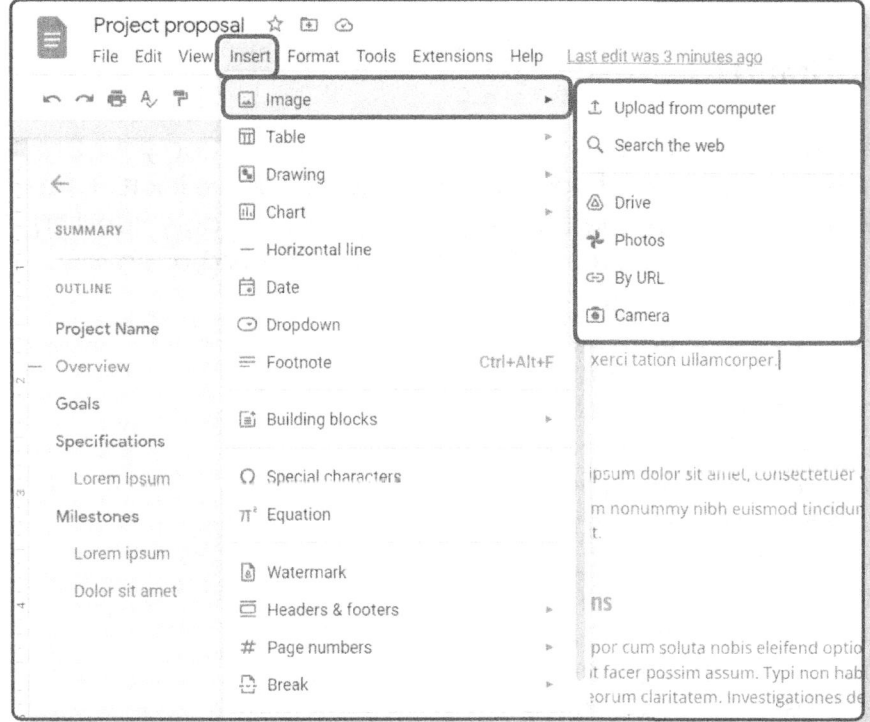

## ADDING TABLES

Open where you want to add the table. Select the exact spot where to add the table in your document by placing the Cursor. After that, click the **Insert symbol** on the task toolbar, then select **Table**. After that, choose the size of the table you want. The size of the Table is determined by the number of rows and columns you need. There is also another option to add or delete rows and columns in case of miscalculations. Do the right-click on your table and the options on how to insert, delete, sort, and distribute the rows and columns will be available for you. Then, you can choose accordingly.

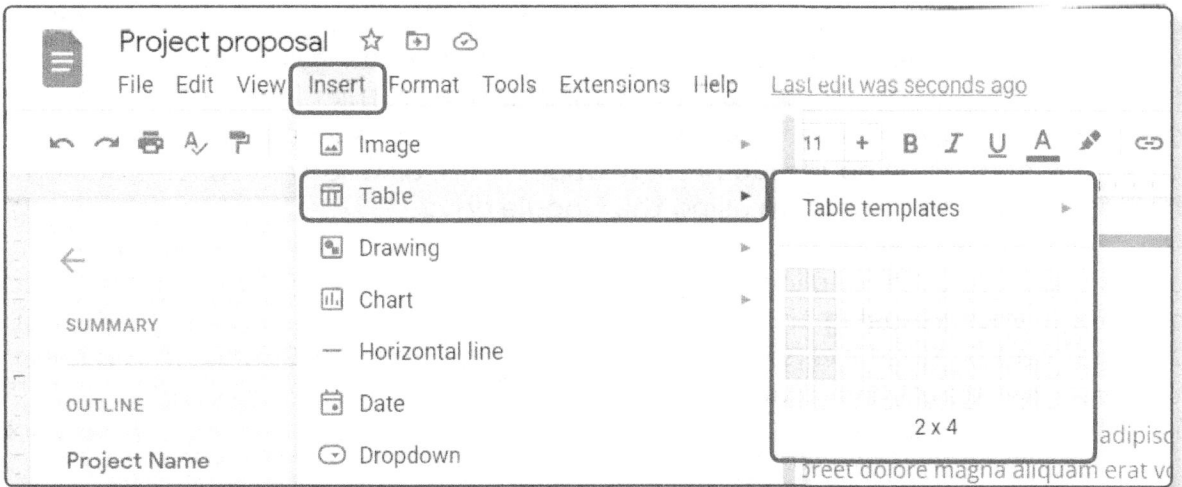

# CHAPTER 7

## SAVING DOCUMENTS

You can save your Google Doc as a Word or PDF document on your Chromebook. Look for **File** at the left top corner of your device's toolbar and click it. Then move the cursor to **Download** and select the file type where you will download the document to from the list on the menu. Choose **PDF or Microsoft word** to save your Google Docs according to your preferences.

If you are using a mobile phone, check for the three dots at the top right side and press them. You will see a drop-down list of options. Select **Share and export**, then **Save as**. Afterward, you need to choose the type of file for your download from the options. Now, you can press Ok and then tap on .docx (Word) or PDF to save your Google Doc according to your preferences. Your documents are now saved.

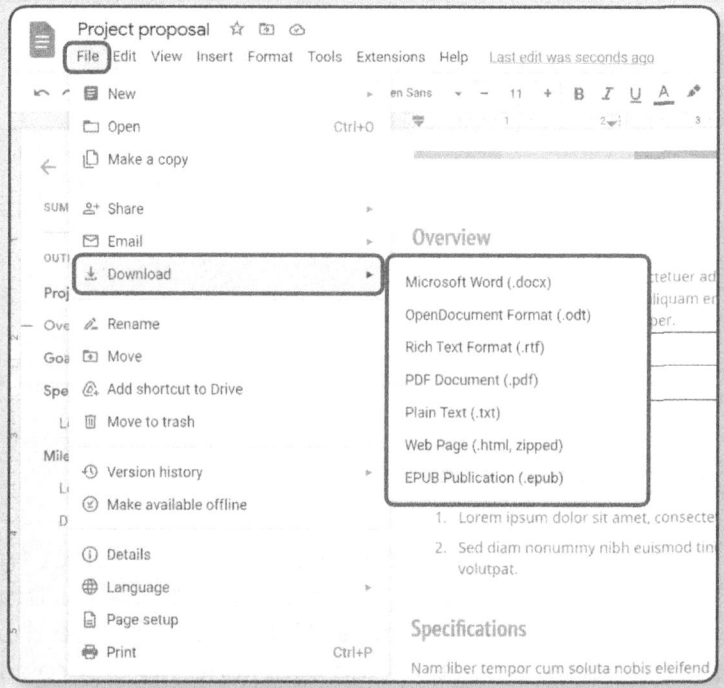

You can also save the Google Doc to Google Drive but you need to activate **Ask first** so that you can save the file prior to downloading Google Drive directly to your device.

### Opening Saved Documents

To open your saved documents, log into your Google account on drive.google.com using your username and password. You should know how to regain your password or username if you can't remember it. Then, double click the file where you saved the documents and open the one you want. The document will open using your Google account despite it being a slide presentation, form, or Google Doc. The audio files, photos, videos, and PDFs open using the Google drive.

You can also use other applications you installed on your device or web apps to open the files. If you are using the installed apps, make sure you have the Application Launcher and a current version of the Backup and Sync by Google. If you meet all the requirements then you can go to drive.google.com and log into your account. Remember to keep your username and password in mind. On a file, do the right-click

# PRODUCTIVITY WITH GOOGLE SUITE

and move your cursor to Open with and select the application of your choice to open your saved document. Make sure you have a default app that is specifically for opening other types of files (Google, 2022).

## PRINTING DOCUMENTS

It is possible for you to print a Google doc on a wireless or wired printer. So to print the document, go to Google Docs. Select and open the document you want to print and go to the top right corner of your device's screen and check for **File**.

Click on **File** so that you will find **Print** on the menu and click on it. You will see a window that will look like a page and you should find your printer and select it but sometimes it might not appear on the list.

If that happens, click on **See More** to search for your printer and get connected to it. Once you get your printer, click on the **Print** button that will be blue in color.

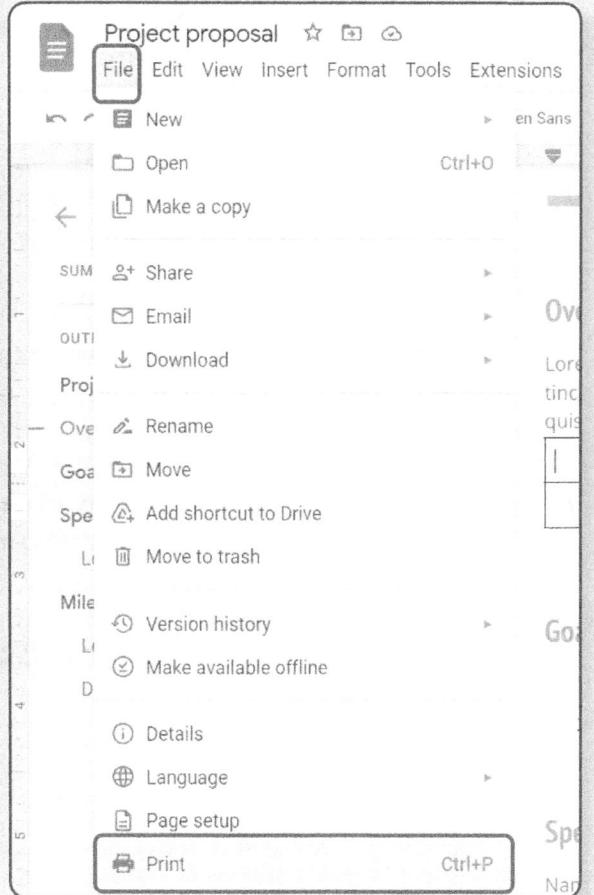

Printing a document on Google Docs from your mobile phone can be done if you have the Google Docs app on your device. Gain access to the document by signing in to the relevant account. Select the document you want to print and press the three dot icon that will be on the top right side of your screen.

Many drop-down options will appear and you should choose **Share and Export**. By clicking on it, another menu will pop-up and that's where you will find **Print**. Selecting the **Print** option will lead you to the window where you are supposed to choose the printer to use.

Upon printer selection, you go on to tap on another **Print symbol** and your document will start printing.

When printing, remember to select the number of copies to be printed and how the document will look like on paper such as portrait or landscape.

# CHAPTER 7

## SHARING DOCUMENTS

When sharing Google Docs, access your Google Drive by typing https://drive.google.com in a web browser. You can also sign in to your Google Docs account. Then, click on the file you are willing to share to open it.

Your document is now open, check for the **blue Share Button** at the upper-right top corner of your document. Click on it and start adding your recipients. Type every recipient's name or the group's name and add it by tapping on it when it appears. If the person or group is not using Google Docs, once you enter their names they are going to receive an invite. The invite will be instructing them to generate a free account so that they can have access to the document sent to them.

Once you click on the recipient's name, the sharing permissions will appear. On the list, choose if the people you are sharing the document with should comment, view, or edit. For example, if you want the person to view the document only, just select Viewer. Check also for more advanced settings by clicking on the tab that is on the top-right corner of your toolbar. By doing this, you will be allowing the recipient like the commenter or viewer to copy, print, or download the document. The editor will also be given the right to share the document with other people or to also change permissions.

Now, you are done with sharing permissions, check for **Notify people** if you are sending via email. Verify that there is a checkmark in the box next to the Notify people option. If you want the recipients to receive a notification that you have shared a document with them, check the box and leave a text in the **Message box** to give more details about the document. Then, click Notify so that your receiver can get an email with a link for them to access the document.

If you don't want them to receive the notification, remove the checkmark. Your document is now ready to be shared so click on Send and the recipient will have access to it.

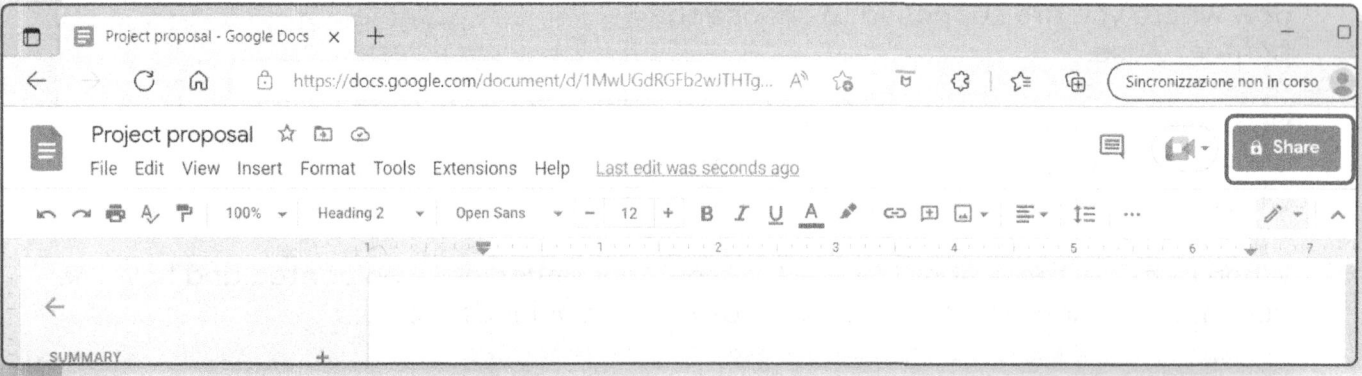

## PRODUCTIVITY WITH GOOGLE SUITE

## GOOGLE SHEETS

**Google sheets** is also a Workspace that is web-based where you can do collaborations, chat, and create videos as a team. There is no limit for the size of the group. The application allows the users to perform different tasks like sharing the data in real time online, updating, modifying, and creating spreadsheets. Google sheets are crucial as you can see the changes while happening, receive notifications for edits that were done in your absence, and also add collaborators easily to projects.

The changes you make on your Google Sheets are automatically saved. You can also sort, delete, and add rows and columns on Google Sheets.

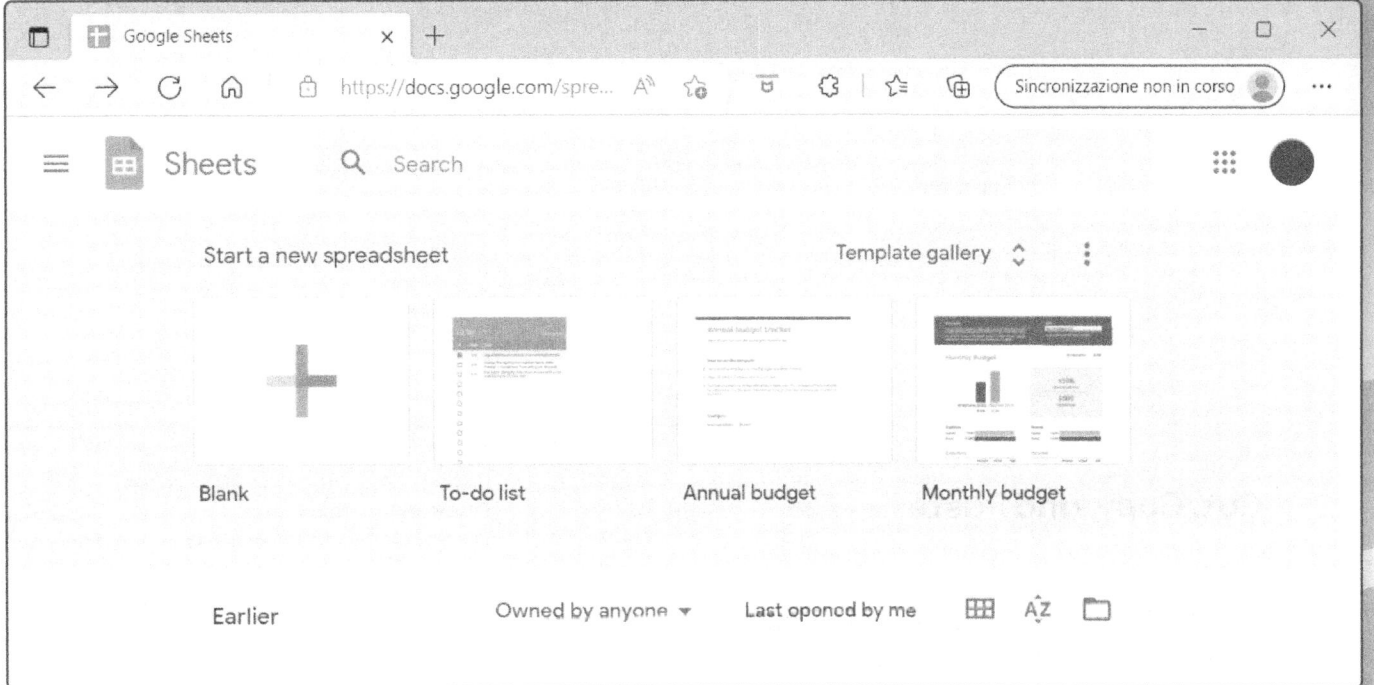

## SPREADSHEETS

A Spreadsheet is also known as a worksheet. This file is created through a combination of rows and columns that enable you to calculate numerical data, arrange, organize, and sort data perfectly. Having a spreadsheet has its own benefit as you will be able to do mathematical calculations of the data in the cells using the formulas.

# CHAPTER 7

## GETTING AROUND GOOGLE SHEETS

Google Sheets plays an important role by making the work of every department easier as you can prepare the invoices, create lists, do budgets, and analyze statistical data. When using Google Sheets, you can work with a variety of functions on your documents and some of them are discussed below.

### Simple Text Formatting

Text formatting can be done by changing the font size, color, alignment, font appearance, and font name. Font appearance involves italic, underline, background font cell color, and bold.

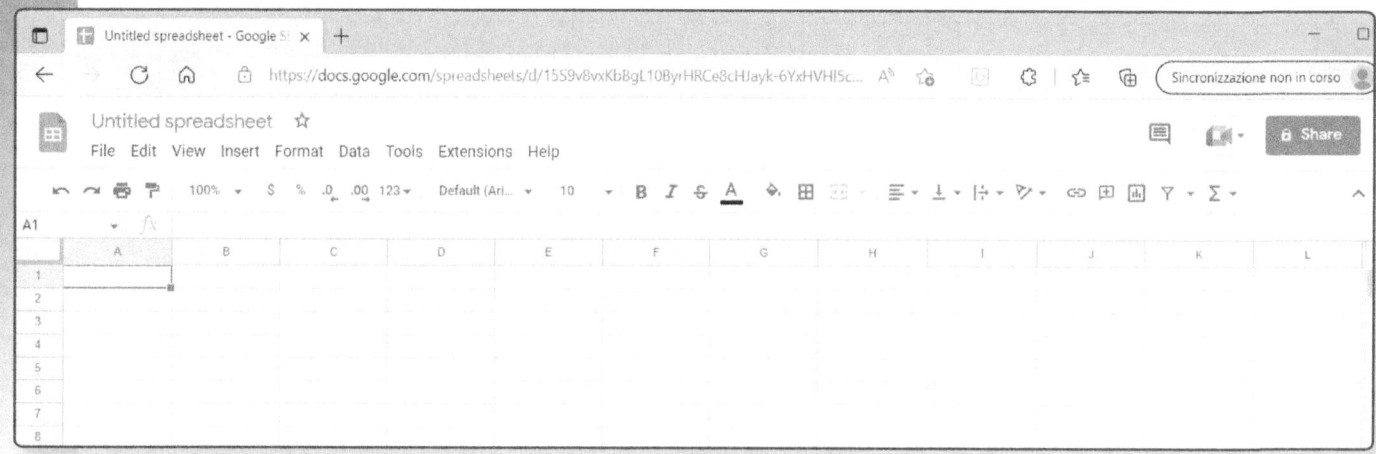

### Cut, Copy, and Paste

The procedure for copying and cutting is the same. The only difference is that when copying, you are creating a duplicate of the original while cutting is when you move the data to a new location.

So to copy the cell contents, start by choosing the cell with the data you want. Then, check for **Edit** on the toolbar and on the drop-down list, choose **Copy** or you can press **Ctrl + C** at the same time and the contents will be copied.

Go on to select the cell you want to paste the contents. Click **Edit** again and select **Paste** from the

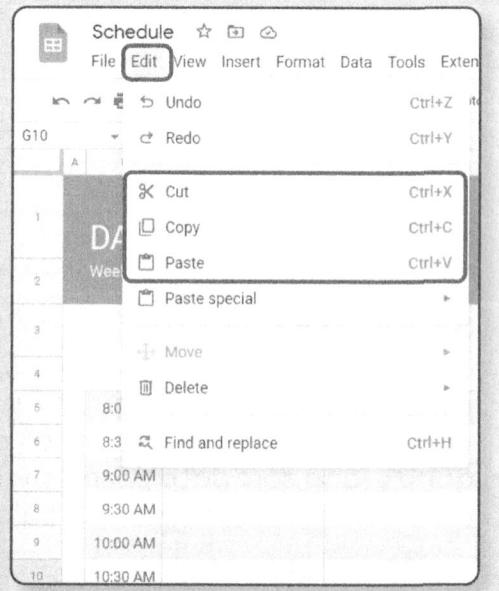

# PRODUCTIVITY WITH GOOGLE SUITE

list. You can also do the shortcut by pressing **Ctrl + V** concurrently to paste the data in the new cell.

## Inserting Rows and Columns

Start by opening the spreadsheets. Next, select the column or row where you want to insert another one. After that, click on the **Insert** on the toolbar and there will be options for you to choose if you are inserting the **Row below** or **Row above**. If you are to choose the **Columns**, it's either **Column right** or **Column left**. By clicking on your selection, you will automatically have a column or row where you chose it to be.

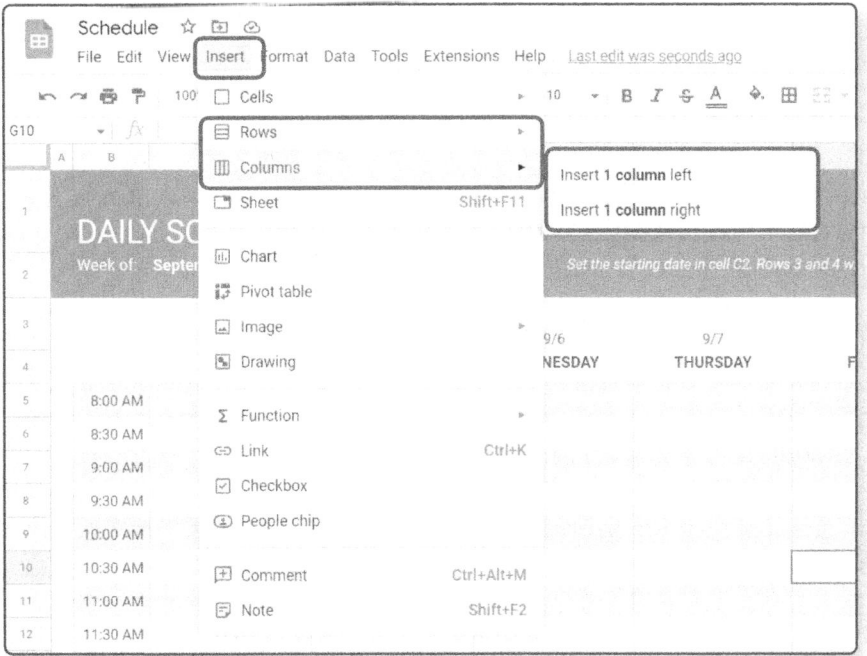

## Cell Alignment

You should choose the cell you want to align either vertical or horizontal.

Click on **Vertical align** or **Horizontal align** depending on your choice and finally choose alignment.

Your cell will be aligned accordingly.

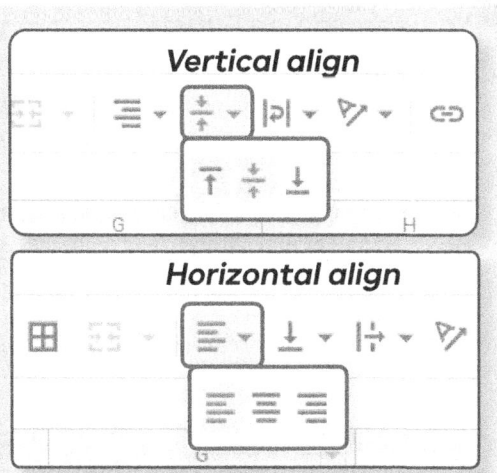

# CHAPTER 7

### Cell Borders

First thing is to open your spreadsheet and then select the cells you want to add borders. The button **Borders** will appear and just click on it. There will be a list of borders available for selection so, you choose the type of border you wish to put on your cell.

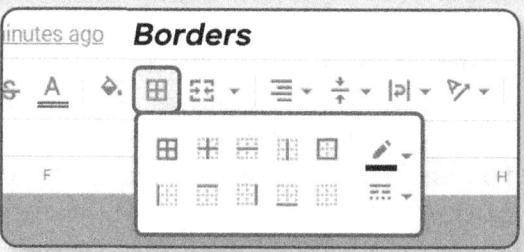

You can also go on to choose the Border style and Border color so that your cell borders will have the specific lines and color that you like. You are now through with all the stages involved and the borders are now on the cells.

### Using Formulas

You should pick the cell that you want to have the calculated value. For example, the cell you are going to put the total value after calculating. Type the **(=)** in the selected cell and then write the cell address after the equals sign.

For example, C10 and it should be the one you want to reference first in the formula. Continue to put the operator you want to use for example, minus sign (-). Type the second reference's cell address for example, C12 and tap on **Enter** on the keyboard. Your results will be displayed in the cell where you put the formula.

To prove if the formula is working, change the value of the cell address, your result should also change.

## USING FUNCTIONS

You should use Functions from the toolbar because it is easy and fast. Pick the cell where you want the calculated result to be and go on to select Functions. A menu of five functions will pop-up and there will be submenus that have every possible function. Finally, select the cells you wish to put in the range and press enter.

Note that when choosing the cells press and hold **Ctrl** and make your choices if you are selecting individual cells. Press and hold **Shift**, choose the initial and last cells in the range for a continuous range.

### Count

Type equals sign in the cell for the formula. Type **C** from your keyboard and you will have a list of options, then choose **Count**. Put the open bracket and write the cell address to be involved, then close the bracket. Press **Enter** so that your result will appear.

### AutoSum

AutoSum is a built-in intelligent function that works automatically by predicting the range you want to do the calculation. Place the cursor on the result cell for example, E15 and press **AutoSum**. The spreadsheet will automatically give you the sum of E2:E14.

### Types of Data

Texts and numbers are common types of data in Google sheets although there is another one called Boolean values. Boolean values include errors, arrays, and true or false. The **TYPE** function can be used to detect the type of data if you are not certain of what is in the cell.

### Adding Charts

Click your Google Sheet to open it. Do the selection of cells you are willing to use in the chart. If you do not have the Google Sheet, go to **sheets.new** and generate it. Do cell selection by clicking on the first one while holding **shift**. Keep holding while choosing the other cells to be included, then tap **Insert** and at last, **Chart** from the options. Your chart will be added and by default, the Google Sheet will choose the chart for you using the data you have provided. To customize the chart, choose from the menu that will appear to your right when you click **Chart**.

## INSERT TABLE

Have a spreadsheet with tabular data on it and format it by doing the center alignment and bolding. You should also remember to freeze the header row while in the sheet's first row so that you will always see it when scrolling. Then, filter the rows by tapping on **Data** and choose **Create filter**, leaving the row for totals unfiltered. Filtering will aid in easy identification of important data. Make sure you apply Indirect Function so that the totals can update automatically whenever there are new columns and rows.

Give your table an identity for easy referencing wherever you use it. Have a name range that will include the header row. Your table is ready to be tested by entering a certain number of rows.

# CHAPTER 7

## GOOGLE SLIDES

**Google Slides** is an online application that can be used for creating new and editing old templates. Google Slides serve the same purpose as PowerPoint. The difference with Google Slides is that you can access your presentation on any device and from wherever you are as long as it was saved on the Google cloud. The changes can also be auto-saved and all the users can have access to Google Sides and do the changes on the presentation simultaneously.

You should know how to use Google Slides for your personal benefit or forf your business. Here are some of the functions you can do on Google Slides to make your presentation worth creating.

### DESIGNING A SLIDE

On the top, right side of your Google's home page, there is a **grid**. Click on it and then on the Drive on the menu. You can also log in to **https://slides.google.com** to quickly get the Slides page. Look for the blue tab and tap it so that you can select **Google Slide**s on the menu to open a slide page. On the toolbar, find a **(+)** to create a new slide. Give your slide a name and a theme of your choice

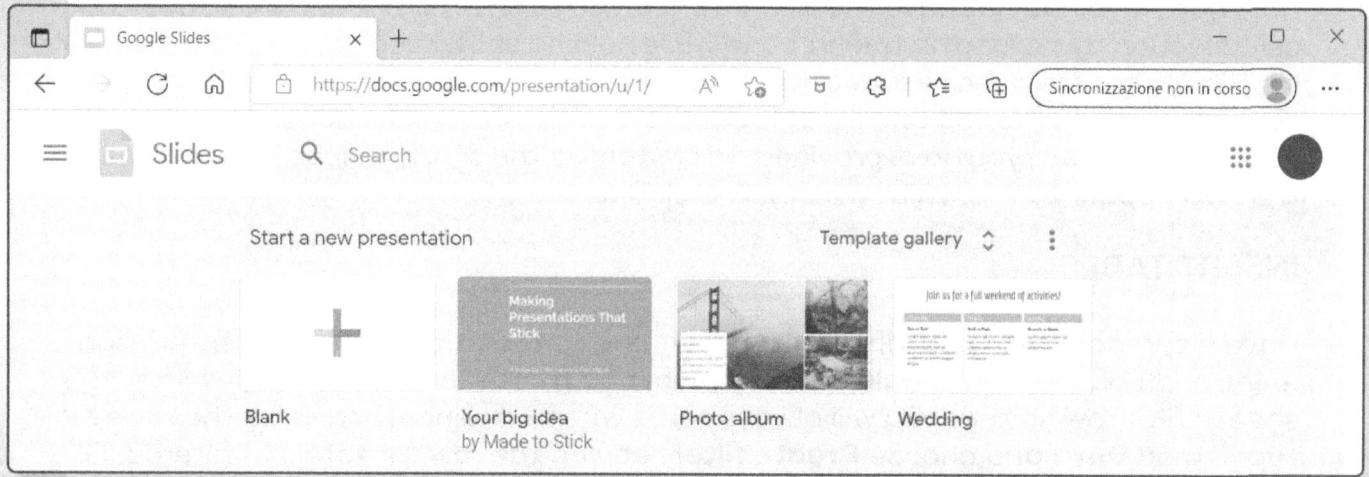

### Add an Image

Go to Google slides presentation and select the slide to add an image on it. Click **Insert**, then go on to look for an image by either searching from the Web or they are in your device. Select the image from the ones appearing. Do double-click to add the image and you are done.

# PRODUCTIVITY WITH GOOGLE SUITE

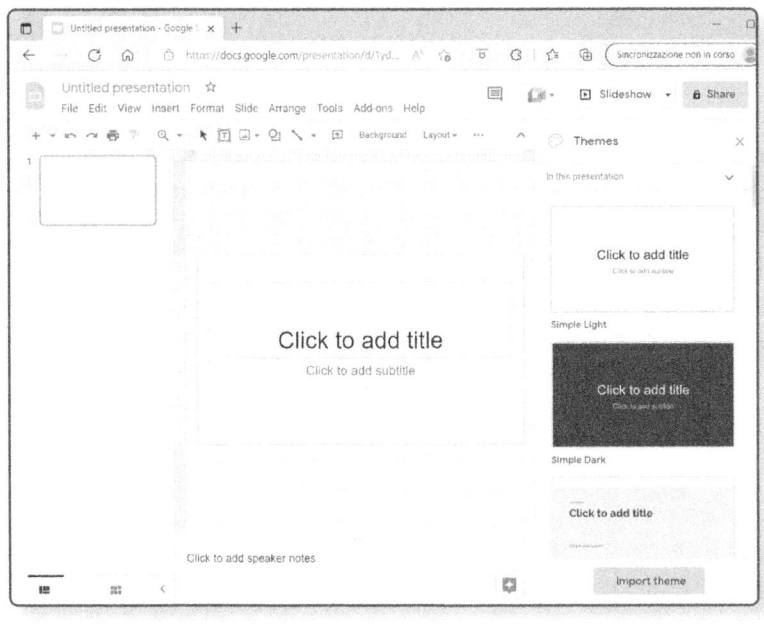
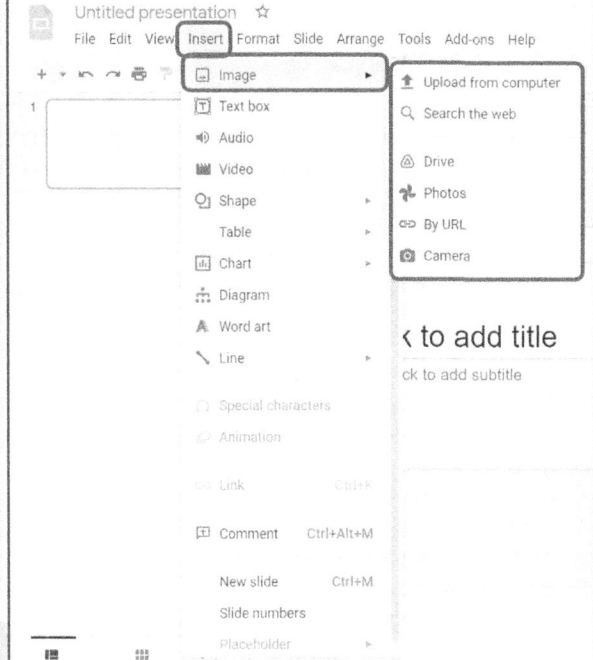

## Resize an Image

The size of the image on your presentation can be adjusted to a larger or smaller size. First, highlight the image by clicking on it. On the squares that are on the edges of your image, press and hold the left-mouse button. Drag the mouse away or toward the image to increase or decrease the photo's size.

## Crop an Image

To begin, open the slide so that you can choose the image to crop. Find the **crop button** on the screen or double-click on the image. You can use the black lines on the image to adjust the cropping by dragging them. Once you finish the adjustments, tap again on the **Crop** or **Enter** to complete the process.

# CHAPTER 7

## Add a Video

Create a new Google slide presentation or open an old one on **slides.google.com**. Start to click **Insert** and on a menu, select **Video**. Find the search tab and type the title or any word that can lead to a successful search of the video you wish to add. Tap on **Enter** to command the search process. Once your video appears on the list, select it and it will be added to your slide. You can resize and reposition the video on the presentation. Use the blue dots on the corners and sides of your slide.

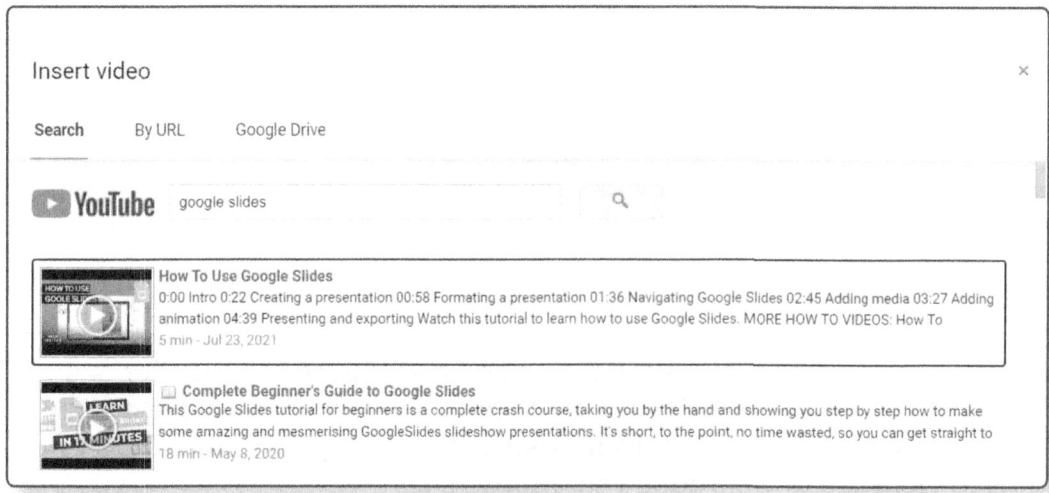

## Slide Layer Arrangement

Open your presentation and click on the object you want to move. Select **Arrange** followed by **Order**. Finally, choose the option that is best for you.

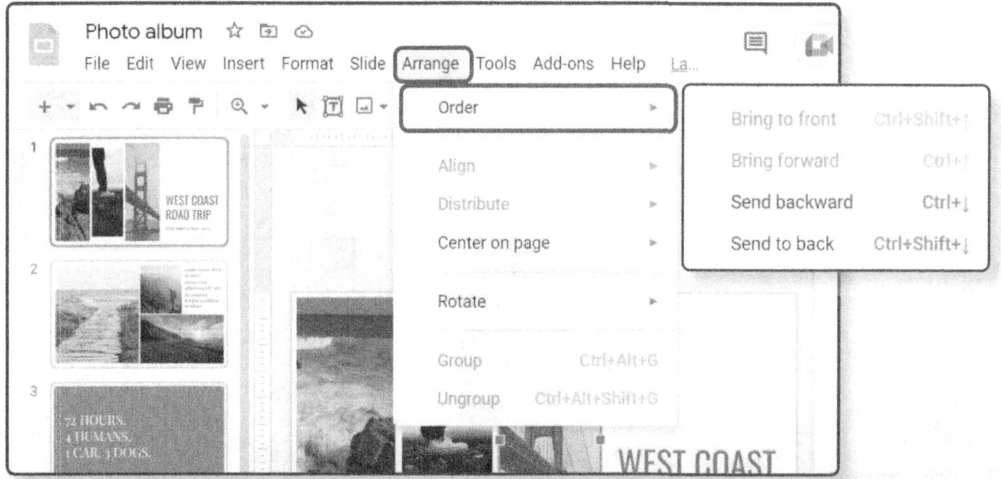

# PRODUCTIVITY WITH GOOGLE SUITE

## Add a New Slide

You can add a new slide to the existing presentation by opening the Google Drive and tap the Google Slides presentation you are to add a slide.

Choose the slide you like from the left column and click **Insert** and **New slide**. You now have a new slide on your presentation.

## Change Slide Layout

The text and images' arrangement can be changed. Begin by opening the Google Slides presentation and pick a slide. Look at the top of your device and click **Layout**, prior to selecting your favorite layout to apply to the presentation.

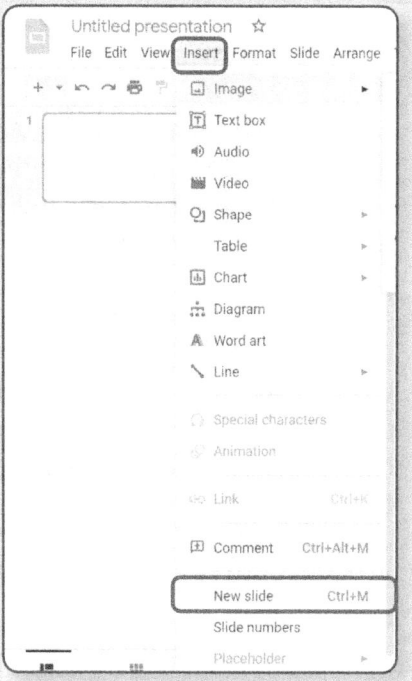

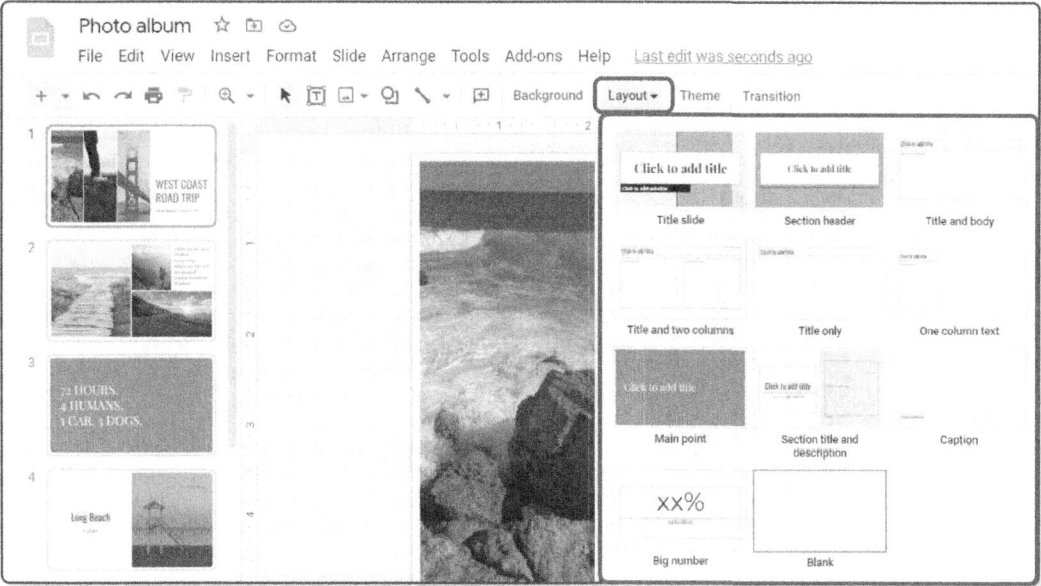

## Slide Masters

On your toolbar, select **View** and then **Slide Master**. Change the color, styles, alignment, and text but you can also choose **Theme** before all the changes to the presentation.

Click **Close Master View** once you've completed all the other stages.

# CHAPTER 7

## Slide Transitions

Look for the slide sorter view at the bottom of your device's screen. The thumbnails of all the slides will appear on the Google Sheet. Click on **Transitions** and the group Transition to This Slide will show up giving you the opportunity to choose the current effect to be used when the transition is taking place.

## Slide Animations

On the **Animation tab,** find the **Advanced Animation group** and click on the **Animation Pane**. The animation options appear on the pane. Click **Add Animation** and you need to apply the effects to four options that include motion, emphasis, exit, and entrance. You can now select a slide and add the animation you like and the results will be seen on the Slide pane. The Animations will permit you to control how the objects or text should appear like on the slide. Speed adjustments can also be done on the speed box.

## PRINTING PRESENTATIONS

Open the presentation to be printed. Select the part to be printed—either the whole presentation or the cells. Click on **File** and select **Print** from the menu. If you are printing the entire sheet, click on the workbook. Also, click on **Current sheet** if you selected the sheet to print and **Selected cells** if you are printing chosen cells only.

## PRODUCTIVITY WITH GOOGLE SUITE

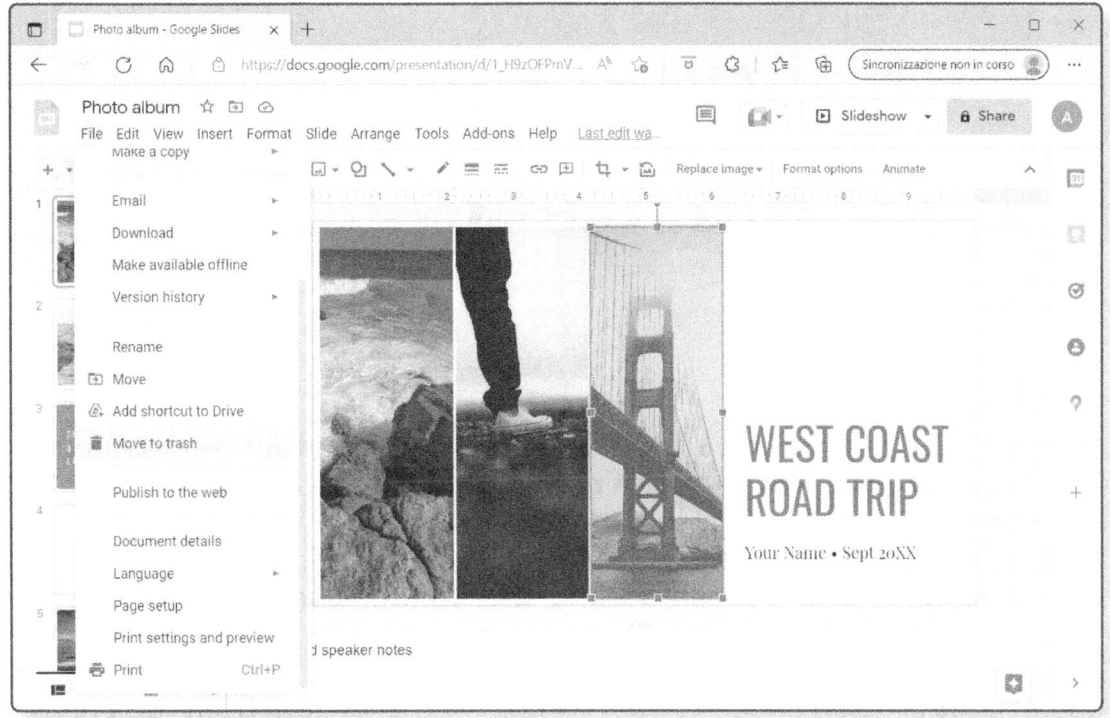

### GIVING YOUR PRESENTATION

You should open your presentation first. Click on the spreadsheet and select option **Share** and add emails of the recipients. Click on the down arrow so that you can set the permissions and if you send a notification, remember to give a brief information about the spreadsheet you sent. After everything, tap **Send** and the recipient can now access it. If you are giving the link, just click on **Share**, then **Copy Link**. You will get the link from **Get link** and paste it on other users' emails.

## PRESENT WITH CHROMECAST

Chromecast enables you to present the spreadsheet on another device using wireless screen sharing, as it is powered by Bluetooth. If you are a chrome browser, you can cast a tab that contains the Google slides, Sheets, and Docs so that you can use it when conducting meetings. A Chromecast uses power and the HDMI to connect to the projector or TV. It also uses Wi-Fi network to perform its functions.

If you want to present with Chromecast, open the information you wish to present. Tap on Google cast extension so that your tab can be casted to the Chromecast.

# Chapter 8: Maintenance

Chromebooks, unlike most laptops, are also simple to maintain and reasonably inexpensive. Your computers' efficiency and functionality, like any other technology, can suffer if they're not properly preserved for long periods of time. The first thing you should do before storing your gadgets is make sure their battery level is at least 80% charged. This means that if your machines are kept unplugged for an extended period of time, they should not run out of power.

Remember that you don't need to entirely unplug the battery from the Chromebook for effective maintenance. Instead, plug in the computer and simultaneously press the "Refresh" and "power" buttons. The battery will be disconnected. If the disconnect was successful, you shouldn't be able to turn the machine on even if you have a good charge.

Maintaining your Chromebooks this way may seem inconvenient initially, but that is one of the greatest ways to maintain their longevity. This will limit battery discharge and keep your battery life from being harmed by frequent charge and discharge rates. If you can't get your Chromebook to the battery detach condition, you may still protect your gadget by disconnecting the charging wire and storing it somewhere dry and cool.

## BATTERY CARE FOR CHROMEBOOKS

One of your Chromebook's most important characteristics is the battery. Many educators choose Chromebooks because of how long they can operate on battery power before charging. Even the greatest batteries, however, do not last indefinitely. The length of time a Chromebook may run between charges may begin to diminish based on your adherence to Chromebook upkeep. Chromebooks are incredibly sturdy and robust since they use lithium batteries. However, these devices can be damaged while being stored. To ensure that your Chromebook investment lasts as long as possible, make sure you:

# MAINTENANCE

1. Over the summer, don't let the battery completely drain. Before putting the device away, be sure it's fully charged and turned off. A battery can be severely damaged if it is left to drain for a long time.

2. A Chromebook should not be left plugged in. Leaving your smartphone hooked into a charger or cart for weeks or months diminishes battery life and raises the chance of various problems.

3. Before storing your Chromebook, turn it off. Making sure the device is properly shut down before storage is an important part of excellent Chromebook maintenance. If you simply close the lid after each usage, the screen will finally turn off in this instance, and the gadget will enter standby mode. While standby only consumes a minimal amount of energy, it nevertheless requires ongoing energy. If you don't want your battery to be drained, make sure your machines are completely turned off. Press and hold the **Chromebook's power button** till the screen goes black. To confirm that your gadget is entirely shut off, the screen should remain blank when you release the power switch. You can start storing the machines once they are entirely shut off.

Google suggests that

1. You make sure that there are no more than 7 Chromebooks stacked on top of each other. The heaviness of the gadgets may cause the displays to fracture.

2. Keeping your Chromebooks out of the way of cleaners and foot traffic is a good idea. This should lessen the chances of them falling over.

3. You keep your Chromebooks in a cool, dry place away from direct sunlight.

## DIAGNOSTICS

Google has included a new tool in recent Chrome OS versions that makes it exceedingly simple for users to run fast tests on their devices.

Diagnostics is the name of the app, and it includes the following tests: Battery\CPU\Memory. So, if you see that your device's battery isn't lasting as long as it should, or if you notice that performance is worsening for no apparent reason, you can run a few of these tests to check if the problem is caused by a hardware issue.

Since the Diagnostics app debuted in ChromeOS 89, you'll need a Chromebook running that version of the OS. Let's have a look at how this tool can be used.

# CHAPTER 8

## OPENING THE DIAGNOSTICS APP

Type diagnostics in the search box on your **Chromebook menu** button at the lower-left corner of the desktop. Once you see the **Diagnostics icon**, press **Enter** on your keyboard or use the trackpad to click on it.

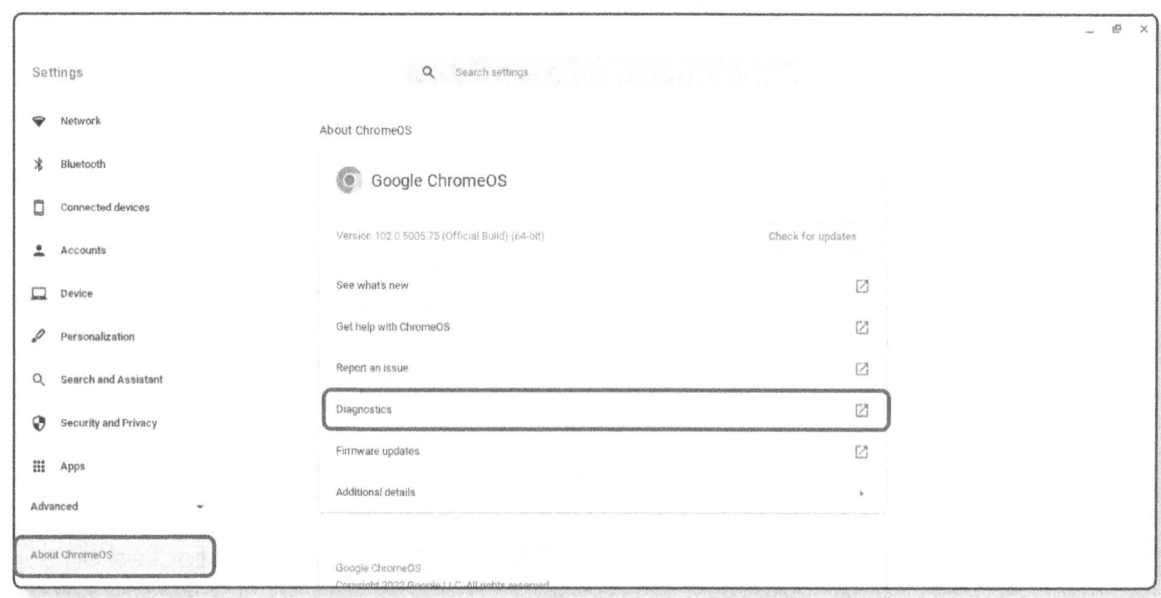

# MAINTENANCE

## UTILIZING THE DIAGNOSTICS APP

You'll see **Run buttons** for the battery discharge, CPU test, and Memory test in the Diagnostics app. To begin the test, hit one of those buttons. The test will begin in the background after you click one of the buttons. The results would then appear at the bottom left of the test card once the test is completed.

A **Learn More** link will be included in each test, which will launch a Chromebook Help window. Unfortunately, the aid page does not provide much assistance. The best option is to use the test findings to conduct your own research. Even so, you should probably contact the supplier of your Chromebook to find out what the battery's usual discharge rate is. However, If the results show "success," you should be fine.

The CPU diagnostic will perform the following tests and this will take approximately four to five minutes:

- Stress examination
- Cache test
- Test of floating-point accuracy
- Prime search test

It's crucial to remember that you shouldn't use your Chromebook while conducting the CPU test. In fact, you'll find it difficult to utilize the device during this test.

The Memory test is the most time-consuming of the three. The completion time should be around 30 minutes. Although the Chromebook can be used during this test, it is recommended to run it when you are not using it. You can save a copy of the testing results by clicking Save session log at the end of the test. Conducting diagnostic tests on a Chromebook is as simple as that. If a reboot doesn't fix the problem, do these three checks to find out whether a hardware defect is the problem.

## UPDATING CHROME OS

Chromebooks are one of the best options because of their great built-in security, integrated encryption features, and specialized hardware. That's why they're popular with schools and other groups. Make sure your Chromebook is up to date; otherwise, security features, as well as other key quality-of-life enhancements, will begin to lag. If you wait too long, you may lose access to Google Cloud.

# CHAPTER 8

## ACCESS SETTINGS

When a new version of the operating system is released, your Chromebook will automatically update in most circumstances. However, this may not always work, or you may want to double-check the update in these circumstances. Here's how to get started.

1. Check that a particular patch has been applied. Make sure your Chromebook is turned on and linked to the internet. On Chrome OS, look down at the taskbar and to the right, you should see the System Tray, which contains the clock. To continue, select the clock.

2. With the System Tray open, tap the gear-shaped Settings icon from the icons at the top of the window.

## CHECK FOR NEW INFORMATION

To check for new information,

1. The **Settings** menu will open, displaying information about your network connections. Look in the lower-left section and pick the final item on the left menu, About Chrome OS, to learn more about your updates.

2. The Chromebook will now provide information about your Chrome OS version. Select the **Check for Update**s button on the far right.

## MAINTENANCE

If an update is detected, your Chromebook should begin upgrading automatically at this point. Here is what you should do:

1. Allow time for the update to download. The percentage of the update that has been completed is displayed under Google Chrome OS. It's critical that your Chromebook doesn't shut off suddenly at this time, so make sure it's plugged in if necessary.

2. Once the download is complete, you'll be prompted to restart your computer to finalize the update. Make sure you don't have any work to save before selecting **Restart**. It may take several minutes for Chrome OS to restart when the operation is completed.

3. If it was a major update, navigate to the Google Chrome OS section and pick **See What's New** from the drop-down menu. This will show you any new features that have recently been added to Chrome OS.

## POWERWASH

It's sometimes great to have a fresh start. You may simply wipe the slate completely and start again with your Chromebook. When you have a lot of garbage on your smartphone, you could find this beneficial. If you wish to reset your Chromebook to its default configuration if you're giving it to someone else. With Chromebook's built-in Powerwash feature, you can wipe your device speedily, easily, and safely. Sign in to your Chromebook and perform the following steps to powerwash it:

- Open the **Shelf's Settings panel** and select **Setting**s.

- Select **Show Advanced Settings** towards the end of the screen.

- In the Powerwash section at the bottom of the screen, click the **Powerwash** button.

- A dialog box displays, informing you that you must restart.

- Click the **Restart** option if you're certain you would like to wipe your Chromebook clean.

You can't undo power washing like you can't undo breaking an egg. Your Chromebook transforms into a safe, power-cleaning machine after you click **Restart**. Nothing will be left on the device. The good news is that nothing on your Google Drive or other web services will be affected.

# CHAPTER 8

## RECOVERY

You can recover your Chromebook's operating system (OS) if it isn't working properly. The recovery process involves deleting and reinstalling the operating system. Backup files if possible before recovering your Chromebook.

Recover is necessary under the following circumstances:

- If you've tried other troubleshooting methods but nothing has worked.
- When you've asked the professionals in your Chromebook assistance forum for advice, they've suggested that you recover.
- After trying less invasive methods before you recuperate.
- When you have tried turning off your Chromebook and then on again.

### THE RECOVERY PROCESS

Remove any devices that are attached to your Chromebook, including a mouse or an external hard drive. Hold down **Esc + Refresh** for a few seconds, then **Power**. Power must be relinquished. Some Chromebook models include: Press **Esc + Maximize** for a few seconds, then push Power. Let go of the other keys when a message appears on the screen. Turn off Chromebox first. With a paper clip or similar instrument, press the recovery button. Press the **Power** button to turn the Chromebox back on. Once you see a message on the screen, release the recovery button.

### TRADITIONAL RECOVERY

To run the traditional recovery process on your Chromebook, follow these easy steps:

1. Install Google Chrome.

2. Install the extension for recovery. To access the recovery extension, click **Extensions** in the top right corner of your browser window. The **Chromebook Recovery Utility** extension should be selected. Make sure the extension pop-up is turned on if it doesn't appear on your screen automatically.

3. Start the recovery process. To begin, select **Get started**. On the Chromebook with the problem, select **Recover using external disk** and follow the on-screen instructions.

## VPNS

By anonymizing your traffic and location, a (Virtual Private Network) VPN was established to preserve your online privacy and make life difficult for hackers. However, it can be used for a variety of purposes, including quick and secure browsing.

A VPN can assist you in a number of ways. VPNs encrypt all of your data before it is sent over the internet. All of your internet traffic is encrypted when you're connected to a VPN server. This means that no one, including your internet service provider, can see what you're doing online (ISP). That implies your ISP won't be able to throttle your connection. Encryption prevents hackers from viewing critical information, such as passwords, that you type onto websites. Because thieves may easily monitor your connection on public networks, this is especially critical if you're utilizing public Wi-Fi. A VPN, on the other hand, ensures that even if your data is stolen, no one will be able to decrypt or comprehend it.

Your privacy is also protected by your VPN. Your IP address is used by websites and services to determine your location. Your IP address is hidden when you connect to a VPN server. They can't see where you are since they can't see your true IP address. Some VPNs block harmful websites, advertisements, and trackers. Without your knowledge, spammers can download malware and spyware into your device. VPNs with built-in security can assist prevent infections by blocking access to certain sites before they can do harm. Ads and pop-ups are also blocked by some VPNs. This prevents malware from entering your device through malicious advertisements.

### HOW DO VPNS WORK?

All of your internet traffic is routed through one of your VPN's servers, where it is encrypted. For example, you could be in the United Kingdom and connect to a server in the United States. The VPN encrypts all of your traffic as it travels from the UK to the US. Your ISP can no longer see your online activity, where you've come from, or track you because it's encrypted. Your VPN server then directs your traffic to the website you've visited. Instead of your device, the site views the VPN server as the source of your traffic. This means it sees your VPN server's IP address rather than your own. The best VPNs have thousands of servers and routinely refresh their IP addresses, making it difficult for sites to block them. As a result, you remain entirely anonymous and untraceable.

### IS A VPN REQUIRED FOR YOUR CHROMEBOOK?

The quick answer is that you almost certainly require one. To understand why, we must first define what a VPN is. A VPN establishes an encrypted connection across

# CHAPTER 8

your Chromebook and a VPN server. When you send your internet traffic via that tunnel, you can rest assured that it will not be intercepted while in transit. Anyone on the same network as you, anyone who can connect that network's router, your ISP, and snoopy intelligence operatives will all be kept in the dark if you use a VPN. Your IP address is also masked, which implies your location is as well.

## INSTALLING A VPN ON A CHROMEBOOK

There are a few options for getting a VPN on your Chromebook. You can use an Android app or a Chrome browser plugin. Although manual VPN setup is possible, we do not encourage it because it frequently requires the use of less secure VPN protocols.

### Install a VPN extension for Chrome

The most straightforward way to safeguard your web traffic is to use a Chrome browser extension. In fact, if you decide to go this route, there is a whole list of Chrome browser add-ons to assist you to choose the best one.

### Make use of an Android VPN application

Using Android VPN software on your Chromebook is the most thorough approach to encrypting your Chromebook's web traffic. Download, login, then turn on the VPN app of your choosing. Android VPN apps appear as connectivity options in your Chromebook's network settings menu. You'll need the most recent version of Chrome OS, as well as permission to access the Google Play store via the **Chrome OS** app settings.

Simply go to the **Settings app**, look for Google Play, and turn it on. However, if you're using a business Google account, you might not be capable of activating Google Play without your system administrator's permission. The majority of Chromebook VPN apps are Android apps. Specific Android apps will not operate with some Chromebooks, and not all Android apps will work on Chrome OS as they do on your mobile devices.

### Android Apps on Your Chromebook

VPNs are supported by Chrome OS. Although using mobile apps on a computer may not be the first thing that comes to mind when considering a VPN, it is the most efficient way to use some of the top VPNs that have been examined, including Editors' Choice picks like NordVPN, ProtonVPN, and TunnelBear VPN.

# Chapter 9: Tips and Tricks for Chromebook

Chromebooks are being preferred all over the world because they are quite simple to use. Despite being simple, not all of their features are being used to their maximum potential. Chromebooks have many tips and tricks that can make them even more simple and interesting. This chapter will look at some of the best 10 Chromebook tips and tricks you will find interesting and useful.

## RUN WINDOWS APPLICATIONS ON CHROME OS

Considering that you can run Linux on your Chromebook, you now have a variety of apps you can install on your device. It is also possible to run Windows-based applications on your Chromebook by using an app called Wine. Windows has a wide and great selection of apps that are not available on Linux, such as Photoshop and Brave Browser. These apps are not available on Chromebook and having them gives you satisfaction in using your Chromebook.

To install Wine, open the Terminal and run the command **"sudo apt – get install wine."** Bear in mind that Wine will only work on Intel-based Chromebooks so if you have an ARM-based Chromebook, this app will not work. Nevertheless, wine can also be installed on any Chromebook as an Android app and runs very well.

## USE AN ANDROID PHONE TO UNLOCK CHROMEBOOK

Most touch-enabled Chromebooks now support tablet mode. However, typing the password in tablet mode is quite hectic since there is a need to use a virtual keyboard. Fortunately, there is an option of changing the password to a PIN in tablet mode.

Follow the guide below to change from password to pin for easy tablet mode use.

# CHAPTER 9

1. Go to **You and Google** on your device and open **system configuration**.

2. Click on **Lock screen and login**.

3. Change the option to PIN and Password.

4. Set a PIN code.

This way, you just have to enter your pin code to unlock your Chromebook when in tablet mode. **This feature makes your Chromebook more user-friendly, especially for beginners.**

Now, when you connect your Android phone in the Connected devices section, you can use it to open your Chromebook easily. This feature works perfectly well just as you use your Apple Watch to unlock an iPhone.

## ACCESS THE OVERVIEW MODE

The overview mode is a feature that allows you to see everything open on the screen at once and it is just like the Expose feature on Mac. Follow these steps to access this feature on your Chromebook.

1. Go to the top row of your keyboard and press the [] || key. You can find it above the '6' button.

2. You can also access the overview mode by swiping down using three fingers on your trackpad or touchscreen.

3. When you access the overview mode, click on any of the available thumbnails to open that window.

4. Clicking on a blank space reverts you to the previous window used.

By using this feature, you will find out that it is a good time-saver considering that you have several apps open simultaneously. Type anything to filter out the windows when you are in the Overview mode, for example, typing 'Google' will prompt your Chromebook to show Google windows that are open.

This way, you will maximize your experience with your lovely gadget.

## USE CHROMEBOOK EXTRAS

Chromebooks run on Chrome OS which makes them more than just mere computers. Chrome OS brings with it more freebies which give more value to your Chromebook with their extra functions. The moment you acquire your Chromebook and get logged in; the first thing is to visit the Chromebook Perks Page to find some awesome offers. These offers expire 60 days from the day you link your Google account with the Chromebook so you have to make full use of them before time runs out.

The offers come in the form of free games, free apps, extended subscription trials, hardware savings, and many others. They are always changing and updating from time to time. The good part of it is that there is always something for you. When you do not find a specific perk that you are looking for, you can find it by following these steps:

1. Open the app Launcher and search **Explore app**.

2. All the active Perks will be shown on the Available Perks tab.

3. When you find your desired app, click on it and you will be asked to verify your eligibility.

4. If available, the perk's promo code will be presented to you and you are good to go.

## SECURITY WHEN SHARING YOUR CHROMEBOOK

A Chromebook is a very private device since it is directly linked to your Google account. This means that if anyone else gains access to your account, that person can view your files, check your emails, view your photos, and many others. Unlike Windows-based computers, Chromebooks may not be that easy to share with someone else. However, there are situations when you need to lend it to a loved one but you do not want them to access your private files. Take advantage of the Guest Mode which allows you to gain access to most of Chrome OS features without logging into an account.

1. Open the Quick Setting menu on the bottom-right corner.

2. Sign out of your profile.

3. To enter a temporary profile, Click **Guest Mode.**

Keep in mind that the Guest Mode is only useful when you need to use apps or functions which do not require you to Log in first.

## OPENING APPS USING KEYS

Bearing in mind that you need apps to perform tasks on your Chromebook, finding and opening them in a quick way helps you to operate it with ease. Opening apps that are on your Chromebook's Dock or taskbar has never been this easy with the use of shortcuts. Clicking **Alt + 1** opens the first app on the left of your Chromebook shelf. Pressing **Alt + 2** opens the second app whereas **Alt + 3** opens the third application and the chain goes on.

These shortcuts help you to search and open apps without wasting much time. You can arrange your apps starting with the most used app to the least used ones for quick access. For example, if your Shelf has Chrome as the first app, you just press **Alt + 1** and you will be directed straight into the Chrome app.

## ADD RESTART BUTTON ON CHROMEBOOK

Chromebooks do not come with restart buttons. This means that when you want to restart your Chromebook, you have to shut it down and turn it on again which is quite boring.

Given that your device encounters performance problems, for instance, graphical issues, slow performance, and mouse latency, among others, restarting it may be a good option. If this is your case, you can create a Restart button manually using the following steps.

1. Press **Ctrl + Shift + O**, go to the top right corner, and click on the three-dot menu.

2. Click **Add New Bookmark** and type **Restart** in the name field. Go to the URL field and type *"chrome://restart"* and save the bookmark.

3. To access the bookmark easily, drag it to the bookmark bar.

Now, when the need to restart your device instantly arises, you simply have to go to Chrome and click on the Restart bookmark.

## TIPS AND TRICKS FOR CHROMEBOOK

## CHROMEBOOK SHORTCUTS

The use of Chromebooks has been made easy by shortcuts, which help you complete tasks quickly. This means that you no longer have to go deeper into your device's functions but rather use the keyboard to instantly open a file, complete a task, and many more.

The underlisted are a few shortcuts you may find interesting and useful.

- To open a file in the browser, press **Ctrl + o**.
- Press **Ctrl + n** to open a new window.
- Press **Shift + Ctrl + n** to open a new window in Incognito mode.
- Press **Shift + Ctrl + w** to close the current window.
- To open a new tab press **Ctrl + t**.
- Press **Ctrl + 9** to go to the last tab in the window.
- Press **Ctrl + Tab** to go to the next tab in the window.
- Press **Alt + Right** arrow to go to the next page in your device's browsing history.

# CHAPTER 9

- Press **Alt + Left** arrow to go to the previous page in the browsing history.

- Press **Shift + Alt + m** to open the Files app.

- Press **Shift + Ctrl and + or –(minus)**.

- Press **Ctrl + search + m or Ctrl + Launcher + m** to magnify the whole screen.

- To take a screenshot, press **Ctrl + Show Windows**.

These are just a few of the many shortcuts available on your Chromebook. These devices are meant to be as user-friendly as possible so they have shortcuts to aid that.

## ENABLE THE OFFLINE MODE FOR GOOGLE DOCS

Enabling the Offline mode for Google Docs and Drive is possible on Chromebook. Given that you want to use it without the internet. The first step is to install **Google Docs Offline Chrome extension.** It allows you to do advanced copy and paste functions in the Google Docs, sheets, and slides.

This extension allows you to create, edit, and view documents, spreadsheets, images, PDFs, and presentations without the use of the internet. Make sure your device has enough space to save your files and turn on Offline access.

Once you have successfully installed the **Google Docs Offline Chrome extension**, you can find files saved for offline access by going to the Settings menu in your Google Drive, Sheets, or Slides app and tapping **Offline**. To save a file for offline views follow these steps.

- Open **Google Drive.**

- Next to the file, click More.

- Tap Make available offline and the file will be ready for offline use.

You can also make a document while offline by going to the **Files** menu and finding the option, **Make available for Offline**. Make sure that all these settings are modified while your Chromebook is connected to the internet.

# TIPS AND TRICKS FOR CHROMEBOOK

## RESET YOUR CHROMEBOOK

Resetting your Chromebook is an option to consider when you are having problems with your Chrome OS. This process is called Powerwash on Chrome OS and the reset process is similar to that on Android. The only difference is that on Chrome OS, all your files are synced to Google Drive so data loss is not a thing to worry about. The following steps will guide you through the reset process.

1. Open **Settings**, go to the left pane menu, and click **Advanced**.

2. Go to **Reset Settings** and click on the **Reset** button.

3. The Chromebook will restart and after that sign in with your Google account and everything will be back to normal just like before.

When a Chromebook has been reset, it will be refreshed thereby speeding its processes and improving its operations.

# **FREE BONUS**

To Download your FREE BONUS
Turn On Your Cellphone Camera,
Focus it on the Code Below
and Click the Link that Appears

OR

Go to:
https://rb.gy/tdvz7c

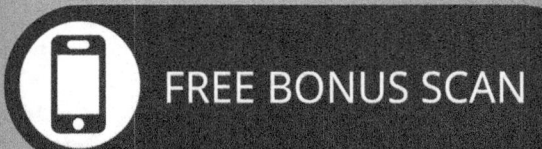

# CONCLUSION

You can also use the Chromebook to do productive tasks. This ranges from creating and editing documents in Google Docs. Furthermore, you can add tables and images to documents, prior to printing or sharing them with others. Apart from documents, you can also utilize Google sheets as well as Google Slides for calculations and different types of presentations, respectively.

This book also talks about how you can maintain your Chromebook. Your operating system will need to be updated every now and then so that efficiency is increased. In case you face some problems and need to reset your Chromebook, it is possible to do it. To sum it all up, this book provides you with handy tips and tricks that you can use on your Chromebook. These allow you to make the most out of your Chromebook so that you will have the best experience in using your device.

If you have managed to read this book up to this point, you now have the necessary bits of knowledge and information on how to use your Chromebook and troubleshoot potential problems. If you do not have a Chromebook, it's time to get yours now and have the convenience, together with an enjoyable experience in using the Chromebook.

# Index

## A

Access Settings.................................. 146
Access the Overview Mode ........ 152
Account Images................................ 14
Add a Contact From Message..... 94
Add a Goal........................................... 92
Add Child Accounts......................... 23
Adding Attachments....................... 88
Adding Bluetooth Devices............. 19
Adding Charts................................. 135
Adding Events.................................. 91
Adding Images............................... 126
Adding Other Email Accounts...... 90
Adding Reminders .......................... 91
Adding Tables................................ 127
Adding Tasks.................................... 92
Adding Users.................................... 22
Add New Contacts .......................... 93
Add Restart Button on Chromebook................................... 154
Allow or Blocks Apps...................... 24
Android Apps........................... 62, 150
Android VPN application.............. 150
App Launcher.................................... 42
App Shelf............................................ 38
App Types........................................... 42
Audacity............................................. 71
AutoSum........................................... 135

## B

Battery Care for Chromebooks................................. 142
Bluetooth Devices .......................... 19
Bookmaking a Site........................... 82
Bookmark Folders........................... 82
Browse Incognito ............................ 80
Browser Tabs.................................... 80
Browsing Chrome App Store ........ 59
Browsing History ............................. 81
Bullet Lists ...................................... 124

## C

Calendar App.................................... 90
Captions........................................... 100
Cell Alignment................................ 133
Cell Borders ................................... 134
Change Background ..................... 100
Change Language........................... 28
Chat Rooms ................................... 103
Check for New Information......... 146
Chrome Apps.................................... 59
Chromebook Screenshots............. 56
Chromebook Shortcuts................ 155
Chromecast.................................... 118
Chrome Operating System ............ 9
Chrome OS......................... 9, 145, 158
Chrome Security ............................. 85
Chrome web store........................... 59
Cloud-Enabled Wireless Printers............................. 17
Color Saturation............................ 111

# INDEX

Conclusion .................................. 158
Configuring Other Settings........... 25
Connected Devices ...................... 19
Connect to Wi-Fi ........................... 20
Connect Your Phone to Chromebook .................................. 19
Contacts Web App ....................... 93
Copying Files................................. 47
Copying Using a Mouse or Touchpad....................................... 48
Copying Using Touchscreen ........ 49
Count ......................................... 134
Create App Folders ...................... 43
Creating a Google Account........... 12
Creating a Meeting for Later ....... 95
Creating a Room and Chatting  103
Creating Folders........................... 44
Cropping and Rotation ............... 112
Cut, Copy, and Paste ........... 126, 132

## D

Deleting Users ............................. 23
Desktop Shortcut ........................ 82
Desktop Wallpaper....................... 12
Diagnostics ................................ 143
Diagnostics App......................... 144
Downloading Apps ...................... 63
Downloads .................................. 83
Dropbox....................................... 30

## E

Enable Google Play Store ............ 63

External Display Settings ............. 27
External Drivers........................... 52

## F

Family Links ................................ 24
FileZilla .................................. 69, 70
Formatting External Drives ......... 53

## G

Getting Around Chromebook....... 34
Gimp Image Editor...................... 72
Gmail App ................................... 86
Gmail on the Web........................ 92
Google Assistant.......................... 58
Google Chat.............................. 101
Google Chrome .......................... 79
Google Docs............................. 122
Google Duo .............................. 103
Google Meet............................... 94
Google Photos ......................... 106
Google Play Books.................... 119
Google Play Store ...................... 63
Google Sheets .................. 131, 132
Google Slides ........................... 136
Google Suite............................. 122
Group Conversation ................. 101
Group Conversation on google duo ............................... 104

## H

HDMI Adapter........................... 118
Holding Space............................ 41

# INDEX

How Do VPNs Work? ...................... 149
How to Install Audacity ................... 71
How to Install FileZilla ..................... 69
How to Turn on Linux? ..................... 67

## I

In-Call Options ................................. 97
Initial Setup ..................................... 11
Inserting Rows and Columns ..... 133
Install Gimp Image Editor ............. 72
Installing a VPN on a
Chromebook ................................. 150
Installing Linux Apps ...................... 68
Install LibreOffice ............................ 73
Install Python .................................. 75
Integrate Dropbox .......................... 30
Integrate One-Drive ....................... 31
Internal Display Settings .............. 26
Invite a Friend on google duo .... 105
Is a VPN Required for Your
Chromebook? ................................ 149

## J

Joining a Meeting ..................... 95, 97
Justify Text .................................... 124

## K

Keyboard ......................................... 36
Keyboard Layout ............................ 29
Keyboard Settings .......................... 29

## L

Library ........................................... 120
LibreOffice ...................................... 73
Linux Apps ................................ 66, 68
Listening to Music ........................ 113
Listening to Music Streaming
Services ......................................... 114

## M

Make Adjustments to the
Exposure ...................................... 110
Management Files in
Chromebook ................................... 44
Manage Web Browsing ................. 24
Managing Apps .............................. 65
Managing Passwords .................... 85
Managing Users ............................. 22
Monitoring Child Accounts
with Family Links ........................... 24
Mouse and Touchpad .................... 25
Moving Files ................................... 46
Music Enjoyment ......................... 113

## N

Netflix ........................................... 118
Network Settings ........................... 30
Notifications ................................... 40
Numbered Lists ............................ 125

## O

Offline mode for Google Docs .. 156
One-Drive ....................................... 31

# INDEX

Onscreen Keyboard Help ............... 36
Opening Apps Using Keys ............ 154
Opening Saved Documents ....... 128
Opening the Diagnostics App ... 144
Overview Mode ............................... 152

## P

Parental Controls ............................. 23
Personalize Your Chromebook .... 12
Photoshop Express Editor .......... 110
Photos in Chrome OS ..................... 107
Pin apps to Your app Shelf ........... 43
Pinned Files ....................................... 41
Playing a Song From a Playlist ... 113
Power Options .................................. 30
Power Up and Power Down ........... 34
Powerwash ....................................... 147
Present and Share Desktops ....... 98
Printers .............................................. 17
Printing a Webpage ........................ 84
Printing Documents ...................... 129
Productivity with Google Suite ... 122
Python ............................................... 75

## Q

Quick Settings Panel ...................... 19

## R

Reading Email .................................. 86
Record the Screen .......................... 57
Recover Deleted Messages .......... 88
Recovery .......................................... 148
Recovery Process .......................... 148
References ...................................... 165
Remote Desktop ............................... 32
Removing Apps ................................ 65
Removing Chrome Extensions .... 60
Removing Linux Apps ..................... 77
Renaming Through Right Clicking ... 49
Renaming Using Keys .................... 50
Reply an email ................................. 86
Reset Your Chromebook ............. 157
Rotate a Photograph .................... 108
Run Windows Applications ......... 151

## S

Saving Documents ........................ 128
Saving Passwords .......................... 84
Schedule Meeting in the Calendar ... 97
Screen Capture ............................... 55
Searching Files ............................... 51
Searching the Store ....................... 60
Search messagges .......................... 89
Security When Sharing Your Chromebook ... 153
Setting up Printers ......................... 17
Setting Up Your Chromebook ...... 11
Set up Parental Controls ............... 24
Share Files on google chat ......... 103
Sharing Documents ....................... 130
Sharing Files .................................... 121

# INDEX

Simple Text Formatting .................. 132
Site Shortcuts ................................. 82
Sorting Files ................................... 51
Spreadsheets ................................. 131
Start a Conversation on google duo ........................................ 104
Starting a Google Meet ................. 94
Starting Google Chat .................... 101
Starting Google Duo ..................... 104
Start Instant Meeting ................... 96
Sync and Google Services ............. 15
System Tray ................................... 39

## T

Talk to Your Chromebook .............. 57
Task Manager ................................. 37
The Login Screen ........................... 34
Time Zone ...................................... 27
Tips and Tricks for Chromebook ................................... 151
TouchPad ........................................ 35
Traditional Printers ....................... 18
Traditional Recovery ..................... 148
Transferring Your File to a Chromebook ................................... 16
Turning Linux off ........................... 67
Types of Data ................................. 135

## U

Updating Chrome OS ..................... 145
Use an Android Phone to Unlock Chromebook ................................... 151
Useful Online Apps ........................ 62

user-friendly .................................. 152
Use the Auto-Correct Feature ...... 110
Using Amazon Prime Video ........... 118
Using Chrome Apps ....................... 59
Using External Drive ..................... 17
Using Formulas .............................. 134
Using Functions ............................. 134
Using Google Drive ....................... 16
Using Linux Apps ........................... 66
Using Online Video Streaming Services ........................................ 117
Using Paragraph Styles ................. 122
Using Spotify to Listen to Music ... 115
Using Your Own Photos ................. 13
Utilizing the Diagnostics App ....... 145

## V

Video Streaming ............................ 116
View Contact Details .................... 93
View Local Photos ........................ 107
VPN extension for Chrome ........... 150
VPNs ............................................... 149

## W

web browser .................................. 79
Web, Email, and Communication .. 79
WebM ............................................. 116
Whiteboard .................................... 99
Writing a New Message ................ 87

## Z

Zoom ............................................... 110

Made in United States
North Haven, CT
27 December 2023

46609493R00091